GENESIS, CREATION, AND CREATIONISM

Lloyd R. Bailey

Paulist Press
New York / Mahwah, N.J.

ACKNOWLEDGMENTS

The Publisher gratefully acknowledges use of the following materials: A reprint of the *Minutes* of the General Assembly, Part I, Journal of the 194th G.A., 7th Series, Volume XVI (1982), pp. 410–414: "Evolution and Creationism." Reprinted with permission of the Office of the General Assembly, Presbyterian Church, U.S.A. Excerpts from *Ancient and Near Eastern Texts: Relating to the Old Testament*, 3rd edition with Supplement, edited by James B. Pritchard, copyright © 1969 by Princeton University Press. Page 107, lines 4–11, reprinted by permission of Princeton University Press. Reprints from *The Genesis Record*, by Henry M. Morris, copyright © 1976, Baker Book House, Grand Rapids, Michigan. Reprints from *What Is Creation Science?* by Henry M. Morris and Gary E. Parker, copyright © 1983, Master Books, Division of Creation-Life Publishers, El Cajon, California. A reprint of "Address to Scientists and Members of the Pontifical Academy of Sciences, by Pope John Paul II," as printed in *Origins*, Vol. 11, No. 18 (Oct. 15, 1981), pp. 277, 279. A reproduction of the Doppler effect drawings from *Cosmos*. Reprinted with permission from Carl Sagan, Cornell University, Center for Radiophysics and Space Research.

Cover art: Crab Nebula in Taurus (NGC 1952, Messier 1). 200-inch photograph, Mt. Palomar. Courtesy of California Institute of Technology.

Library of Congress Cataloging-in-Publication Data

Bailey, Lloyd R., 1936–
    Genesis, creation, and creationism/Lloyd R. Bailey.
      p. cm.
    Includes bibliographical references and index.
    ISBN 0-8091-3255-9 (pbk.)
    1. Creationism—Controversial literature. 2. Bible. O.T.
    Genesis I—Criticism, interpretation, etc. 3. Bible and evolution.
    I. Title.
    BS651.B235   1993
    231.7′65—dc20

                    92-33185
                    CIP

Published by Paulist Press
997 Macarthur Boulevard
Mahwah, New Jersey 07430

Printed and bound in the
United States of America

CONTENTS

iii

TABLES AND ILLUSTRATIONS

Tables

Illustrations

ABBREVIATIONS

AB	Anchor Bible Commentary Series
AJSL	*American Journal of Semitic Language*
AFO	*Archiv für Orientforschung*
ANET	*Ancient Near Eastern Texts* (2nd ed.; Pritchard, ed.)
ArOr	*Archiv Orientální*
BASOR	*Bulletin of the American Schools of Oriental Research*
B.C.E.	Before the Common Era (i.e., B.C.)
CAD	*Chicago Assyrian Dictionary* (multi-volumes; in process)
C.E.	Common Era (i.e., A.D.)
C/E	*Creation/Evolution*
HUCA	*Hebrew Union College Annual*
IB	*The Interpreter's Bible*
ICR	The Institute of Creation Research (San Diego, Calif.)
IDB	*The Interpreter's Dictionary of the Bible,* 4 vols.
IDBS	*IDB, Supplementary Volume*
IEJ	*Israel Exploration Journal*
IO-VC	*The Interpreter's One-Volume Commentary On The Bible*
JAOS	*Journal of the American Oriental Society*
JB	The Jerusalem Bible (English translation)
JBC	*The Jerome Biblical Commentary*
JBL	*Journal of Biblical Literature*
JNES	*Journal of Near Eastern Studies*
JPS	Jewish Publication Society (translation of the Bible)
JRAS	*Journal of the Royal Asiatic Society of Great Britain*
JSS	*Journal of Semitic Studies*
JTS	*Journal of Theological Studies*
KJV	King James Version of the Bible
LXX	Septuagint (ancient Greek version of the Bible)
MT	Masoretic Text (of the Bible)
NAB	New American Bible (translation)

NEB	New English Bible (translation)
NJB	New Jerusalem Bible (translation)
nv	"I have not seen (the source cited)"
OT	The Old Testament
PEFQS	*Palestine Exploration Fund Quarterly Statement*
RSV	*Revised Standard Version* (translation)
SI	*The Skeptical Inquirer*
SP	Samaritan Pentateuch (ancient version of the Bible)
SVT	*Supplements to Vetus Testamentum*
TB	Babylonian Talmud
TDOT	*Theological Dictionary of the Old Testament*
TEV	Today's English Version of the Bible
v., vv.	verse(s)
VT	*Vetus Testamentum*
W-B	Weld-Blundel Text of the Sumerian King List
ZAW	*Zeitschrift für die Alttestamentliche Wissenschaft*

PREFACE

THE PURPOSE OF the present volume is to investigate the message (agenda, goal) of the biblical story of creation in Genesis 1:1–2:4a and to compare the result with the interpretation of that same story by "young earth" creationists. Such creationists believe that the earth (and indeed the universe) is only a few thousand years old and that their conclusion is in accordance with biblical data.

Readers of the present volume will be struck by the fact that I have purposefully neglected a basic tool for the determination of the meaning of a text. Ordinarily one would want to ask: Who was the author (or authors), when did they live, what were the circumstances, and who were the intended audience? For example, was Moses the author (or collector) of the Genesis material, or was it some other(s)? If the former, did he live in the fifteenth century B.C.E., or was it the thirteenth? The environment and mentality of the audience might be quite different in each case. On the other hand, if Moses was not the collector (or author), then by whom, and in how many stages, and to what situations and mentalities addressed?

About these and other matters there have been and are yet major differences of opinion. Generally, a "main line" Protestant approach, based upon the documentary hypothesis and often characterized as "liberal," has been opposed by an approach whose advocates characterize themselves as "evangelical," or "conservative," or "fundamentalist." Often this divergence has led to an intolerance of opposing opinion, or to the suspicion that a book (even before it is read) has been poisoned by the pre-conceived notions of a "Fundy" or a "stinking liberal." The following declaration is illustrative of this tendency.

Most so-called liberal theologians and commentators, along with not a few conservatives, have followed the theory that a number of unknown writers and editors, during the period of Israel's history . . . compiled and edited several old legends and traditions . . . into the Book of Genesis. . . . This is the "Documentary Hypothesis" . . .

ix

Adherents of this odd idea have attempted to justify it on the basis of supposed peculiarities of language and style, references to customs and cultures, and other internal evidences. . . . No doubt their real reason, however, was their basic commitment to the evolutionary concept of man's development. . . .[1]

Undoubtedly, the underlying reason for this documentary hypothesis was the evolutionary prejudice of liberal scholars, who were unwilling to concede that monotheism and a high culture could have prevailed during Moses' day.[2]

One might wonder how this recent author could know, beyond any "doubt," the "real reasons" for the conclusions of thousands of interpreters, most of them dedicated Christians and Jews, stretching across the span of two centuries. One might also wonder if it would be equally fair (and accurate) to state that beyond doubt, the real reason for *rejecting* the documentary hypothesis has been a prior commitment to the non-evolutionary concept of human origins and development. Such rhetoric, however, accomplishes very little.

In any case, the present volume will set aside the entire controversy concerning authorship and date of the materials in Genesis-Deuteronomy. There will be little appeal to some of the tools of historical-critical inquiry (and to "source criticism" in particular). Perhaps in the loss there will be a gain: an invitation to all sides of the debate to read the text carefully and without prior commitment for or against "the theory of evolution." My concern herein is to let the Bible speak for itself, insofar as it can do so given our distance from its own time and mentality. If the agenda of the biblical creation story coincides with the conclusion of modern "young earth" creationists, so be it! If the agenda is opposed to that modern conclusion, then so be that as well! My primary purpose, as an ordained, "Bible believing" Christian (incidentally, with a degree in physics), is to enhance the ability of the Bible to speak for itself.

While much has been written by scientists about the adequacy or inadequacy of "scientific" creationism, much less is available about its proposed counterpart, "biblical" creationism. Critics of the latter (especially in its "young earth" manifestation) have couched their analysis of the biblical text in terms of the aforementioned documentary hypothesis.[3] The present volume, therefore, is to my knowledge unique in its approach.

It should be stated at the outset that creationists are serious, Bible-believing Christians, and for that they are to be lauded. Any dissatisfaction that I may have with their interpretation of scripture must be seen within that context. I hope that I may be accorded the same courtesy.

Notes to the Preface

1. Henry Morris, 1976, pp. 22–23.
2. *Ibid.* p. 24.
3. An extremely well done volume of this type is Conrad Hyers, 1984.

PART ONE

What Is "Creationism"?

CHAPTER I

The Problem of Terminology

THE TERM "creation" is ordinarily used in English in two senses. On the one hand, it can describe the product of human inventiveness, as when fashion designers introduce their "latest creation." Here the "creator" has presumably used existing materials in a new way. On the other hand, the term can describe God's primal act of bringing the world into existence. Jews, Christians, and Muslims have traditionally been "creationists" in the latter sense.

Advocates of God as creator have not been unanimous as to the manner and chronology of such activity. Did it involve the creation of matter (and the attendant categories of time and space) "out of nothing," which theologians (ever fond of Latin terminology) refer to as *creatio ex nihilo*? Or did it involve the restructuring of prior chaotic (possibly eternal) matter, the bringing of order where none previously existed? (The first three verses of Genesis have often been the center of debate about this issue, as will be discussed below.) In either case, it has been traditional to speak of an ongoing divine creativity in the realm of nature (whether miracles or seemingly accidental events), and in human response (conversion and nurture in the faith).

With respect to the origin of life, was the divine creativity a series of interruptions of nature which resulted in instantaneous appearances of a sequence of forms? Or did the creator work through the processes of nature as life evolved from the substances of the earth and then progressed to ever more complex forms? (The former perspective is sometimes designated "special creation" and the latter "theistic evolution.")

Whatever the nature of the creation of the universe and of life, did it take place billions and millions of years ago respectively or only a few thousand years ago?

Difference of opinion about these and related matters is a reflection of the diversity of thought in contemporary theology. The problem of terminology becomes evident when some groups claim to be the sole true "creationists," and when the term "creationism," in popular usage, has come to refer primarily to a single group. This has happened in recent decades in the case of "special creationists" of the "young earth" type.

With the advent of modern scientific estimates of the age of the universe (billions of years), and especially with the publication of Charles Darwin's *Origin of Species* (1859), a rift began to develop within the Christian community. The issue was: How much of the new science is compatible with the Bible and with the tradition of the church? Rather than an outright rejection of "the theory of evolution" (and its attendant vast age of the earth), there arose in some quarters an adaptation which has come to be known as "theistic evolution": God, rather than having enacted separate special creations over a recent period of six days (Gen 1), might have guided, over vast ages, those astronomical, geological, and biological activities which the imperceptive interpreter might regard only as the result of "blind chance." In effect, one could compromise with the new sciences by accommodating the Bible to them, but only at those points which were considered to be non-essential to the biblical faith. For example, God as creator (however that be defined) must be maintained, but matters of chronology and mechanics could be seen as mere culture-bound attempts to express that creation faith. At the same time, it could be affirmed, and rightly so, that the question of ultimate origins ("Is the universe a creation, demanding a creator?") is beyond the scope and methodology of the scientific method to answer.

Although generations of innovative and devoted Christians and Jews have warmly affirmed creation along the lines of "theistic evolution," their religious detractors have refused to recognize them as "creationists."

Staunch biblical literalists initially refused to recognize the validity of scientific assertions about the great age of the earth and especially about the "evolution" of human beings. Most of them eventually made a more limited accommodation of the Bible to the sciences, especially in the realm of chronology. One might accept, for example, that the age of the earth was in the millions of years, and yet maintain belief in separate creative acts such that life did not evolve and humans did not biologically descend from "lower creatures." More importantly, one could even claim that this was not an accommodation, but rather reflected new insights about the ambiguous chronological language of the early chapters of Genesis. Otherwise put: perhaps the vast ages of the geologists have been implied all along in the Bible (or, at least, are an allowable interpretation of the Bible). Thus the scientific estimates would merely have opened the eyes of interpreters to the reality of the Bible as an advanced scientific document.

The primary way that the biblical chronology was brought into line with the vast geological ages was the supposition (discovery?) of "gaps" in the Genesis record. One or more of the following types might be sufficient to bring about agreement.

1. A vast gap, perhaps billions of years, between Genesis 1:1 and 1:2. (This so-called "gap theory" is discussed in detail in Appendix I.)

2. Vast gaps, perhaps millions of years each, between each of the eight creative acts in Genesis 1. Otherwise put: perhaps the word "day" in the text actually designates an age or a geological epoch. (This so-called "day-age theory" is discussed in detail in Appendix II.)

3. More modest gaps, perhaps thousands of years, between the lives of the individuals who are listed in the genealogies of Genesis 5 and 11. Thereby, Adam remains the first human, but he could have lived at a far more remote age than the text takes care to make explicit. (This so-called "generation gap theory" is discussed in detail in Appendix III.)

The "gap" theorists advocate "special" creationism, as opposed to secular (naturalistic, materialistic) evolution and to theistic evolution (or evolutionary creationism). Another way to describe them would be to say that they are theistic anti-evolutionists.[1] Since they are willing to affirm that the earth is very old (in keeping with the estimate of geologists), they are sometimes known as "old earth creationists" or as "old earthers." Their approach was quite popular in the early nineteenth century (pre-Darwin), and held in more recent times by (among others) Cyrus Scofield (editor of the widely used Scofield Reference Bible), Herbert W. Armstrong[2] (whose monthly magazine, *The Plain Truth,* has a circulation of eight million), Charles C. Ryrie (editor of *The Ryrie Study Bible*), the Jehovah's Witness movement (whose advocates have distributed about eighteen million copies of a 1967 book, *Did Man Get Here by Evolution or by Creation?*), and a number of radio and television evangelists (e.g. Kenneth Hagin and Jimmy Swaggart).

Within the last few decades, a new group of creationists has come to popular attention.[3] These are the so-called "young earthers," who disdain equally secular evolutionists and theistic evolutionists, and who regard the "old earth" approach as an unnecessary concession to evolutionary science.[4] Rather than accommodate part of the Bible to science, they propose that the sciences, when properly understood, affirm the cosmology and cosmogeny of the Bible. That is, "biblical creationism" and "scientific creationism," although distinct disciplines, lead to the same conclusions. It is they who have popularized the term "creationism" for their point of view and with whom the title has come to be associated in the popular press.

The result of this terminological assignment is an unfortunate linguistic twist in which the terms "creationist" and "creationism" have come to designate a small segment of the entire spectrum of Jewish and Christian thought on the matter of origins. Thereby the majority of such theologians is excluded, even though they may be firm advocates of creation by the deity. (As an illustration of this reality, see Appendix V for formal statements by some denominations in renunciation of the "young earth" approach.)

In recognition of this linguistic reality, I will hereafter use the terms "creationism" and "creationists" (in quotation marks) to refer to such "young earthers." This I do, not with negative connotation, but in order to preserve a legitimate distinction between creationists and "creationists," and thereby remind the reader of a larger and proper use of those terms.

Chapter I   Notes

1. A helpful discussion of such terminology may be found in Howard J. Van Till, 1986, pp. 216–219.

2. Founder of the Worldwide Church of God and of Ambassador College (with branches in California, Texas, and England). His ideas may be found in numerous publications, including *Did God Create a Devil?* (1959) and *Mystery of the Ages* (1985).

3. For an interesting discussion of its antecedents, see John Reginald Armstrong, 1988, pp. 151–158. The title is whimsical, since this group is virulently anti-evolutionist. See also Martin Gardner, 1986, pp. 202–205.

4. The inadequacy of the various "gaps," from a biblical point of view, is discussed by "young earther" Henry Morris, 1970, pp. 58–68.

CHAPTER II

"Creationism": Biblical and Scientific

"CREATIONISM" IS a perspective on the origins of all things: not merely the universe and the planet earth, but also life (plant and animal) as well. It proposes (a) that the universe is relatively young (a few thousands of years old), (b) that the history of the earth has been characterized by violent, formative geological and meteorological catastrophes (including a universal flood) as opposed to the uniformitism of traditional geology and biology, and (c) that the basic "kinds" of life-forms appeared suddenly rather than having evolved slowly from "lower" to "higher" forms.

"Creationism" has two foci (approaches), each of which, it is proposed, leads to the same conclusion: "biblical creationism" and "scientific creationism." Dr. Henry Morris, President of the Institute for Creation Research (hereafter ICR) defines them as follows:

> BIBLICAL CREATIONISM: No reliance on scientific data, using only the Bible to expound and defend the creation model. SCIENTIFIC CREATIONISM: No reliance on Biblical revelation, utilizing only scientific data to support and expound the creation model.[1]
>
> Even though the tenets of scientific creationism can be expounded quite independently of the tenets of Biblical creationism, the two systems are completely compatible. All the genuine facts of science support Biblical creationism and all the statements in the Bible are consistent with scientific creationism. Either can be taught independently of the other or the two can be taught concurrently, as the individual situation may warrant.[2]

Although the two approaches may be pursued independently, with entirely compatible results, they are far from equal in the details which result:

The fact is that scientific creationism is perfectly compatible with Biblical creation. The latter, of course, is of higher priority to the true Christian, giving information that cannot be determined by scientific research (e.g., creation in six days), but it certainly does not contradict any scientific facts.[3]

The two foci (or approaches to understanding the origin and nature of all things) may be combined as

SCIENTIFIC BIBLICAL CREATIONISM: Full reliance on *Biblical revelation* but also using *scientific data* to support and develop the creation model.[4]

The Book of Genesis thus is in reality the foundation of all true history, as well as of true science and true philosophy.[5]

Even though the term "creation" is used for both approaches, this need not imply that the scientific model *mandates* a theological conclusion (or at least has as its basis a theological presupposition[6]). Whereas the classical "argument from design" (associated with St. Anselm in the eleventh century C.E.) insists that "creation demands a creator," scientific creationism only points to evidence of the abrupt appearance of the universe and of life, but within itself cannot explain the origin of either. Scientifically speaking, one can only say that "the universe . . . must have been created by processes which are not continuing as natural processes in the present."[7] One is thus "left in the dark," apart from biblical creationism. The term "creation," then, in a scientific context, merely describes the coming-to-be of things, in contrast to the use of that term in the history of theological reasoning.

We must now examine each of these foci. More space will be given to biblical creationism, in keeping with the title of the present volume. Even so, the discussion will be brief, since the primary goal is not to examine "creationism" per se, but rather to study the biblical text in order to determine whether or not its agenda conforms to that of the "creationist" understanding (see Part Two).

1. "Biblical Creationism"

The basics of this focus are outlined in Henry Morris' article, "The Tenets of Creationism,"[8] and are as follows.

1. "The creator of the universe is a triune God—Father, Son and Holy Spirit." There is no other divine source of being or meaning.

2. The Bible (sixty six books in the Protestant canon) "is the divinely-inspired revelation of the Creator." That inspiration is "unique, plenary, verbal," guaranteeing that it is "infallible and completely authoritative on all

matters" with which it deals, "free from error of any sort, scientific and historical as well as moral and theological." (By the text of the Bible, one means "as originally and miraculously given.")

3. Creation of all things took place in six literal days (each of twenty-four hours' duration). Thus "all theories of origins or developments which involve evolution in any form are false." The creation included Satan and his angels, who subsequently rebelled and are "attempting to thwart his [God's] divine purpose in creation."

4. Adam and Eve were the first humans, and all other men and women are their biological descendants.

5. The primeval story (Gen 1–11) "is fully historical and perspicuous."

6. Human sin, having alienated humans from the creator, "can only be remedied by the Creator himself," through Christ's substitutionary death as redemption, as affirmed by Christ's bodily resurrection.

7. Immediate restoration of fellowship with the creator is possible solely through personal trust in the Lord Jesus Christ. Those who fail to do so "must ultimately be consigned to the everlasting fire prepared for the devil and his angels."

8. The purpose of creation will be ultimately realized "at the personal bodily return to the earth of Jesus Christ to establish his eternal kingdom."

9. "Each believer should participate in the ministry of reconciliation" through evangelism and Christian living as an example.

From these statements it should be clear that "biblical creationism" is a far more comprehensive system than a position on "first things." It involves a theological interpretation of the entire Bible, although the writings and speeches of "creationists" and the focus of media attention are upon the early chapters of Genesis. It should be evident, furthermore, how very far this focus goes beyond that of the other one ("scientific creationism"), since several of the tenets are beyond the scope of scientific investigation.

Among the conclusions which apparently follow from these tenets, and from "creationist" interpretations of the text of the Bible, are the following.

a. The earth is only a few thousand years old, given the literal biblical chronology of the early chapters of Genesis, and given the unacceptability of the "gap theory" and the "day-age theory." Only the possibility of a few modest instances of the "generation gap theory" prevent a firm acceptance of the chronology as it stands.[9]

. . . there is no good reason not to accept the simple literal Biblical chronology. This is not necessarily [Archbishop James] Ussher's chronology; but it will be of the same general magnitude, since Ussher did base his calculations on the Biblical data. There are many uncertainties in such calculations, as noted above.[10]

b. The serpent who conversed with the first woman (Eve in the garden of Eden—Gen 3) was in fact an "evil spirit using the serpent's body." This means that members of an angelic host (created "probably on the first day of creation") had rebelled and been cast out of heaven. This happened sometime between Genesis 1:31 and 3:1.[11]

c. Types of plants and animals were created with the ability to reproduce, each "after its kind" (Gen 1:11, 21, 24). This assures a "stability of kinds" and precludes the evolution of new "kinds," i.e. mico-evolution but not macro-evolution.

A great deal of "horizontal" variation is easily possible, but no "vertical" changes.

. . . .

Whatever precisely is meant by the term "kind" (Hebrew *min*), it does indicate the limitations of variation. Each organism was to reproduce after its own kind, not after some other kind. Exactly what this corresponds to in terms of the modern Linnaean classification system is a matter to be decided by future research. It will probably be found eventually that the *min* often is identified with the "species," sometimes with the "genus," and possibly once in a while with the "family."[12]

As for the vast geological ages which scientists have usually assigned to the earth, this has resulted not so much from scientific data as from a prior belief that such ages were necessary for evolution to have taken place: "The hypothesis of vast geologic ages is the absolutely indispensable condition for a viable theory of evolution." From the standpoint of the Bible, this hypothesis is false and "can only lead to eventual apostasy."[13]

d. Since all "kinds" of animals were created within a two-day span (days five and six of the creation week of Genesis 1), they all co-existed with humans on the earth. This means that dinosaurs, rather than becoming extinct millions of years before humans appeared (so the "evolution" model and the "old earth gap theory"), actually shared the environment with humans for a time.

The frequent references to dragons in the Bible, as well as in the early records and traditions of most of the nations of antiquity, certainly cannot be shrugged off as mere fairy tales. Most probably they represent memories of dinosaurs handed down by tribal ancestors who encountered them before they became extinct.[14]

All animals were originally plant-eaters, since "there was no death before Adam and Eve rebelled against God."[15]

e. The astonishing ages of the pre-diluvians (some approaching one thousand years) are a reliable chronological framework for computing the time when human life emerged. Such great ages are "evidently . . . connected with the antediluvian climatological and environmental conditions . . . sober history in every way."[16]

f. The flood was an historical, worldwide event, from which pairs of each "kind" of land animal were saved by Noah. Thus it was not necessary to save pairs of each species that is known today, and thus the available space in the ark was quite adequate. This included dinosaurs, but likely as young adults ("no bigger than a cow perhaps").[17] "Creationists" also generally believe that remnants of Noah's ark yet survive.[18]

g. All of humanity, originally speaking a single language ("perhaps even Hebrew"), has descended from Noah's family, spreading from Mount Ararat in Armenia no more than a few thousand years ago.[19]

> If a generation was thirty-three years . . . there would then have been eleven such generations by the time Abram went to Canaan. . . . If each such generation were to experience a 500 percent increase, slightly less than did the first generation . . . then the world population at this time [Abraham's journey] could have been at least 300 million people . . . large enough to account for all the evidence of civilization at that time throughout the world.[20]

Many more aspects of "creationist" interpretation of Genesis 1–11 could be given, and in greater detail. Those who desire greater detail may pursue the matter from the literature cited and with the assistance of Appendix IV.

How, in Henry Morris' perspective, did the materials in Genesis 1–11 originate? In *The Genesis Record,* he proposes that, while Moses actually wrote Exodus-Deuteronomy (which describe events during his own lifetime), "he served mainly as compiler and editor of materials in the Book of Genesis" (which describes events prior to his lifetime). Such materials, handed down to Moses, "give further testimony to the authenticity of the events recorded in Genesis, since we can now recognize them all as firsthand testimony" (p. 26).

By "firsthand testimony" Morris points to eleven passages which begin or end with the expression, "These are the generations of (so-and-so)." Rather than an indication of the subject matter, this indicates to Morris the identity of the author. That is, "This is the book of the generations of Adam" (Gen 5:1) indicates not so much a list of Adam's descendants (which it in fact contains), as it does that Adam himself wrote the material.[21]

Such an approach presents a certain difficulty, of course, in the case of the first instance of the phrase: "These are the generations of the heavens and the earth" (Gen 2:4). Rather than let this be the indication for how all the other instances of the expression are to be understood, "It must either have been written directly by God Himself and then given to Adam, or else given by revelation to Adam, who then recorded it" (p. 28). The former possibility has the advantage of explaining why chapter 1 does not attempt to refute polytheism "or to prove the existence of the true God." Since the text was written prior to human life, "there was no need to argue about the reality of God and Creation, since no one doubted!" (p. 39).[22]

Occasionally, curious departures from such authorship are felt to be necessary. Adam, describing his companion, could write: "And Adam called his wife's name Eve" (Gen 3:20), rather than the natural "I called my wife's name Eve." But how could he then continue, "because she was the mother of all living," using the past tense, when she in fact had not yet given birth to children? Concludes Morris: "This statement was added later as an editorial explanatory insertion, possibly by Moses" (p. 129).

How does the "creationist" understanding of Genesis 1–11 relate to that of the wider spectrum of Christianity? Mention has already been made (in Chapter I) of opposition from "old earthers," and in the present chapter of opposition by "young earthers" to "theistic evolution." (The point here is not to suggest that correctness of interpretation depends upon a plurality of numbers, but rather as a matter of information to enable the reader to locate "creationists" in a larger context.) "Main line" Protestant denominations do not define the inspiration of the Bible (which they do not doubt) in terms such as "verbal" or "infallible in scientific matters." United Methodists, Presbyterians, Episcopalians, and Lutherans generally do not, but Southern Baptists are divided over the issue. To this consensus may be added Roman Catholics, the Orthodox churches, and branches of Judaism. In fact, some of these groups have issued official statements in explicit repudiation of "creationism" (see Appendix V).

In addition to these groups (most of which "creationists" tend to regard as "liberal" or "evolutionist"), "creationists" distinguish themselves from a great many groups which consider themselves to be "conservative" or "evangelical."

> Nevertheless there seem to be an increasing number of evangelical scholars today who are advocating the notion that this section [Gen. 1–11] is only a great hymn, or liturgy, or poem, or saga—anything except real history.[23]

Why is it that the vast majority of interpreters of scripture have not followed the "creationist" route and instead have adopted theistic evolution as compatible with Genesis? As "creationist" Henry Morris explains it:

For almost 150 years now, Christians have been following a strategy of compromise and retreat on these issues. The result of this century-long *effort to purchase a pseudo-respectability* in academic circles at the cost of undermining the Biblical foundations . . . has been a post-Christian world. . . .[24] (emphasis added)

It is high time that Christians face the fact that the so-called geological ages are essentially synonymous with the evolutionary theory of origins. The latter in turn is, at its ultimate roots, the *anti-God conspiracy of Satan himself!*[25] (emphasis added)

Whatever one may think of "creationism" as an interpretation of the Bible, one should not accept the first of these two characterizations. It says, in effect, that if one is not a "creationist," then one is not merely mistaken in the reading of scripture, but also may be lacking in personal integrity, merely desiring the accolades of a certain circle. Such a charge is aimed at a multitude of people, in various denominations, throughout the world, over more than a century of time. Upon what basis does such an astonishingly strident evaluation rest?

What is the evidence, furthermore, that this alleged "compromise" is the cause of a "post-Christian world"? How does one define such a "world"? Large areas of the world have never been Christian to begin with (e.g. the lands of Islam, Hinduism, and Buddhism, among others). How "Christian" were the various areas which are nominally designated "Christian," prior to the reported "compromise and retreat"? What is the entire range of factors which might have contributed to this specified decline? Was it evolution alone? At all? Is it not just possible that such "literalist" interpretations as those of "flat earthers," "old earthers," and "young earthers" have played some role in turning people away from the Bible?

The second characterization (quoted above) appears to be even more problematic. If one wants to oppose evolution, there is no dishonor in saying so, or in presenting the facts as one sees them and letting others decide for themselves. One need not seek to cloak oneself in the guise of piety and inerrancy by characterizing one's opponents as part of an "anti-God conspiracy" when in fact those opponents are overtly theists and Christians at that. Not only is such a statement devoid of any demonstrable basis in fact, but also might be taken as an indication that a weak case is being bolstered by emotion-ridden language.

As illustrations of the range of unwitting participation in Satan's "anti-God conspiracy," namely the acceptance of "the so-called geological ages" (Henry Morris' words), note the following:

1. The widely used *Introduction to the Old Testament* by avowedly "conservative" Protestant R.K. Harrison (professor of Old Testament at Wycliffe

College, University of Toronto): The ages in the early chapters of Genesis "cannot be employed in a purely literal sense as a means of computing the length of the various generations mentioned in the text. Nor is it satisfactory to assume that the various names are those of dynasties or peoples . . ." (p. 152). He goes on to cite archaeological evidence of human habitation dating back 150,000 years (p. 153).

2. The "Chronological Table" in the New Jerusalem Bible (bearing the imprimatur of Cardinal George Basil Hume) begins with *homo habilis* (see Table No. 2) and a date of "2,000,000 BC" (p. 2055). See also the statement by Pope Pius XII (Appendix V) that God's creative act took place "milliards of years ago" (i.e. billions).

"Creationism," then, is one manifestation among others of a literalist interpretation of scripture. It is not the purpose of the present volume to examine the adequacy (or inadequacy) of literalism in general. Rather, in Part Two, the early chapters of Genesis will be examined in a straightforward reading in order to see if "creationism" is in fact in accordance with the intent of scripture, even from a literalist's perspective.

2. "Scientific Creationism" (Also Called "Creation Science")

The near consensus of physical scientists is that the universe is billions of years old, that life emerged gradually from chemical combinations under the right environment (temperature, pressure, radiation, etc.), and that complex organisms evolved from simpler ones by mutation and natural selection (resulting in the emergence of humans a few million years ago).

One may view such an understanding from either a naturalistic or a theistic point of view.[26] A "naturalistic" perspective is secular or materialistic: autonomous matter "behaving according to self-caused and self-governed patterns."[27] This perspective is reflected in the opening words of astronomer Carl Sagan's popular book *Cosmos:* "The cosmos is all that is or ever was or ever will be."[28] By contrast, a "theistic" perspective would affirm that God was creator of the universe (although not necessarily "out of nothing"), that divine governance was responsible for the beginnings of life (even if the chemical combinations therein may be described as "laws" or depicted in equations), and that the increasing complexity of life-forms (resulting in humans) was a manifestation of a divine plan.

The two perspectives are antitheses: the latter is theistic, but the former is a-theistic; the latter is creationist, but the former is non-creationist. Nonetheless, "creationists" ignore the antithesis and equate the two as evolutionist. The true antithesis of both, they say, is anti-evolutionism, and belief in an evolutionary process is tantamount to atheism.[29]

In any case, the traditional scientific ages for the universe (twenty to ten billion years old) and the earth (perhaps five billion years old) collide with a literal reading of Genesis which may indicate that all things were created as recently as six thousand years ago. Can such a divergence be resolved with a literal reading of the Bible intact? "Creationists" vigorously proclaim that it can.

All the genuine facts of science support Biblical creationism and all the statements in the Bible are consistent with scientific creationism.[30]

The fact is that scientific creationism is perfectly compatible with Biblical creation. The latter . . . certainly does not contradict any scientific facts.[31]

There is scientific evidence for creation from cosmology, thermodynamics, paleontology, biology, mathematical probability, geology, and other sciences.[32]

The contrasts between the "creation model" and the "evolution model" include the following (Table No. 1).[33]

TABLE 1. Antitheses Proposed by "Creationists"

"Creation Model"	*"Evolution Model"*
1. Universe created suddenly	Universe "emerged by naturalistic processes"
2. Sudden creation of life	Life emerged from prior non-living substances by "naturalistic processes"
3. All living "kinds" (both plants and animals) have "remained fixed"; genetic variations happen only within "kinds"	Simple living organisms evolved into complex ones: from single cells to vertebrates, including humans
4. Humans and apes "have separate ancestry"	Humans and apes emerged from a "common ancestor"
5. The earth's geologic features (e.g. mountains) were largely fashioned by catastrophes of a global scale (e.g. flooding) over a short period of time	The earth's geologic features were formed largely by gradual processes over extremely long period of time
6. The origin of the earth was "relatively recent"[34]	The formation of the earth was billions of years ago

Since the claims for "scientific creationism" have been adequately investigated by other writers[35] and since the focus of the present volume is upon "biblical creationism," these antitheses will be but briefly examined here.

Antitheses 1 and 2 present the well known "creationist" claim that an evolutionary process is of necessity to be understood as a naturalistic one. This understanding is spelled out by Duane Gish:

> Since evolutionary theory is an attempt to explain origins by a process of self-transformation involving only naturalistic and mechanistic processes, God is unnecessary and so excluded from the process. . . . By definition, evolution is a strictly mechanistic, naturalistic, and, therefore, atheistic process.[36]

In actuality, such a definition is nothing other than the in-house convention of "creationist" literature. This is clear from generations of scientists and theologians who have advocated theistic evolution[37] and from official proclamations by major factions of Christianity which decisively repudiate "creationism" on biblical and theological grounds (see Appendix V). Van Till states the opposing point of view with clarity:

> The biblical theist knows that to affirm the authenticity of the regular patterns of material behavior that we can empirically discover in the Creation does not entail the denial of the reality of divine governance. The biblical theist perceives, through the spectacles of Scripture, that these orderly patterns of behavior are in fact a revelation of the faithful and lawful governance of the material world by the Creator. The patterned behavior of matter must not be viewed as a substitute for or an alternative to divine action; it must be perceived as evidence for divine governance.[38]

From the standpoint of biblical theism, "evolutionary processes are not distinguishable from other material processes. . . . And we know that no natural process ought ever to be viewed as inherently naturalistic."[39] Thus to contrast "creation" (presupposing deity and governance) with naturalism (autonomous matter) is not the same as to contrast "creation" and "evolution." To do so is to use words in defiance of their commonly understood meaning in the community of theologians.

A "creation model" need not necessarily presuppose, contrary to "creationists," that such divine activity came about "suddenly." From the biblical evidence, on the one hand, it is not at all clear that creation of matter was "out of nothing" (*ex nihilo*) or that it was instantaneous (see below, Chapter VI and Appendix X). From a scientific point of view, on the other hand, whether the universe is "creation" or not is beyond the goal or ability of the scientific method to address. The physical sciences, as they pertain to the history of the universe, are properly concerned with physical properties, physical processes, and formative events, all within a system whose existence is taken for granted.[40] The universe simply "is," and it is no more scientific to call it "creation" than it is to deny that it is "creation." The question of ultimate origins lies beyond the domain of scientific method, although scientists may make plausible conjectures about this matter and come to opposing conclusions. Thus, when the astronomer Carl Sagan remarks that "The cosmos is all that is or ever was or ever will be,"[41] one might ask of him no less than of a "scientific creationist": "Scientifically speaking, how do you *know* that?"

The description (in the "evolution model") that the universe "emerged" presumably derives from the fact that the "steady-state theory" of cosmic history, once confidently proposed, has now been abandoned. That theory, usually associated with the thought of British astronomer Sir Fred Hoyle, proposed that the universe (consisting of matter-energy totality which may shift from one type to the other) has no beginning or end. Matter is continuously being spontaneously formed (in innerstellar space) and being destroyed (in stellar evolution).[42] This view has been replaced, in the thought of most astronomers, with the "big-bang theory," wherein the universe suddenly emerged from the gigantic explosion (some twenty to ten billion years ago) of an immensely compact collection of matter (which may have resulted from the collapse of a previous universe).[43] "Creationists" reject this approach (as well as the former one), in part because of the immense time involved (which contradicts a literal biblical chronology)[44] and in part because (to their thinking) it "flatly contradicts the Second Law of Thermodynamics."[45]

It is concerning *Antithesis 3* that "creationists" and their detractors have "spoiled the most ink." The issue is whether all living things have evolved from single-celled ancestors over vast periods of time or whether distinct "kinds" were created and all co-existed in the last few thousand years.

"Creationists" assert that transitional forms ("missing links" which evolutionary biologists presuppose to have existed) have in fact not been found in the fossil record, and thus that concrete evidence of evolution from "lower" to "higher" forms of life ("macro-evolution") does not exist.[46] The kinds of evolution that can be observed ("micro-evolution") are far more limited and apparently remain within a "type," where there is enough genetic potential to allow for all known variations (e.g. skin coloration in humans or subgroups of fruit flies).

Real evolution (macroevolution) requires the *expansion* of the gene pool, the *addition* of new genes and new traits as life is supposed to move from simple beginnings to ever more varied and complex forms ("molecules to man" or "fish to philosopher").[47]

"Creationists," like evolutionists when they speak of "species," associate the term "types" with groups that normally interbreed. The equivalent assertion, in "biblical creationism," rests upon the statement that God created animals "according to their kinds" (Gen 1:21, 24–25). This has occasionally given rise, in "creationist" publications, to the term "baramins" for distinct types.[48]

"Creationists" also affirm that the great ages (millions and even billions of years) which "evolutionists" assign to the earth were not derived from detached scientific evidence, but rather have been postulated in order to provide sufficient time for supposed macro-evolution to take place.[49] Subsequent techniques for placing such ages on a solid scientific basis are not regarded to be reliable.

The sparcity of transitional forms has indeed led a few proponents of "traditional" evolutionary understandings to remark that "The fossil record with its abrupt transitions offers no support for gradual change. . . ." They propose sudden "jumps" in order to account for macro-evolution,[50] a process which they have designated as "punctuated equilibria."[51]

This new approach is likewise being rejected by "creationists," since they are willing to acknowledge micro-evolution only. Macro-evolution would require "profound structural transitions," as opposed to mutations which produce "only minor variations." No accumulation of mutations ("hopeful monsters") can lead to the former.[52]

> At least the hopeful monster concept avoids the problem of missing links. But notice: this new concept of evolution is based on fossils we *don't* find and on genetic mechanisms that have never been observed. The case for creation is based on thousands of tons of fossils that we *have* found and on genetic mechanisms (variations within type) that we do observe. . . .[53]

Readers of the present volume who wish to pursue this aspect of the debate should do so with the assistance of the secondary literature previously cited and especially by reading Strahler, Part VI.

Antithesis 4 concerns the biological relationship (or lack thereof) between humans and animals of all types. This is a very complicated issue, focusing upon paleontology (comparison of fossils), comparative anatomy, and molecular biology (chemical similarity).

The paleontological and comparative anatomy issue is whether hominoids (the genus *Homo,* "man") can be fitted developmentally into the family Hominidae and thus part of the primate order (which includes the greater and lesser apes). (See Table No. 2.) Most recently, attention has been focused upon the discovery of remains that reportedly are millions of years old and which have been assigned to a new genus, *Australopithecus*. Popular awareness of this group of Hominidae has focused upon a female skelton assigned to the (new) species *Australopithecus afarensis*, whom the discoverer (Johanson) named "Lucy" because he had recently been listening to a Beatles' song entitled "Lucy in the Sky with Diamonds."[54] Those readers who wish to pursue this aspect of the debate will find a "creationist" perspective in Morris and Parker[55] and the "evolution model" (with detailed rejection of "creationism") in Strahler.[56]

The other area of research and debate (molecular biology) examines the possibility of evolutionary development of species (phylogeny) by compar-

TABLE 2.

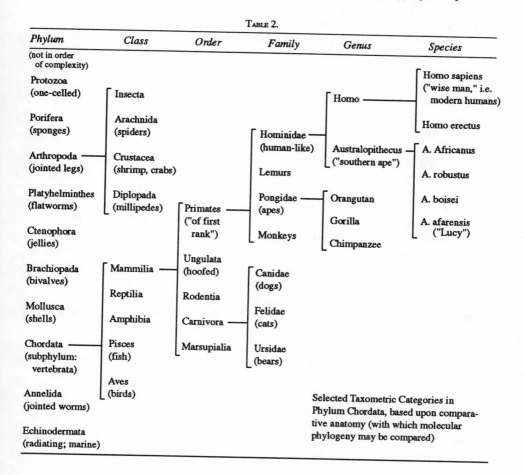

Phylum	Class	Order	Family	Genus	Species
(not in order of complexity)					
Protozoa (one-celled)	Insecta			Homo	Homo sapiens ("wise man," i.e. modern humans)
Porifera (sponges)	Arachnida (spiders)		Hominidae (human-like)		Homo erectus
Arthropoda (jointed legs)	Crustacea (shrimp, crabs)		Lemurs	Australopithecus ("southern ape")	A. Africanus
					A. robustus
Platyhelminthes (flatworms)	Diplopada (millipedes)	Primates ("of first rank")	Pongidae (apes)	Orangutan	A. boisei
Ctenophora (jellies)			Monkeys	Gorilla	A. afarensis ("Lucy")
				Chimpanzee	
Brachiopada (bivalves)	Mammilia	Ungulata (hoofed)	Canidae (dogs)		
Mollusca (shells)	Reptilia	Rodentia	Felidae (cats)		
	Amphibia	Carnivora			
Chordata (subphylum: vertebrata)	Pisces (fish)	Marsupialia	Ursidae (bears)		
Annelida (jointed worms)	Aves (birds)				
Echinodermata (radiating; marine)					

Selected Taxometric Categories in Phylum Chordata, based upon comparative anatomy (with which molecular phylogeny may be compared)

ing aspects of their body chemistry. For example, all proteins are made of building blocks known as amino acids, of which there are about twenty kinds in nature. Each species differs slightly in the structure and sequence of its amino acids, even from others in the same genus (e.g. presumably *Homo sapiens* from the extinct *Homo erectus*). The difference is greater when comparison is made with a species from another genus (e.g. *Homo sapiens* vs. a gorilla), and greater still when comparison is made with a species from a different family (e.g. *Homo sapiens* vs. a lemur).

A number of such chemical analyses (not only amino acid sequences, but also immunological response comparisons and DNA comparisons) can be used to construct phylogenetic "family trees" of the organisms tested (now numbering in the thousands). The results are not only compatible with each other, but also they match rather well the older "tree" that has been constructed on the basis of fossils and comparative anatomy (Table No. 2). For example, the so-called "binding ratio" of human DNA strands (a measure of similarity) is one hundred percent for the chimpanzee (taxonomic difference only back to the family level), eighty-eight percent for the rhesus monkey (superfamily level), forty-seven percent for the lemur (suborder level), twenty-one percent for the mouse (order level: primate vs. rodent), and ten percent for the chicken (class level: mammal vs. aves/bird).

Those readers who desire to pursue the debate about what such differences and similarities mean in terms of evolution will find a "creationist" position presented by Knaub and Parker[57] and a non-"creationist" response (in great detail and with many helpful charts) in Strahler.[58]

Antithesis 5 is one of the more interesting of the series of "creationist" opposites. It includes the conclusion that the various sedimentary (water deposited) layers (strata) of the earth's rocks were formed rapidly in succession, one after the other, by "a constant set of hydraulic factors which cannot remain constant very long."[59] (By "a constant set of hydraulic factors" is meant something approximating the flood as related in the Bible.) By contrast, the "evolution model" concludes that individual strata may have been formed by distinct processes and that considerable time may have passed between the conclusion of one and the onset of the next. Such "distinct processes" include slow deposition (as in the case of coral reefs); lake deposits (which are formed by slow fine-grained sedimentation as opposed to swift course-grained river deposits); glacial deposits that have subsequently cemented into firm rock (tillite); eolian (wind laden) deposits (dunes) that result from the slow abrasion of bedrock; and evaporite deposits of such water soluble minerals as halite (salt), gypsum, and anhydrite (formed, for example, when the sea retreats and leaves behind vast pools of mineral laden water). Thus one might conclude:

The sedimentary rock record is replete with rocks that formed in glacial, lake, desert, reef, evaporite, and other environments that are utterly impossible to reconcile with the Flood hypothesis. These deposits all formed in environments that take considerable time to develop. They all point to the fact that the Earth is far more than just a few thousand years old as creationists would have us believe.[60]

It is especially important to notice whether the surface of a given stratum blends smoothly into the one above it, or whether it evidences erosion. Such erosion, if present, would suggest that there was a chronological break between the two formations rather than both resulting from a continuous rather uniform process. Extended discussion of this issue, with multiple instances of such erosion, may be found in Wonderly's volume. He is an "old earth" creationist who berates the ("young earth") "creationists" for lack of field training and awareness of geological realities. Speaking of the issue under discussion, he remarks:

Even longer periods of erosion occurred *between* the deposition of *formations.* That is, we find, within the rock record, areas where there was extensive ancient erosion of the *upper* layers of various formations before the next formations above them were added. In some cases, there was even a change of slope of the depositional basin floor before the next formation was added. . . . It should surely be obvious that such erosional surfaces represent long periods of time, not only for the erosion process, but also for the cementation of the rock layers that were eroded. This cementation requires long periods of time, as will be explained in the sections which follow.[61]

Related to this antithesis (and also to no. 6) is the chronological implication of how fossils of plants and animals are distributed throughout the superimposed strata of the earth's rocks (the so-called geological column). Such fossils, rather than occurring at random in the tremendous depths (sometimes thousands of feet) of the strata, are in fact found in related groups (geologic systems) that change as one progresses vertically from one stratum to the next. In general, the change is from lesser to greater complexity of living organism as the column is studied from bottom to top. There are thirteen such systems (periods), as illustrated on the accompanying Table (No. 3). These strata are found across the surface of the earth, although one or more of them may be missing at a given location. (Perhaps the most visible illustration of the superimposed strata occurs in the Grand Canyon, where five of the twelve layers are in evidence.)

According to the evolutionary model, the various strata represent stages

TABLE 3. Postcambrian Time Scale
(Phanerozoic Eon)

Era	Period	Epoch	Years Ago	Characteristics
Cenozoic	Quaternary	Holocene	10,000–present	warming of climate, beginning of agriculture, village life, civilization
		Pleistocene	1.6 million–10,000	glaciation, paleolithic culture, *Homo sapiens* appears
	Neogene (Tertiary)	Pliocene	5.3–1.6 million	Australopithecus appears
		Miocene	23.7–5.3 million	*Ramapithecus* appears
		Oligocene	36.6–23.7 million	saber-toothed cats appear; *Aegyptopithecus*
	Paleogene (Tertiary)	Eocene	57.8–36.6 million	early horse and carnivores
		Paleocene	66.4–57.8 million	dinosaurs extinct; first primates
Mesozoic	Cretaceous		144–66.4 million	Rocky Mtns. formed; flowering plants
	Jurassic		208–144 million	breakup of Pangaea; conifers
	Triassic		245–208 million	trilobites extinct; dinosaurs; volcanoes
Paleozoic	Permian		286–245 million	
	Pennsylvanian (Carboniferous)		320–286 million	warm climate; swamps; coal beds form; large reptiles and insects
	Mississipian (Carboniferous)		360–320 million	land mass increases; coal beds; ammon-ides; winged insects; amphibians
	Devonian		408–360 million	forests; fishes
	Silurian		438–408 million	land plants
	Ordovician		505–438 million	invertebrates flourish
	Cambrian		507–505 million	"explosion" of life in the seas

Ages based upon Faure, *Principles of Isotope Geology,* Appendix I. See also Strahler, *Science and Earth History,* Figures 20.30, 31.2, and 32.12.

in the development of the earth and of life in particular: from simple (early) to complex (recent), over vast periods of time. For example, trilobites belong mostly to the Cambrian and Ordovician Periods, and became extinct before the dinosaurs appeared (evolved) in the Triassic Period. To descend into the time: from the ages of mammals (Quaternary and Tertiary), through those of dinosaurs (Cretacious, Jurassic, and Triassic), and beyond. Ultimately, one would descend beyond the time of the "Cambrian Explosion" of life and reach the pre-Paleozoic Era where simple life-forms existed, and beyond (below) that to igneous rock where no life-forms are evident.

According to the "creationist" model, all known types of plants and animals co-existed on the earth only a short time ago, but they inhabited different ecological zones (with some overlap, of course). That is, sea creatures were limited to a given realm, there were plants and animals particular to lowland swamps or to the highlands, and so on. Otherwise put: trilobites, dinosaurs, and humans were contemporaries on the young earth, but were not necessarily in regular contact with each other. Consequently, one would not expect to find their fossilized remains to be intermingled, but rather to be separated vertically as a consequence of their separate eco-systems. The stratigraphic record, then, does not reflect a sequence of vast chronological eras (ages), but rather divergent but contemporary living-zones. "A walk through the Grand Canyon, then, is *not* like a walk through evolutionary time; instead [from bottom to top], it's like a walk from the bottom of the ocean, across the tidal zone, over the shore, across the lowlands, and on into the upland regions."[62]

The "creationist" model, then, involves two major departures from the evolutionary model: (1) life did not evolve, whether gradually or by sudden leaps ("punctuated equilibria"), in the sense of macro-evolution, and (2) there was no time-lapse from the appearance of one plant or animal "type" to another, regardless of their relative complexity. Although the two departures are linked in "creationist" thought, it is important to realize that they are not necessarily related, as if one were the necessary corollary of the other. That is, in theory one could propose that the sudden emergence of a distinct "type," in the absence of transitional forms, suggests "creation" (or at least denies evolution), and yet allow for vast amounts of time before the next such appearance. This means that in order to bring the two departures into congruence, the methods by which evolutionists and "old earth" creationists have assigned great ages to the various strata must be denied scientific accuracy and furthermore that the number of catastrophes (capable of producing fossilization of a vast scale) must be reduced to a minimum (preferably one).

The evolutionary model proposes that a number of factors (largely regional) have been at work, over vast periods of time ("uniformitarianiam"), in the production of the geological column: continental drift, climatic changes (e.g. glaciation), local flooding (e.g. in Mesopotamia which have given rise to stories of "the flood"[63]), volcanic activity, uplift of the earth's crust (creating mountains and driving back the sea), and so on. The various stages can be placed in a relative historical sequence and given an absolute date.

By contrast, "creationists" propose changes on a worldwide scale ("catastrophism") and flooding in particular as the key to fossil formation. How many such catastrophes were there, and to which of them may the various strata of the earth be assigned? About this "creationists" disagree, but the idea of a major cataclysm is common.

The concept of a single global hydraulic cataclysm accounting for all or most of the geologic column . . . would in effect not only eliminate the geologic-ages concept, but destroy the entire chronological framework of the basic Evolution Model. . . . Consequently, evolutionists of all stripes vigorously resist the idea of a worldwide hydraulic cataclysm, even though they are now quite amenable to any number of intermittent regional catastrophes.

Nevertheless, the Cataclysmic Model can be shown to be a very effective model for explaining all the real data of the geological column.[64]

(The biblical "cat" may not be "out of the [scientific] bag" here, but the feline features of Noah's flood are beginning to be discernible!)

How might the present arrangement of fossils in the geological column have come about as the result of a single catastrophic flood? Why does one not find the remains of trilobites, dinosaurs, and humans intermixed, since they would all have perished at the same time? The "creationist" proposal is that plant and animal remains came to rest in discernible layers of sediment according to (1) the elevation of natural habitat (e.g. the waters reached the domain of mountain goats a bit later than that of marsh dwellers), (2) ability to flee from the rising waters (e.g. humans might climb to presumably safer heights that a dinosaur could not reach), and (3) "increasing resistance to hydrodynamic forces and therefore an increasing tendency to be transported farther and deposited more slowly" (presumably this means that some creatures could "tread water" longer than others and that some corpses floated more readily than other types).[65]

A few moments of detached reflection may reveal the tremendous difficulties which this proposal for fossil distribution entails. I here list only a few of a general and obvious nature, but a great number involving specificity of species could be given.[66]

1. Human remains are limited to the uppermost strata (the Quaternary Period). While it is true that, as the waters of a flood arose, many might have fled to higher ground and would have been able to swim for a while before drowning, surely some lowland dwellers would have been overcome (especially the aged, deformed, and infants) and thus their remains be found in deeply submerged strata. In any case, what of the remains of those who died and were buried prior to this supposed cataclysm? (Or is it *necessary* to suppose that all corpses had been carried to the heights for interment?)

2. Why are the remains of dinosaurs concentrated in the Cretaceous, Jurassic, and Triassic Periods, regardless of their body shape, size, or natural habitat? Would we not expect those which were acclimated to the sea (e.g. Elasmosaurus) to survive a cataclysm of water at least as well as humans and for remains of the two groups to be intermingled? It is unreasonable to expect that at least *one* dinosaur (especially those which inhabited the lowlands at the border of the oceans) would have been swept onto the floor of the sea and that the *total* accumulation of sediment from a great flood would be deposited above it (e.g. it would be found in strata no higher than the Cambrian Period)?

3. Why are mammalian porpoises found only in the upper strata, whereas fishes of similar size and strength are found much lower (and some such species *only* much lower)? While all such carcasses might have floated in flood waters for a week or so (especially with the aid of buoyancy caused by internal gases as the flesh decayed), they would with equal facility have plunged to the bottom when their abdomens ruptured and would now be intermingled at the same level.

The matter is succinctly put by Strahler (p. 454), speaking of the fact that rock strata which evolutionists designate "Cretaceous" and "Tertiary" (see Table No. 3) contain fossilized remains that are unique to themselves.

> For reasons unknown and perhaps impossible to imagine [in the "creation-ist" perspective], the new taxa represented by the Tertiary strata would have had to remain in suspension in the floodwaters while the taxa that failed to pass the K-T [Cretaceous-Tertiary] boundary would have an op-portunity to settle out first. This selective settling must have been perfect, for there are no representatives of the extinct Mesozoic reptilian and other groups above the K-T boundary. If hydraulic stratigraphy was governed by differences in settling velocity, the separation we observe would be totally impossible. Corpses of titanotheres and mastodonts (and all the Tertiary animals) would have had to remain suspended until every last corpse of the Mesozoic reptiles (and of all other Mesozoic organisms, including the Me-sozoic marine zooplankton) was laid to rest in bottom sediment. This segregation requirement would have had to be repeated for every one of the major and minor extinctions in the geologic record and for all occurrences of individual extinctions at various times throughout the record.

For a while, some "creationists" affirmed that stratigraphic evidence of the simultaneous existence of dinosaurs and humans had actually been found.

> Even more dramatic are the finds of fossil footprints in the Paluxy River bed near Glen Rose, Texas. These prints are much more obviously human than Mary Leakey's [found in East Africa by her in the late 1970's and dated to be about 3.6 million years old, but still millions of years later than the age of dinosaurs by the same dating system]. . . .
>
> And that's the problem: Where they were found. I almost hate to bring this up. All of us were taught, from grade school onward, to believe that dinosaurs died out millions of years before man appeared. But sure enough, here are those human-like footprints in the Paluxy River bed— you guessed it—crisscrossing the tracks of dinosaurs! . . .
>
> Now I've done it. You can just drop the book, saying, "Some crazy, crack-pot Californian wrote that the Flintstones were real!"[67]

The author then encourages readers to check the evidence for themselves, mentions published volumes on the topic[68] as well as films (one done "as part of a post-graduate degree in film arts"), reports that casts of the footprints may be viewed in ICR's Museum of Creation and Earth History in San Diego, observes that "anti-creationists are beginning to take pot shots" at the well known tracks (e.g. Harvard University geologist Stephen Jay Gould), and concludes with satisfaction that the doubts (of genuineness) are not substantial.

In retrospect, it appears that the entire episode is a dismal chronicle of marred and removed "evidence," changing accounts by observers, misinterpretation of natural features, and "artificially chiseled giant mantracks."[69] The case has become so weak that even John Morris (son of the author quoted above) observed:

> In view of these developments, none of the four trails at the Taylor site [on the Paluxy River] can today be regarded as unquestionably of human origin. . . . Trails and prints elsewhere along the Paluxy . . . may be insufficient to stand alone. . . .
>
> Even though it would now be improper for creationists to continue to use the Paluxy data as evidence against evolution . . . continued research is in order.[70]

The reason why mainstream geologists and biologists (under the "Evolution Model") assign increasingly great ages to strata as one descends the geological column is not merely to provide sufficient time for evolution to have taken place (contrary to the "creationist" charge which is reported above). Long before the publication of Charles Darwin's *On the Origin of Species* (1859), even devout members of the church were aware that the various rock strata had not been deposited at once but rather that much time had passed between the formation of each.[71] Niels Steensen (1638–1686) observed cases where erosion had taken place in a given stratum prior to the superpositioning of the next one. Jean Etienne Guettard (1715–1786) observed an abundance of extinct volcanoes in central France, for which there was no written record, and wondered if they preceded human history. Nicholas Desmarest (1735–1815) observed that hardened lava flows in the same area of France had been subsequently deeply eroded by streams of water before being covered by another eruption, thus mandating an extensive period of time between the flows. Georges Louis Leclerc, Comte de Buffon (1707–1788), supposing that the earth had been torn from the sun by a passing comet, set about to calculate its age based upon observable rates of heat loss: spheres were heated to a white heat and the time of cooling noted, and then extrapolations were made for a sphere the size of the earth, with the result being about 75,000 years. Be this estimate accurate or not, the point is that such early calculations of age had nothing to do with "allowing time for evolution to take place." A bit later, in the nineteenth century, however, that factor seems indeed to have been taken into account. Nonetheless, specific figures, in the millions of years, were based upon rates of observable erosion, thickness of deposited sediments, the concentration of dissolved elements in sea water, the rate of heat loss from a cooling earth, and so on.

It was the discovery of radioactivity by the French physicist Henri Antoine Becquerel in 1896 that would lead to modern standard scientific estimates of the age of the earth. Certain elements (initially uranium) were observed to decay at a constant measurable rate which was independent of external conditions (e.g. pressure and temperature). By measuring the amount of such decay that had taken place in a given specimen of mineral or rock, it was proposed that an absolute age for that specimen could be calculated. Since the formation of rocks goes back to the early history of the earth, a possible means was at hand for determining a minimal age for "when it all began." Initial estimates were in the range of tens to hundreds of millions of years, but recent refinements of the technique have centered upon an age of four and a half billion years (regardless of whether the specimens be from earth, the moon, or meteorites).

Readers who desire to understand how radiometric techniques are carried out, what the "creationist" objections to their accuracy are, and how mainstream geologists respond to those objections, may pursue the matter with the aid of Appendix VI and the sources cited there. The present discussion will be limited to a single demonstration that radiometric dates are a *reliable* indication that the ages of the earth's strata increase as one proceeds downward. (That is, such strata are not the result of a single cataclysm, even if the individual radiometric ages should not be precisely accurate.)

Consider the fact that the Geological Survey of Canada has used the potassium-argon method (based upon micas in igneous and metamorphic rocks) to construct a time scale for the Precambrian Period. (For the Cambrian and later periods, characterized by sedimentary rocks and fossils of plants and animals, see Table No. 3.) The dates have been refined by the rubidium-strontium and the uranium-thorium-lead methods, so that there is independent attestation of their accuracy (see Appendix VI). The results are shown in Table No. 4.

"Creationists" affirm that the earth is only a few thousand years old (ten thousand being about the maximum figure). Thus, they would propose that a radiometric date for igneous rock just prior to the Cambrian Period (570 million years ago) is in error by a factor of 5700! (That is: divide the radiometric age by 5700 to get the "true" age.) Such a rate of error would be truly astonishing, but let us grant for the moment that it is so. We now turn to a rock

TABLE 4. Precambrian Time Scale

	Eon	Era	Sub-era	Years Ago	Characteristics
Cryptozoic Eon	Proterozoic	Hadrynian	Late	620–570 million	ozone layer begins to form;
			Early	1000–620 million	multi-celled animals diversify in the seas
		Helikian	Neo	1.4–1 billion	blue-green algae form stromatolites; continental lithosphere growing;
			Paleo	1.75–1.4 billion	Gondwana being formed; carbonate rocks being formed
		Aphebian	Late	1.87–1.75 billion	development of oxygen-releasing algae; continental lithosphere growing
			Middle	2.14–1.87 billion	
			Early	2.51–2.14 billion	
	Archean		Late	2.67–2.51 billion	
			Late Middle	2.9–2.67 billion	oldest undoubted fossils (algae);
			Late Middle	3.4–2.9 billion	primitive atmosphere (no oxygen); oldest questionable fossils;
			Early	(5?)–3.4 billion	oldest known earth rock (3.8 billion); earth's crust forms; primitive oceans form; oldest moon rock (4.6 billion)

Terminology and dates from Geological Survey of Canada (Faure, *Principles of Isotope Geology*, Figure 6.6). Descriptions based on Strahler, *Science and Earth History*, Figure 20.30.

sample from the older Proterozoic-Archean boundary, radiometrically dated to 2.51 billion years. However, its "true" age, applying the aforementioned correction factor (i.e. dividing by 5700), should be 44,000 years. "Not so!" a "creationist" must object. "The correction factor must have changed for this rock, being now 251,000!" For the sake of argument let us grant this as well and turn to the earliest known rock (radiometrically dated to 4.6 billion years). Is its "true" age now 8,070,000 years (first correction factor), or is it now a mere 18,000 (second correction factor)? "Neither!" the "creationist" should now say. "You must now correct the radiometric date by a factor of 460,000!" Similarly, and more dramatically, the correction factor would change for each Period of the Postcambrian Time Scale (for which see Table No. 3).

Now, if "creationists" believed that the superimposed strata of the earth's rocks had been formed in many individual stages over a considerable period of time, they might be able to argue that the rate of radioactive decay (half-life) of the elements upon which radiometric dating is based had changed repeatedly with time. (They might be hard pressed to demonstrate how this could be, given current knowledge of nuclear physics, however.) But since they believe, instead, that the strata were formed in a very short time (the sedimentary ones as a consequence of perhaps a single cataclysm of the Noah's flood type), there is no conceivable reason why the "correction factor" should shift by multiples of thousands from one moment to the next (shifting in such a way as erroneously to indicate greater age as one descends the geological column, save for instances of overlapping strata, broken and dislocated strata, folding of strata, and so on).

In short, radiometric dating does indicate increasing great ages as one descends the geological column, just as "mainline" geology proposes that it should. There seems little doubt, then, that radiometric dates are a genuine measure of the age of rocks: clearly a reliable *relative* chronology (sequence: "this" is earlier than "that"), if not an *absolute* one. For such an instrument of measure to err by a small factor (10?) might not be surprising—but by hundreds of thousands?

Antithesis 6 is related to the previous one, in that the method of dating is the same (radiometric). A related matter is the age of the universe, often discussed in "creationist" literature, where quite different methods apply.

Of the several lines of evidence that astronomers propose for determination of this span of time, it is perhaps the so-called "red shift" that is best known to non-specialists in the field.[72] Since this is commonly understood to be a type of Doppler Effect,[73] it can be used in accordance with well-known principles of physics to calculate distance, velocity, and time.

The method begins with the observation that light travels at a finite and measurable speed, roughly 186,000 miles per second in a vacuum. It thus takes a given particle of light about eight minutes to travel from the sun (which is about 93 million miles away) to the earth. The consequence is that one cannot see the sun itself, but only the light that arrives from it, i.e. the sun as it appeared eight minutes previously. Were the sun suddenly to disappear, viewers on earth would continue to see it for that period of time. This is sometimes called the "lookback time." Thus, if one could determine the "lookback time" of more distant celestial objects, one would know a minimum time for their existence. For example, if we could know that the only galaxy outside our own (the Milky Way) that is visible to the naked eye (M31 in the constellation Andromeda) is 11.6 million trillion miles distant (the distance that light travels in two million years, known as two million light-years), then we could say that the "lookback time" of the galaxy (and the minimum age of the universe) is two million years. As it turns out, M31 is relatively close and many objects are at vastly greater distances. Today's newspaper (November 20, 1989), for example, contains a report of the discovery of the most distant object yet detected: a radio-source (quasar) that is fourteen billion light-years away, formed about a "billion years after the beginning of the universe."

Briefly stated, this method of determination of distance and age works as follows. The color of a light is a reflection of its wavelength or speed of vibration: the faster the vibration (or the shorter the wavelength), the more it will be toward the blue end of the visible spectrum; the slower the vibration (or the longer the wavelength), the more it will be toward the red end of the spectrum. (Waves of red light are in the vicinity of .000065 centimeter [6500 angstrom units] each, while those of blue light are .000047 [4700]. Otherwise put: the red source is vibrating about 46 trillion times per second, and the blue one about 64 trillion times per second.)

If a source of light is approaching a viewer, the wavelength will be compressed (shortened) and thus it will appear to shift toward the blue end of the spectrum (appear to be bluer than it actually is). On the other hand, if the source is moving away, the wavelength will be lengthened so that the color will appear to shift toward the red end of the spectrum. Hence the designation "red shift" for the latter situation.

Two analogies will perhaps make the matter clear. First, consider the well known case of the person who stands beside a railway track and listens to the whistle as the locomotive approaches, passes by, and moves away: the pitch will suddenly drop as the train passes. The higher pitch, as the whistle approached, is comparable to the compressed wavelength (blue shift) of an oncoming light; the lower pitch as it departs is comparable to the elongated wavelength (red shift) of a receding light.

A second analogy would be the consequences of pebbles that drop sequentially into a container of water. If the source of pebbles is stationary, the result would be a series of concentric waves (crests) that spread evenly from the single point of impact. Wherever an observer stood, the appearance would be the same as that shown in Figure 1. If, however, the source of pebbles were approaching a stationary observer (at point A on Figure 2), then the center of each successive ring (wave) (numbered 1–6) would be closer to the observer and the incoming crests would appear to be compressed (shifted toward a briefer interval between arrivals at the rim of the container). An observer at point B, on the other hand, would see that the period between the crests had grown longer.

Next, one must know that each element or compound, when heated, emits light with a characteristic color. The wavelength/frequency is so specific that it serves as a signature of the elements present. With the assistance of a spectroscope (essentially a prism which enables an incoming beam of light to be broken into its color components), the wavelength of each element will be marked at a specific place on a graph. (That of calcium, for example, is 3933.664 and 3968.470 angstrom units.) The resultant spectro-

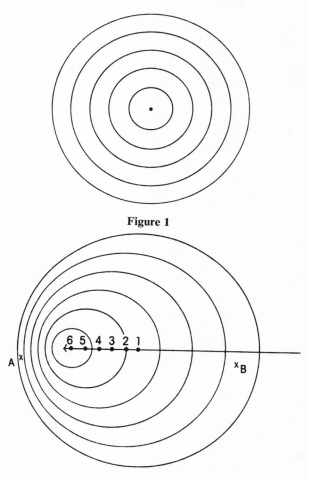

Figure 1

Figure 2

Figures 1 and 2. An Analogy Illustrating the Doppler Effect. In Figure 1, a series of pebbles is dropped into a container of water, producing a series of wave crests that spread toward the edge. Regardless of where an observer is stationed, the space between the waves will be the same. In Figure 2, however, the point from which the pebbles are released (numbered 1–6) grows closer to an observer at point "A" and farther from an observer at point "B." As a consequence, the wave crests approaching "A" will have less time between them than those approaching "B." (From Carl Sagan, *Cosmos,* p. 252, who uses the diagrams to illustrate the same consequence for a source of light or sound.) If the "red shift" (of light) is a Doppler Effect, then an observer at "B" would know that the source (a star or galaxy) was moving away (from points 1–6 and beyond) at a measurable rate of speed and distance.

graph is thus a record of the constituent makeup of the light source (e.g. a star or galaxy). One can thus learn that the sun contains calcium, hydrogen, iron, magnesium, sodium, and so on.

When light from quite distant stellar objects is subjected to spectroscopic analysis, the signatures (Fraunhofer lines) shift toward the red end of the scale by a measurable amount. According to the Doppler Effect, this indicates that the light source is receding from the earth. For example, the spectrum of the faint star Delta Leporis (in the constellation the Hare) has the K-line of calcium displaced by 1.298 angstroms toward the red. This indicates that the star's speed is a modest 61.4 miles (or 99 kilometers) per second.[74]

Finally, this velocity can be used to calculate the star's distance from the earth: 6.6 million light-years.[75] This, then, is the star's "lookback time": we are seeing it as it appeared 6.6 million years ago, so it (and the universe) is at least that old.

Such indications are devastating to the "creationist" proposal that the universe is "relatively recent." Otherwise put: "If the stars are only six to ten thousand years old, as we 'creationists' think they are, the light from these distant galaxies would not have even reached us yet." Consequently, "solutions" are necessary.[76]

1. Perhaps the speed of light (now about 186,000 miles per second) has not always been constant. "One suggestion is that the speed . . . (was) 5×10^{11} (500 billion) times faster [than now] 6000 years ago. If this is true, light from a 5 billion light-year star . . . would have reached us in 3 days!" [Unfortunately for the case being made, the "one suggestion" is cited to another "creationist" source, and baseless "suggestions" do not constitute scientific evidence.]

2. "Light may take a 'shortcut' as it travels through space," arriving from near infinite distances (following Riemannian curvature of space) in about fifteen years. [The previous evaluation applies.]

3. "There are Biblical indications that the earth and the universe were created with the *appearance* of age" (emphasis added). Examples include those plants, animals, and humans that "were created fully mature" in Genesis 1–2. This non-scientific argument is taken to suggest that the stars, whatever their distance from the earth at their moment of creation, "were seen on the first day of their existence" (or could have been seen, were there humans to do so). "Therefore, the stars and the light beams connecting them visually to the Earth were both created at the same time." [This hardly helps the "creationist" case, since such light would presumably be the normal spectrum rather than a "red shifted" one caused by massive velocity away from the earth. A "creationist" could go on to say, of course, since there are no boundaries upon *speculation,* that God adjusted the incoming wavelength of each of the untold billions of stars in accordance with the velocity it was to

assume, just *as if* it had originated from a central cosmic explosion ("big bang") billions of years before.]

This third "solution" takes one from the domain of "scientific creationism" to that of "biblical creationism." One may suspect, of course, that the latter is the driving force behind the former at this point (and in general, for which see Appendix IX).

The difficulty which the Doppler Effect poses for the "creationist" is not quite over, however. What is one to make of supernovae, the incredibly violent and massive explosions of certain stars when they reach a critical state of their history? (The developmental sequence or aging process of stars, according to their initial size, has long been worked out according to the laws of physics and based upon observation of stellar types.[77] Such explosions were noted by writers in the past (e.g. the Crab Nebula, 6,000 light-years distant, whose sudden flareup was noted by the Chinese in 1054 A.D.), remnants of them have been photographed in the present at the location where ancient writers reported (see photo on book cover), and they have been observed at the moment of their appearance in the present (1987).[78] The records of such explosions, at specific moments in time, millions of light-years distant, have been carried to earth by the resultant light-waves. This is quite a different matter from the steady in-coming light of a star which can be said always to have remained the same since creation. The problem is stated by Henry Morris:

> Some have objected to this concept [of a young universe] on the basis of the evolutionary changes *supposedly* taking place in stars. The fact is, however, no one has ever observed such changes taking place. . . . The only *possible* exception of any consequence to this statement *might* be the novas or supernovas that are occasionally observed in the heavens when stars *apparently* heat up or explode. Some of these have been observed in galaxies *supposedly* hundreds of thousands of light-years from the earth; the argument is, therefore, that the stellar event producing the nova or supernova must have taken place the corresponding number of hundreds of thousands of years ago.[79] (emphases added)

The "creationist" answer is quickly at hand:

> Finally, there is no reason why God could not, if He had so willed, create "pulses" in the trails of some of the light waves created traversing space from the beginning. When such pulses reach the earth, they would then be interpreted as, say, novas, when they were in reality merely created bursts of energy in the light trails connecting the various stars. Though the reason for God doing such a thing is not yet clear, that in itself is no argument

against it. God may have reasons . . . which we do not yet understand. . . .
In any case, our uncertainty . . . cannot offset the clear Biblical testimony
to such recent creation.[80]

In the first place, it is pointless (in a scientific context) to speak of what
God could do "if He had so willed." Indeed, it is fruitless even in a theological context, since what God "could do" is no indication of what God has in
fact done. Anything and everything then becomes "possible," and one learns
nothing as a consequence. It is just as possible that God created the universe
twenty to fifteen million years ago (just as non-"creationists" propose), that
God revealed only religious truth in the Bible, leaving the human authors of
scripture to express that truth in the finite language (including the obsolete
worldview) of the time. "There is no reason why God could not, if He had so
willed," done so. So, where does that leave us?

In the second place, it may be doubted that an injected "pulse" of light
would be mistaken for a supernova (unless, of course, the divine mind goes
to extreme lengths to mock just such an event). Supernovae result when
massive stars (of a calculable mass and temperature) use up their nuclear fuel
and erupt in a violent expulsion: streams of gaseous matter are hurled in all
directions in a flash of light that may be brighter than all the stars in a galaxy
combined. As the fireball expands, it dims in intensity,[81] and leaves behind
the core of the star in the form of a rapidly rotating pulsar (neutron star). All
of this happens in accordance with known laws of physics. Furthermore, the
light from the explosion contains all the spectral lines that one would expect
from a star. (Or is it necessary to say that the injected "pulse" has been
adjusted to provide the spectra of known stars?)

Several such celestial events have been observed and recorded in the last
thousand years. The most celebrated is that of July 1054 A.D., as recorded by
chronicles of the Chinese Sung Dynasty. It is now known as the Crab Nebula
(M1) in the constellation Taurus. The description of location is so precise
that there is no doubt that the event of 1054 is the one still visible today:

> In the 1st year of the period Chih-ho, the 5th moon, the day chi-ch'ou, a
> guest star appeared approximately several inches south-east of [the star]
> Tien-Kuan. . . . After more than a year it gradually became invisible. . . .[82]

A related source gives further information:

> The guest star has become invisible. . . . Originally . . . it was visible in the
> day like Venus, with pointed rays in all four directions. The color was
> reddish-white. . . . It was seen altogether for twenty-three days [as a day-
> light object].[83]

That the event described by the Chinese is the same as the presently observable Crab Nebula (supernova) is clear not only from its position (just "south-east" of the star Zeta Tauri),[84] but also from the rate of expansion of the latter. Successive photographs of the Nebula reveal that (from the vantage of earth) it is expanding at a rate of about 0.2″ (2/10 of an arc-second) per year. By triangulation (at its distance as provided by "red shift," a recent figure being about 6,300 light-years), the result is 50 million miles per day (600 miles per second), with the resultant total diameter of the Nebula now being about six light-years. At this rate of expansion, the original event (explosion) would have been sighted approximately nine hundred years ago (i.e. between 1050 and 1100 A.D.).[85] At the center of the Nebula is the surviving remnant of the original star: a pulsar (designated NP0532), blinking each time it rotates on its axis at the rate of thirty times per second.[86]

The photograph of the Nebula shows the violence of the original explosion and the continuing turbulence as filaments of gases stream outward from the center in all directions. Successive photographs (taken over decades) show the continuing movement of such filaments outward from the center against the background of exterior "fixed" stars.[87] Thus, a proposed amorphous "pulse" of light, tossed into "the trails of some of the light-waves . . . traversing space," does not accord with the known and clearly evident physical realities of supernovae.

In the third place, such alleged "pulses" could not have been injected at the point of departure from a stellar body, since they would then still take millions of years to reach earth. Rather, the deity would need to have injected them in transit, always so calculating that it be at a point *no more than* about 6,000–10,000 light-years distant from earth (i.e. at the "creationist's" estimate for the age of the universe).

One might wonder if, in the "creationist's" opinion, radiation from the star continues to arrive along with the "pulse" and thus give *two* sources for spectroscopy which would then be separable. (Or has God adjusted the two so that they have the same spectra and thus are indistinguishable?) Is the "pulse" eternal, or does it fade away, leaving the original source (star) unchanged? (In actuality, the fireball created by a supernova does slowly fade in intensity and the gases disperse into space, with the original star reduced to a small nucleus. This would not be the case, were a "pulse" injected into the beams of light from a steadily burning star.)

Surely by now only the most ardent of "creationists" would continue this line of thought. Not only has the idea of divine freedom (capriciousness?) been stretched to the limit, but all pretext to scientific endeavor has been abandoned. Contrary to the assertion that scientific creationism has "no reliance on biblical revelation,"[88] the biblical "cat is now clearly out of the bag."

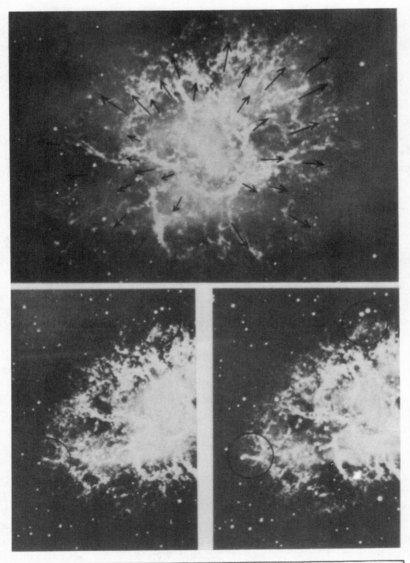

EXPANSION OF THE CRAB NEBULA. Top: The arrows indicate the outward motion of the filaments in about 250 years. Below: Two photographs made 34 years apart, illustrating the outward motion of the nebulous filaments.

From *Burnham's Celestial Handbook* (New York: Dover Publications, 1978), Volume III, p. 1847, used with permission of Robert Burnham, Jr.

An adequate final evaluation of "scientific creationism" may be found in the words of Kitcher:

> Creation "science" is spurious science. To treat it as science we would have to . . . abandon large parts of well-established sciences (physics, chemistry, and geology, as well as evolutionary biology . . .).[89]

> Creationism does not merit scientific discussion. . . . It is not integrated with the rest of science, but is a hodgepodge of doctrines, lacking independent support. It offers no startling predictions, no advance in knowledge. We cannot commend it for any ability to shed light on questions that orthodox theories are unable to answer. . . . Finally, there is no excusing it on the grounds that its resources are, as yet, untapped. . . . Where the appeal to evidence fails so completely, the appeal to tolerance cannot succeed.[90]

No little additional injury is done to the "creationists' " cause by continuing misuse of sources[91] and of data that has been discredited. Years after "mainline" scientists have published corrections to their observations, data, and conclusions, "creationists" continue to put forward such material in support of their own cause. Cases include the claim that a "shrinking sun," lack of an accumulation of lunar dust,[92] and the rate of influx of various elements into the oceans all argue for a young earth. Following a devastating analysis of the first two of these claims, Van Till, Young, and Menninga conclude:

> The continuing publication of these claims by young-earth advocates constitutes an intolerable violation of the standards of professional integrity that should characterize the work of natural scientists.[93]

Chapter II   Notes

1. Henry Morris, 1980, p. i.
2. *Ibid.* p. iv.
3. ICR *Acts and Facts,* December 1987, p. 4.
4. Henry Morris, 1980, p. iv.
5. Henry Morris, 1976, p. 21.
6. However, opponents of "creationist" vigorously insist that there is such a theological presupposition (as will be discussed below).
7. Henry M. Morris and Gary E. Parker, 1982, p. xii.
8. Henry Morris, 1980.
9. Henry Morris, 1970, p. 67. See 1976, p. 284, where the drop in ages from Peleg downward (Gen 11:19ff) may indicate such a gap.

10. Henry Morris, 1976, p. 45. Ussher's date for creation was 4004 B.C.E. (see Table No. 20), but Morris' maximum estimate is 10,000 B.C.E.

11. *Ibid.* pp. 106–107; 1970, p. 63.

12. Henry Morris, 1976, pp. 63f.

13. Henry Morris, 1970, p. 71.

14. Henry Morris, 1976, p. 69. See also John D. Morris, 1980; ICR *Acts and Facts* (May 1989).

15. ICR *Acts and Facts* (May 1989).

16. Henry Morris, 1976, pp. 154–155.

17. ICR *Acts and Facts* (May 1989).

18. This claim has been thoroughly investigated and found wanting by Lloyd R. Bailey, 1989, Chapter 4.

19. Morris, 1976, pp. 267, 275.

20. *Ibid.* p. 284. But see 1970, pp. 79f, where the estimate is but 2,800,000 persons. The pre-flood estimate is a population of seven *billion,* according to *The Genesis Record,* p. 144.

21. He says that the "weight of the evidence" supports this (p. 27), although no such evidence is presented, and in fact there is none available.

22. Below, I will suggest that a refutation of polytheism is at the center of the text's agenda (Chapter V, Part 4).

23. Henry Morris, 1970, p. 57. Note that Morris has published a rejection of Davis A. Young's *Creation and the Flood* (1977) and of *Christianity and the Age of the Earth* (1982), although Young is "an avowedly evangelical Christian." Young prefers the "day-age theory" to account for an "old earth." Morris characterizes him as among the "evangelical accommodationists" (p. 8). Here, the distinction between a creationist (Young) and a "creationist" (Morris) is clear.

24. Henry Morris, 1970, Preface. The same type of characterization may be found in an ICR insert to *Acts and Facts* ("Back to Genesis," June 1989, by Ken Ham). He speaks of Christian scholars who do not accept "creationism" as characterized by "feigned scholarship" and "motivated by a desire for acceptance and respect from their secular peers." His overall point is that "creationists" are like poor little pious David, beset by bad Goliath-like non-"creationists." The former, he suggests, have obeyed Paul's warning about not being "corrupted" (2 Cor 11:3). "Like David, with God on our side . . . we can defeat these 'giants.' "

25. Henry Morris, 1970, p. 71.

26. See the helpful discussion of the distinction between "behavior and governance," "nature and naturalistic," and "natural and supernatural" in Howard J. Van Till, 1986, Chapter 11.

27. *Ibid.* p. 222.

28. Page 4. For the observation that such a conclusion is beyond the power of scientific method, and rather reflects "scientism," see Howard J. Van Till, Davis A. Young, and Clarence Menninga, 1988, p. 16.

29. For this claim and the proposal that belief in evolution is the basis for many of the world's problems (e.g. racism), see Humber, 1987. For a forceful denunciation of such "creationist" claims, see Philip Kitcher, 1982, Chapter 7 ("The Bully Pulpit").

30. Henry Morris, 1980, p. 5.

31. ICR *Acts and Facts,* 16 (December 1987), p. 4.

32. Gish and Bliss, June 1981, p. 3.

33. Summarized from Gish and Bliss, May and June 1981. A similar statement may be found in Henry Morris, 1980, entitled "The Tenets of Creationism" which are part of the by-laws of ICR.

34. Although the list of "tenets" does not supply a specific figure, "young earthers" place it in the range of a few thousand years (a maximum of 10,000, taking into account the possibilities of the "genealogical gap theory"). See Henry Morris, 1976, p. 45.

35. See Philip Kitcher, 1982, and especially Arthur N. Strahler, 1987.

36. Gish, October 8, 1982, at pp. 28–29.

37. Among the recent specimens are the aforementioned works by Van Till (1986) and Young (1982).

38. Van Till, 1986, p. 234.

39. *Ibid.*

40. For extensive discussion, see Howard J. Van Till, Davis A. Young, and Clarence Menninga, 1988.

41. Sagan, 1980, p. 4.

42. Fred Hoyle, 1956, Chapter 4.II (pp. 77–86).

43. A poplar presentation may be found in Sagan, 1980, Chapter X. Greater detail may be found in Steven Weinberg, 1988.

44. For a full discussion, see Chapter IV of the present volume.

45. So Henry M. Morris and Gary E. Parker, 1982, Chapters 4 and 6. See also Henry Morris, March and April 1978; March 1985. This ubiquitous claim concerning the second law is rejected by most scientists, for which see Kitcher, 1982, pp. 89–96; Strahler, 1987, Chapter 13; and John W. Patterson, 1983, pp. 99–116.

46. See Morris and Parker, 1982, Chapter 3, and many other sources.

47. *Ibid.* p. 84.

48. The term is functional, although a grammatical monstrosity: Hebrew *bara'* ("he created," as in Gen 1:1), plus Hebrew *min* ("kind"), plus the English sign of the plural ("s").

49. Henry Morris, 1970, Chapter II, and many other places.

50. Stephen Jay Gould, 1977, pp. 22, 24, 28, 30; 1980, pp. 119–130.

51. Stephen Jay Gould and Niles Eldredge, III, 1977, pp. 115–151.

52. Morris and Parker, 1982, pp. 111–116.

53. *Ibid.* p. 116.

54. See Martin K. Nickels, 1986–1987, pp. 1–15. Perhaps the most famous species is *Australopithecus afarensis,* for which see D.C. Johanson and Maitland A. Edey, 1981.

55. Morris and Parker, 1982, pp. 116–129.

56. Strahler, 1987, Chapters 49 and 50.

57. Clete Knaub and Gary Parker, 1982. For the claim of a horrendous misuse of scientific data of this type by Parker, see Frank Awbrey, 1980, 40–43; Awbrey and Thwaites, 1982, pp. 14–17.

58. Strahler, 1987, Chapter 36 ("Molecular Biology and Phylogeny"). See also Chapter 34 ("The Genetic Code—A Review of Mainstream Molecular Biology").

59. A set of six statements concerning the formation of geological strata (attributed to Henry Morris, *Scientific Creationism,* General Edition, Creation-Life Publishers, 1974, pp. 115–116; *nv*) may be found in Daniel E. Wonderly, 1987, p. 3.

60. Young, 1982, p. 91. See also Kitcher, 1982, pp. 106–120; Strahler, 1987, Part IV. Especially interesting (and difficult from a "creationist" point of view) are the varves of the Green River formation. (A varve is a distinct layer of sediment that has been deposited by water, ordinarily within the course of a year.) The formation, covering "tens of thousands of square miles," contains places where millions of varves have been superimposed (twenty million in one location). Apparently this reflects sedimentation in fresh water lakes, since it is a process that can be observed in such bodies of water in the present. Thus the formation would reflect twenty million years of the earth's history. "If the Green River shales were laid down during the Flood [of Noah's time], there must have been forty million turbidity currents [coarse, light sediments during the summer; dark, fine sediments during the winter], alternately light and dark, over about three hundred days [of the Flood's duration]. A simple calculation (which creationists have avoided for twenty years) shows that the layers must have formed at the rate of about three layers every two seconds . . . (which) seems a bit unlikely." (So Robert J. Schadewald, 1982, pp. 12–17.)

61. Wonderly, 1987, p. 5.

62. Morris and Parker, 1982, p. 131.

63. Geological and archaeological evidence, versus popular claims of a world-wide flood, are examined by Lloyd R. Bailey, 1989, Chapter 3.

64. Morris and Parker, 1982, pp. 212–213.

65. Henry Morris, 1976, pp. 212–213; 1974, pp. 118–119 (*nv*); Morris and Parker, 1982, p. 214.

66. Great detail is given to the matter in Strahler, 1987, Chapter 39. Brief, but far more scathing, are the remarks of Kitcher, 1982, pp. 127–134 (under the heading, "Room at the top for the upwardly mobile?").

67. Morris and Parker, 1982, p. 127.

68. Among those available is John Morris, 1980, published by ICR.

69. See the series of articles by "creationists" and non-"creationists" alike in a special issue of the periodical *Creation/Evolution,* XV (Vol. 5, No. 1), entitled "The Paluxy River Footprint Mystery—Solved," edited by Cole and Godfrey. See also XXI (1987), pp. 30–42, "Tracking Those Incredible Creationists—The Trail Goes On," by Ronnie J. Hastings.

70. John D. Morris, 1986.

71. A good summary, from which illustrations herein have been taken, may be found in Young, 1982, Part One.

72. Van Till, 1986, pp. 176–180; Sagan, 1980, pp. 252–256; for detail, see Allan Sandage, 1956, chapter 5.I; Timothy Ferris, 1983, *nv;* Steven Weinberg, 1988, pp. 20–30, 168.

73. Queries about this identification may be found in Sagan, 1980, pp. 255–256 and Weinberg, 1988, pp. 28–29. The problem arose in the 1970s when astronomer Halton Arp called attention to galaxy NGC 5296 in the constellation Canes Venatici,

"the hunting dogs" (magnitude of redshift .0074). Apparently silhouetted in front of it (i.e. nearer to the observer) was a small unnamed galaxy with a much greater red shift (.0863) and supposedly therefore much greater velocity and distance away. This would be an open violation of the cosmological principle associated with Hubble's Law that the greater the red shift the greater the distance and velocity. However, recent photographic evidence by astronomer Nigel Sharp suggests that the silhouetting (proposed by Arp) is illusory ("a chance alignment and the fortuitous presence of an irregular brightness variation in the outer part of NGC 5296 that resulted in an indentation adjacent to the high-redshift galaxy" (News Notes, 1990). If this new evidence is correct, then a minor problem with the red shift-Doppler Effect equivalence is removed.

74. The velocity is derived by dividing the displacement by the normal (at rest) wavelength, then multiplying by the speed of light: $1.298/3933.664 \times 186,000$.

75. The distance is derived by multiplying the velocity (in kilometers per second) by Hubble's constant, yielding a result in light-years. The "constant" is named for the astronomer Edwin Hubble (in the 1920s) who suggested the value 1.6×10^{-4}. (For a brief account of how he did this, from the apparent luminosity of stars, supposedly related to their distance, see Weinberg, 1988, pp. 25–28.) Subsequent refinement has defined the constant as 1.5×10^{-5}. Another way of defining the constant (H) is that it allows a velocity of 50 kilometers per second for each megaparsec (3.26 million light-years) of distance. Thus: $d = v \times (1/H)$, or, $99/(1.5 \times 10^{-5}) = 6.6 \times 10^6$ light-years.

76. Niessen, 1983 ("Starlight and the Age of the Universe").

77. Van Till, 1986, Chapter 8; Sagan, 1980, Chapter 9.

78. For a description of the process by which the star Sanduleak $-69°$ 202 (in the Large Magellanic Cloud) became Supernova 1987A, see Woosley and Weaver, 1989.

79. Henry Morris, 1976, p. 66.

80. *Ibid.*

81. For photos of the supernova in the constellation Coma Berenices, taken eight months apart and showing how the source had greatly dimmed, see Schramm, 1974, p. 69.

82. As quoted in Robert Burnham, Jr., 1978, p. 1846.

83. *Ibid.* p. 1849.

84. There is a small discrepancy in location, since the Nebula is one degree northwest of the star rather than southeast (*ibid.* p. 1851).

85. *Ibid.* p. 1846.

86. *Ibid.* p. 1858; Sagan, 1980, p. 259.

87. Burnham, 1978, p. 1847 for photos.

88. Henry Morris, 1980, p. 1.

89. Kitcher, 1982, p. 164.

90. *Ibid.* pp. 171–172.

91. In addition to the instance cited in note 57 (Awbrey), see John R. Cole, 1981, pp. 34–44 (seven different scientists involved).

92. Frank T. Awbrey, 1985, pp. 21–29; Steven N. Shore, 1984, pp. 32–35.

93. *Science Held Hostage,* p. 82.

CHAPTER III

A Multi-Faceted Movement

"CREATIONISM" IS not merely a clearly defined theological perspective on the origin of all things, but it also involves ideas and actions in a number of purportedly related areas. This makes it possible to speak of a "creationist" movement, some of the aspects of which will now be discussed.

1. *"Creationism" features a socio-political analysis and resultant agenda.* This is succinctly put by one of the foremost advocates:

> Evolution is the root of atheism, of communism, nazism, behaviorism, racism, economic imperialism, militarism, libertinism, anarchism, and all manner of anti-Christian systems of belief and practice.[1]

Such a sweeping charge has been taken to suggest that the fundamental objection which "creationists" have to evolutionary biology does not lie intrinsically in objective scientific analysis but rather in a perceived evil consequence of the teaching of evolution.[2] The proposed consequence may be calculated to sway an audience apart from an objective look at the scientific evidence.

> Those who have been beguiled into thinking that a high school course in evolutionary biology is the gateway to a life of violence and depravity are not likely to ponder the scientific credentials of the theory of evolution.[3]

There is, of course, a chronological problem with such alleged connections, since such ideas and practices as atheism, racism, economic imperialism, and militarism were certainly in full vigor long before the writings of Charles Darwin or his immediate antecedents. This has led Henry Morris (who is quoted initially above) to posit that "Modern evolutionary materialists are not so modern after all. Their system is essentially the same as the pre-Socratic Greek cosmology of 2500 years ago!"[4] Even that antecedent is not early enough to cover the raft of resultant evils, so an earlier connection is made with ancient Babylon just after the time of the flood which is mentioned in Genesis. And what is the ultimate antecedent of evolutionary biology?

> It is therefore a reasonable deduction, even though hardly capable of proof, that the entire monstrous complex was revealed to Nimrod at Babel by demonic influences, perhaps by Satan himself.[5]

Poor Nimrod! The biblical text describes him briefly (Gen 10:8–12), without a hint of criticism. He is merely said to have been a "mighty hunter before the Lord" and to have ruled over several named cities in Mesopotamia. Morris, without a word of explanation (or shred of linguistic justification), changes the translation to "mighty tyrant in the face of Yahweh."[6] He does cite a late source as critical of Nimrod: the Jerusalem Targum (an Aramaic expansionist paraphrase of the biblical text) speaks of his "wickedness."[7]

Why has Morris sought to saddle Nimrod with this proposed Satanic plot called "evolution"? Seemingly only because he must hang it *somewhere* soon after the flood, if his charge that it is the "root" of a vast conglomerate of evil is to have any substance! Thus, to describe Morris' proposal as a "shaggy-dog story," as does Kitcher,[8] is surely an understatement. (For related instances of "creationist" abuse of the Bible, see Appendix IV.)

It should go without saying (although Morris' claims make it necessary) that belief in biological evolution does not intrinsically mandate any specific system of values. ("Theistic evolution," in the context of the Judeo-Christian faith where the term has come to be used, arguably does entail a value system, but it would be the antithesis of the evils which Morris lists. This cannot be acknowledged, however, since Morris has lumped "theistic evolution" together with "anticreationism.") That some interpreters have used the idea of evolution to base purpose[9] does not reflect upon the theory itself any more than the base purposes to which Christian thought has been put (e.g. antisemitism and the inquisition) negate the essence of Christianity.

> Yet although the Christian church has a checkered history, it is evident that . . . the evils result from perversions of religious doctrine: Evil or misguided men have twisted the Gospel to evil ends. Morris himself seems to appreciate this point; 'If certain Christian writers have interpreted the Bible in a racist framework, the error is in the interpretation, not in the Bible itself' (*The Troubled Waters of Evolution,* 162). But if charity ought to be extended to Christian doctrine, then it is equally appropriate for evolutionary theory. Both the Bible and evolutionary theory can be misread and

their principles abused. Hitler's anti-Semitism is no more a fruit of evolutionary theory than it is of Christianity.[10]

2. *"Creationism" features a well developed educational program.* In view of the litany of perceived evils which "creationists" attribute to evolutionary theory, this is hardly surprising.

The forms of the program (limited to examples from ICR alone) include: publication of a large number of books (Henry Morris alone has written more than forty); production of video tapes (e.g. seven in "The Creation Knowledge Video Library"); weekly radio broadcasts on stations throughout the United States; well-attended workshops, summer institutes, and speeches across the country (e.g. a recent two-day "Back to Genesis" seminar in Portland, Oregon, had an attendance of 2,500); debates with academicians who advocate evolution, on college campuses and other locations (e.g. recently at Southern Illinois University and Fresno State University);[11] a family magazine entitled *Creation* (produced in Australia); and curriculum materials for home-school and Christian-school use (e.g. a K-6 plan entitled, "Good Science—Under the Attributes of God").[12] In addition, mention should be made of Christian Heritage College and the related ICR Graduate School (offering the degree M.S. by approval of the California State Department of Education).[13]

3. *"Creationism" features a political and legal aspect,* largely a consequence of the desire to introduce the "creationist" perspective into the public schools. This agenda, more than anything else, has brought the movement to public awareness. In this regard, it has antecedents in earlier anti-evolution legislation at the state level which was eventually struck down by the federal courts. Subsequently, bills to empower state boards of education to implement "balanced treatment of creation-science and evolution"[14] were introduced in a number of state legislatures. Some succeeded but were struck down by the U.S. Supreme Court in 1987. (A partial list of such legislative actions may be found in Appendix XIV.)

The stated rationale for the inclusion of "creationism" in the public school science curriculum includes the following points.[15]

a. "Scientific creationism is *not* based on Genesis or any other religious teaching."[16] Thus it is not prohibited by the "establishment of religion" clause in the U.S. Constitution.

b. Macro-evolution is not a proven fact of science and should not be taught as such, "since there is no conceivable way that it can be tested" and since the fossil record does not directly support it.

c. Since macro-evolution cannot be tested (to say nothing of proven), "it can only be believed" and as such is a form of religion. Hence, from a constitutional point of view, it is as objectionable as is the teaching of the Bible.[17]

d. Scientific objectivity requires an openness to all points of view on a given problem. Thus, the "balanced treatment" bills neither forbid the teaching of evolution nor compel the teaching of "creationism": neither may be taught, or both may be taught, but not one without the other.

e. It is a violation of students' academic and religious freedom (and unfair to parents who support the public schools through taxation) to forbid the presentation of a point of view ("creationism") which many of them desire to discuss.

By way of evaluation of these rationales, let it *first* be noted that it is clear that "scientific creationism" *can be presented* apart from mention of Bible or deity. In fact, some ICR publications have accomplished this very task (e.g. the public school edition of *Scientific Creationism,* by Henry Morris). Whether or not "creationism" is based on the Bible, on the other hand, is quite another matter and one that has been hotly debated.[18] From a legal point of view, however, the matter would seem to have been settled by decisions of the U.S. District Court (concerning the Arkansas statute) and the U.S. Supreme Court (concerning the Louisiana statute). In the former case, the court concluded that the statute "was simply and purely an effort to introduce the Biblical version of creation into the public school curricula." (For the text of the decision, see Appendix XV.) On the other hand, the minority opinion in the Louisiana case (by Justices Scalia and Rehnquist) included the statement that "We have no basis on the record to conclude that creation science need be anything other than a collection of scientific data supporting the theory that life abruptly appeared on earth."[19] (Readers of the present volume may get a clearer perspective on the intent of scientific "creationism" with the assistance of the statements collected in Appendix IX.)

Evaluation and sources concerning the *second rationale* have been presented above.

As for the *third rationale,* it is true that the word "religion" has come to have a meaning devoid of any implication of a supreme being: "Any objective attended to or pursued with zeal or conscientious devotion: *A collector might make a religion of his hobby.*"[20] Be that as it may, it may be doubted that the framers of the Constitution had such a definition in mind when they forbade "an establishment of religion." What motivated their prohibition was not fear of random agendas or ideas which were merely "believed" (as opposed to proven), and certainly not fear of any objective that was "pursued with zeal." Rather, the danger was from state-imposed and state-supported overt theism (e.g. the Roman Catholicism, Anglicanism, and Lutheranism of the time) to which the European ancestors of the framers of the Constitution had been subjected. This third rationale, then, stands eighteenth century English "upon its head."

As for the *fourth rationale,* it must be stated that openness to all points of view is not to be equated with the conclusion that a given point of view is worthy of attention. It is not merely the vast majority of secular scientists who have found "creationism" wanting, but also great numbers of "evangelical" Christian scientists as well. Indeed, the "old earth" creationists (perhaps more numerous than the "young earth" group) include scientists who find the conclusions of the latter group to be unacceptable.[21] Kitcher's conclusion would thus seem to be the point: "Once it has become clear that a proposal makes no contribution to our understanding, we are not compelled by tolerance to give it further attention."[22] That is, the scientific "establishment" need not intrinsically be denounced as closed-minded merely because they have rejected "creationism." On the contrary, there are voluminous publications which evidence a careful study of "creationist" claims and which outline the reasons for rejecting them. This the non-specialist (general public) does not realize, and thus the *fourth rationale* continues to have popular appeal. Conversely, it may be pointed out that many statements in "creationist" literature are hardly models of open-mindedness.[23]

As for the *fifth rationale,* there is every reason to precipitate open discussion in the educational process and much to be said in favor of parental involvement in public school learning. It is quite another matter, however, to determine what constitutes valid science by means of a popular referendum. This is especially to be avoided in the United States, where the already existing public school curriculum has produced generations of persons who are scientifically illiterate and whose graduates lag far behind any other country in the industrialized western world. A recent survey, for example, revealed that a high percentage of persons in our society (thirty percent or more, I think) did not know that it was the earth's orbiting the sun that determined the length of the year. Likewise, substantial numbers of persons believe that some UFO's are of extraterrestrial origin ("manned craft"), or in astrology, "channeling," "Bigfoot" and related monsters, unusual powers of the Bermuda Triangle, and a raft of "paranormal" claims (to list but a few particulars). This clearly marks the failure of our society to produce scientifically literate persons. To leave the definition of future curricula to such a population is educational insanity!

While ICR does not itself lobby legislatures for "balanced treatment" enactments, it has published "model resolutions" for use of school boards and state legislators upon request.[24] It also has personnel who are "willing . . . to serve as consultants or expert witnesses on the scientific, educational or legal merits of creationism."[25]

With implementation of "balanced treatment" at the state level blocked by court decision, the agenda has now shifted to the local school districts. This has resulted in fierce struggles concerning the adoption of textbooks (indeed, this was already the case prior to the legal reversals). The situation in Texas has been especially notorious, where procedural regulations have allowed a small group of "creationists" to determine the nature of biology textbooks. Since this state purchases the largest number of volumes of any state in the nation, catering to it by publishers has resulted in the near expulsion of references to evolution in high school curricula. Recent developments, however, have indicated a shift from such control.[26] Textbooks by major publishers (e.g. Prentice-Hall) were judged so inadequate by school boards (e.g. in New York City) as to be unacceptable for purchase. The entire problem of inadequate coverage of evolution has even been the subject of a National Academy of Sciences workshop (1983).[27]

An ICR pamphlet ("Introducing Creationism in the Public Schools") suggests that parents and students form community organizations with such names as "Civil Rights for Creationists," "Committee for the Improvement of Education," and so on.[28] Readers are advised to "poll the views of their community" and to inform ICR of those school districts that "permit teachers to implement the two-model approach to origins."[29] That is, since the U.S. Supreme Court decision does "not preclude teaching the *scientific* evidence for creation," school boards and their teachers should "be strongly encouraged to do so." The court is denounced for coming "perilously close to identifying the United States as an atheistic nation and, as it were, telling our Creator His presence in our national life and public schools is no longer wanted. This does not bode well for the future of our country."[30]

Much of this rhetoric, of course, is similar to the language of certain politicians (who seek to use it to their advantage). It is thus not surprising to find the Rev. Jerry Falwell's Moral Majority soliciting contributions to assist in the fight against evolution,[31] and even a candidate for the presidency of the United States (Ronald Reagan) endorsing public school instruction in "creationism."[32]

Chapter III Notes

1. Henry M. Morris, 1972, p. 75. See also his articles dated 1977, 1978, 1987, 1988; Humber, 1987, 1988; John N. Moore, 1977.

2. Kitcher, *1982,* Chapter 7.

3. *Ibid.* p. 187.

4. *The Troubled Waters of Evolution,* 1974, p. 67 (*nv*).

5. *Ibid.* p. 74.

6. *The Genesis Record,* pp. 251–252.

7. On Targumim, see the *IDB* article, "Versions, ancient" (Vol. IV, at p. 750).

8. *Abusing Science,* p. 193.

9. For example, the claim that the black race is less evolved than is the Caucasian (as cited by Humber, 1987).

10. Kitcher, *1982* p. 198.

11. Reports of such debates (favorable to the ICR team) are regularly featured in *Acts and Facts.* The ICR debaters are quite skilled, but only initially were underestimated by their opponents. See Frederick Edwards, Spring 1982, pp. 30–42. For a glimpse of such debates, see the P.B.S. television program *Nova* for February 21, 1989. ICR's negative reaction to the broadcast may be found in *Acts and Facts* (April 1989, p. 5).

12. See Bliss, 1988.

13. See ICR *Acts and Facts* (February 1989 and subsequent issues) for impending reevaluation of the school's accreditation.

14. An excellent and detailed summary may be found in Edward J. Larson, 1985. The "creationist" origins of such legislation are discussed on pp. 147–151.

15. I have not found a systematic treatment of this topic, but rather gathered information from Morris and Parker, 1982, Appendix A; Henry M. Morris, December 1988; ICR *Acts and Facts* (May 1980).

16. Morris and Parker, 1982, p. 263.

17. Henry M. Morris, 1982. See p. iii: "The schools are already saturated with the teaching of religion in the guise of evolutionary 'science.'" From this perspective it was logical that a California congressman introduce a bill to end funding for the Smithsonian Institution!

18. See e.g. Langdon Gilkey, 1983, pp. 55–69.

19. Quoted in Bird, 1987, p. ii.

20. This is the third definition of "religion" in *The American Heritage Dictionary of the English Language* (1978). See *Creation Evolution* XXIII (1988), pp. 44–46.

21. In the realm of geology, for example, see Daniel E. Wonderly, 1987.

22. Kitcher, 1982, p. 168 (part of a chapter entitled "Exploiting Tolerance").

23. See e.g. the sweeping charge concerning non-"creationist" Christian desire to "purchase pseudo-respectability" (above) and the repeated charge that belief in evolution is an "anti-God conspiracy of Satan himself." See also the quotations in Appendix IX, where those who share the "creationist" point of view are described as "instructed Christians" and believers of the Bible (in apparent contrast to believers in "theistic evolution").

24. ICR *Acts and Facts* (May 1980), p. 2. The resolutions themselves were published in ICR *Impact* Series Nos. 26 and 71.

25. *Acts and Facts* (May 1981), p. 2.

26. See references to Mel and Norma Gabler in the volumes by Kitcher and

Larson; "News Briefs" in *Creation/Evolution,* XII (Spring 1983), pp. 34–35; XIV (Fall 1984), pp. 52d–53.

27. Stuart W. Hughes, 1983, pp. 33–34.
28. Cited in Kitcher, 1982, p. 2.
29. ICR *Acts and Facts* (May 1980), p. 5.
30. Bird, 1987, p. iv.
31. See Kitcher, 1982, pp. 2, 4, 165, 174.
32. See Larson, 1985, pp. 126–127 (citing *Time* magazine for March 16, 1981, p. 80).

PART TWO

Genesis and Creation

CHAPTER IV

Indications of What the Biblical Agenda Is Not

IF THE AUTHOR (or authors[1]) of the creation story in Genesis could be present in our day and explain their agenda in modern terms, what would they say?

Would they say that their goal had been to answer what we would now call "scientific" questions concerning the beginning of all things: When? From what? How long? To relate the sequence of creation, the relationship between animal "kinds," and to set the entire thing within an absolute chronological framework? Would they then observe that there are interpreters in the present ("creationists") who have correctly understood their agenda?

Or would they say that, although their goal had indeed been a "scientific" one, their achievement was only within the limits of the best knowledge of their time and hence their perspective would now need supplementation and correction? Would they then rejoice in the advancement of knowledge, agreeing with Kepler (Leibnitz?), "Surely, O God, I am but thinking your thoughts after you"? Would they then see as their successors those scientists in the present who believe in theistic evolution?

Or would they say, as ancient scientists, that subsequent discovery of the interrelatedness of the physical world and the increasing discovery of the "laws of nature" have diminished the need for a deity to the vanishing point? Would they then conclude, perhaps reluctantly as some modern theists have done, that humans come-of-age must give up ideas of a creator and divine providence?

Or would they deny that their goal had been to address "scientific" issues in the first place? Would they assert instead that they had been addressing the issue of monotheism versus polytheism in their own day, with whatever implications it might have for subsequent thought? Would they say that the essential questions are "Who?" and "For what purpose?" rather than those

53

of sequence and chronology? Would they affirm those interpreters in the present who separate "scientific questions" from "theological questions" and who place the biblical creation story in the latter category?

Modern diversity of opinion indicates the difficulty of deciding what the author(s) of the Genesis account intended for their own time, much less how they might express themselves in the present. This difficulty is the result of the following realities, among others.

1. The linguistic gap between "then" and "now." There is always some loss of meaning when translation from one language to another takes place (as expressed in the Italian proverb, "A translator, a traitor"). There is the fact that our knowledge of the vocabulary and syntax of the biblical languages is not exact. There is a loss of meaning when language is transformed from speech to written text as one now finds it in the Bible. (For example, inflection of the voice, knowing those whom a speaker faces, and "body english" all contribute to communication.) There is the possibility that the original speakers or writers did not express themselves unambiguously.[2]

As a consequence of such difficulties, contrast "In the beginning God created the heavens and the earth" (Gen 1:1, RSV, KJV) with "When God set about to create heaven and earth—the world being then a formless waste . . ." (AB; compare the footnote in NJB, JPS). The former translation suggests an absolute beginning; the latter affirms the existence of matter prior to the initial creative act. The "meaning" of the verse cannot be resolved on linguistic grounds alone. (For full discussion, see below, Chapter V and Appendix X.)

2. Inability to identify the audience for which the text was intended. For example, were the creation accounts in Genesis the product of Moses' inspired perceptions in the thirteenth century, B.C.E., as some modern interpreters think, or, was it in the fifteenth century, as others think? Or is the present text the result of a long process of inspired editing, stretching from perhaps the eleventh to the sixth centuries, B.C.E. (as the documentary hypothesis proposes[3])? The correct answer to that question matters little for our purpose in the present discussion, since the issue is the same for each possibility: What was the mentality of the initial audience, their religious questions and needs, the realities of their world to which the text provided needed insights? That is, if we knew the situation, we could better understand the message that was intended for it. However, if there is some uncertainty about the date, and even if we knew it for sure, the recovery of the realities of that time (historical, economic, social, and religious) is not always easy and the sources for doing so are not always numerous.

Alternatively, should one assume that the biblical materials were not addressed with the ancient (initial) audience primarily in mind? Were they an historically detached revelation, intended for all times and places, such that we should strive to hear them directly rather than seeking to understand them in their context and then ask what it might mean for us? ("Just read the text: it'll speak to you.")

In the former approach, one could notice that most of the created objects in Genesis 1 (for example, light, darkness, seas, stars, animals) were regarded by Israel's neighbors as manifestations of divine powers, and thus one might wonder if there is an intended "point" to their being reduced to mere physical objects. Thereby, the focus of the chapter would be primarily in the realm of religion. In the latter approach, the focus might be thought to be primarily in the realm of the physical sciences.

3. The cultural gap between "then" and "now," consisting of such elements as worldview, anthropology, and behavior patterns. We may, for example, consider it to be nearly self-evident that space extends indefinitely in all directions, and fail to realize that for ancient Israel "all things" were concentrated inside a tiny enclosed space which was almost within the reach of human architecture (Gen 11:1–5). (See Appendix XI.) Failure to perceive this gap may lead, on the one hand, to distortion of the text by making it conform to modern ideas, or to distortion of the present by making it conform to the text.

The difficulty in deciding what the authors of the creation story might say in the present is more than a theoretical problem caused by the three issues I have just raised. It is an actual problem, evident in the opinions of modern interpreters of the Bible. The existence of "creationism" with its polemics against "mainline" biblical interpretation is sufficient to establish the point. How, then, do we proceed to resolve the issue?

Before inquiring as to the agenda of the creation story (for which, see Chapter V), it may be helpful (and certainly easier) to speak of some aspects of what the agenda was not. The procedure for doing so is straightforward: an analysis of the text on its own terms. No prior assumptions will be made concerning its authorship, data, situation, or the nature of the "inspiration" of the text. Such considerations, ordinarily important, but which have the potential for divisiveness, need not enter our deliberations at this point. (See my statement concerning this in the Preface to the current volume.) Likewise, text which can quickly lead to disputes about interpretation should be avoided. For example, it is to no avail, in some quarters, to suggest textual evidence that the "firmament" in Genesis 1:6–8 was a hard dome of sufficient strength to hold up the heavenly reservoirs which were thought to contain the water which produced rain, snow, and sleet (Appendix XI), if it be objected that the evidence does not apply here and if it be projected instead that the "firmament" is a "vapor canopy of some sort.[4] I propose, instead, to deal with six issues which are seemingly more straightforward.

1. The Ages of Persons in Israel's Primeval Story[5] (at Chapters 5 and 11)

Even the most casual reader of the Bible will be struck by the astonishing ages of individuals as reported in its early chapters. This is especially true of the so-called pre-diluvians (i.e. prior to the flood), as reported in Genesis 5. They range from a mere 365 to a maximum of 969, with the average being 858 years. Similarly elevated are the ages at which these individuals fathered their first child, ranging from 65 to 500, averaging 156 years. (See Table No. 5.) How does one account for such astonishing longevity, if this is an historical report (as "creationists" affirm that it is)? How does one account for the individual figures, and their departure from the later biblical norm (perhaps forty years)?[6] One modern interpreter undoubtedly speaks for a host of others when he remarks:

> Every commentator on Genesis, including the present writer, has spent hours over pencil and paper, and recently with a pocket calculator, trying to wrest some sense or pattern out of the figures with which the MT supplies us. The best conclusion drawn from this effort is that there are other pursuits more rewarding. There undoubtedly is, or was, a key to these numbers . . . but whether it has disappeared in transmission or simply now eludes us is impossible to determine.[7]

Perhaps the most conspicuous characteristic of the ages, in all three categories, is that they are not randomly distributed. This is in contrast to what we would expect from a genealogical list of historical ages. Rather, the vast majority of them are divisible by five (i.e. they end either in 0 or 5). Note that the total number of independent entries is fifty-one (excluding the "life-span" column since it is merely the total of the "first-born" and "remaining years" columns for Genesis 5 and 11). Of those, thirty-five end in 0 or 5. Of the remaining entries, ten of them end in either 7 or 2. The two categories consume the entirety of the pre-diluvians. Only six ages stand outside this scheme when the post-diluvians are included.

By contrast, note the randomness in the lengths of reign of the kings of Israel and Judah (mostly in years), as recorded in 1 and 2 Kings, beginning with Rehoboam (see Table No. 19 for Judah alone): 17, 3, 41, 2, 24, 2, 7 days, 12, 22, 25, 2, 8, 1, 28, 40, 17, 16, 29, 52, 41, 6 months, 1 month, 10, 2, 20, 16, 16, 9, 29, 55, 2, 21, 3 months, 11, 3 months, and 11.

TABLE 5. Early Biblical Ages

name	age at marriage	age at time of first-born	remaining years	lifespan [ ] = not actually given in text
The Pre-Diluvians (Gen 5)				
Adam		130	800	930
Seth		105	807	912
Enosh		90	815	905
Kenan		70	840	910
Mahalalel		65	830	895
Jared		162	800	962
Enoch		65	300	365
Methuselah		187	782	969
Lamech		182	595	777
Noah		500	450	950

(The flood begins in Noah's 600th year = Shem's 100th year)

The Early Post-Diluvians (Gen 11)				
Shem		100	500	600
Arpachshad		35	403	438
Shelah		30	403	433
Eber		34	430	464
Peleg		30	209	239
Reu		32	207	239
Serug		30	200	230
Nahor		29	119	148
Terah		70	135	205

The Patriarchal Figures (Gen–Deut)				
Abraham		100		175
Sarah		90		127
Isaac	40	60		180
Ishmael				137
Jacob				147
Esau	40			
Joseph				110
Moses				120
Joshua				110

It may easily be observed that there is a possible connection between the ages ending in 0 or 5 and those ending in 7 or 2: the addition of 7 to the former type yields the latter type (7 + 5 yielding 12). For example, Sarah's 127 years is 120 + 7 and Lamech's 182 is 175 + 7. If such a procedure has in fact been operative, then forty-five of the fifty-one entries belong to a divisible-by-five scheme. If the "lifespan" column is now included, three of the remaining aberrations then follow the same scheme: 969 for Methuselah, and 239 for Peleg and Reu, have a 9 at the end because it is the sum of 2 and 7 from the other columns. In the case of Methuselah, however, another explanation for his age is possible: the elapsed time at his death coincides with the year of the flood, as if he died in that catastrophe.

It is interesting to note that almost all of the remaining figures in the primeval story fit this same scheme (in contrast to the remainder of the biblical materials). As for divisibility by 5, note that the human lifespan is set at 120 years (Gen 6:3); the dimensions of Noah's boat are 300 × 50 × 30 (6:15); rain fell for 40 days and 40 nights (7:12), covering the mountains to a depth of 15 cubits (7:20) and enduring for 150 days (7:24); the mountains emerge at the beginning of the 10th month (8:5); and a window is opened on the 40th day (8:6). Furthermore, some animals come aboard in 7 pairs (7:2); the flood begins after 7 days (7:10); the waters endure until the 17th day of the 7th month (8:7); birds are sent out at 7-day intervals (8:8–12); and the earth becomes dry on the 27th day (8:14).

The possibility must now be seriously entertained (some would find it a compelling conclusion) that these numbers are not random, historical periods of time, but rather represent a biblical concern or value (which is yet to be defined). This is by no means to suggest that the figures are not "true." Rather, it is to raise the possibility that they were meant to depict a dimension of "truth" that does not coincide with a modern concern for chronology. At the very least, the task of the interpreter is to try to understand what the text intended to convey by such (apparently) stylized, regularized numbers. If such non-literal, non-chronological usage seems strange to us, that is *our* problem and our challenge to understand. The text is, after all, our teacher.

The question now becomes: Have the ages which end in 7 or 2 in fact resulted from the addition of 7 to ages that were originally divisible by 5? An apparent instance of such practice relates to the reported number of provinces in the Persian empire. According to the book of Daniel (6:1), there were 120 of them at the time of Darius. However, at the time of his successor Ahasuerus (Est 1:1), there were 127 of them. It is possible, of course, that the empire expanded in the meanwhile, but the curiosity remains that it would be precisely by that ubiquitous number 7. That such expansion was not the case, but rather that the figures are symbolic, is suggested by the fact that the Egyptians regarded 110 and 120 as the ideal age,[8] and the Bible accepts the latter as a maximum: ". . . his days shall be a hundred and twenty years" (Gen 6:3). Curiously, the only persons (from Table 5) who attain precisely those ages have been residents of Egypt: Joseph and Joshua at 110, and Moses at 120. (Did it "just happen" that way, or is the text saying that "They lived life to the full" regardless of their actual ages?)

As for the number 7, in Ancient Near Eastern literature it attained a near mystic sense and was often used to signify fullness, completeness, and perfection (rather than a literal 6 + 1; see Appendix VII). Note, then, the age of Sarah, also a resident of Egypt: 127 years (120 + 7), as if to say: "She lived life to the full, and then some! Absolute perfection! They don't make 'em like that anymore!" As for the extension of the Persian empire from 120 to 127 provinces, admiration may thereby be being expressed for its extent and its efficiency ("Now, there's a government for you!"). Even the number 120 is suspect, since it is 60×2, as will be discussed below.

One may now ask: What is the significance of the fact that the ages are usually divisible by 5? Is this merely an approximation, a matter of "rounding off," as sometimes happened when cuneiform texts were broken?[9] This is a complicated problem, the solution to which emerges when the ages of the pre-diluvian monarchs of Mesopotamia are charted (Table No. 6). According to Sumerian literature, there was a great deluge, prior to which rulers lived to exceptional ages. Various copies may differ as to individual length of reign, but a common mathematical base is in evidence.

Note that individual names may vary from one list to the next (i.e. be listed in one text but not in another), that the total number of names may vary (eight in W-B 444, but ten in the others), and that the individual ages vary radically from one text to the next (e.g. that of Alalgar is 72,000, or 36,000, or 10,800). However, regardless of variations, an eye has been kept on the total of ages: in each case it is a multiple of 60^2 (i.e. of 3600). This is especially conspicuous in the case of W-B 444, where two of the ages are not exact multiples of 60^2 but also involve multiples of 60 (Enmenduranna and Ubartutu). The total of the two, however, is engineered to be 39,600 ($60^2 \times 11$).

It is apparent, then, that these figures are not intended to depict actual lengths of reign, but are highly stylized creations in which the number 60 and its multiples have a symbolic significance. The list is similar to that of pre-diluvians in Genesis in two regards: adherence to a numerical scheme (involving the same "base," as we shall see), and unreality from a biological point of view of the ages.

Why should the Mesopotamian list be based upon multiples of 60? Because base-60 (the so-called sexigesimal system) was the basis of place-notation in Babylonian mathematics! Note that the English system of calculation is constructed on base-10. That is, our basic "units" are 1–9, and in order to

TABLE 6. The Sumerian King List

Name	Length of Reign (years)		
	W-B 62[10]	W-B 444	Berossos[11]
Alulim	67,200 (to be corrected to 68,400?) (60^2 x 19)	28,800 (60^2 x 8)	36,000 (60^2 x 10)
Alalgar	72,000 (60^2 x 20)	36,000 (60^2 x 10)	10,800 (60^2 x 3)
Enmenluanna	21,600 (60^2 x 6)	43,200 (60^2 x 12)	46,800 (60^2 x 13)
Enmengalanna	not listed	28,800 (60^2 x 8)	46,800 (60^2 x 18)
. . . kidunnu	72,000 (60^2 x 20)	not listed	not listed
. . . alimma	21,600 (60^2 x 6)	not listed	not listed
Evedoragxos	not listed	not listed	64,800 (60^2 x 18)
Ammemon	not lissted	not listed	43,200 (60^2 x 12)
Dumuzi	28,800 (60^2 x 8)	36,000 (60^2 x 10)	36,000 (60^2 x 10)
Ensipazianna	36,000 (60^2 x 10)	28,800 (60^2 x 8)	36,000 (60^2 x 10)
Enmenduranna	72,000 (60^2 x 20)	21,000 (60^2 x 5) + (60 x 50)	not listed
Ubartutu	28,800 (60^2 x 8)	18,600 (60^2 x 5) + (60 x 10)	28,800 (60^2 x 8)
Ziusudra	36,000 (60^2 x 10)	not listed	64,800 (60^2 x 18)
TOTALS	457,200 (corrected) (60^2 x [120 + 7])	241,200 (60^2 x [60 + 7])	432,000 (60^2 x 120)= (60^3 x 2)

count beyond that one uses place-notation: one then "starts over," one column to the left, the result being "1–0." Each succeeding column, leftward, is $10\times$ the previous one.[12] Thus, the configuration 111 means: $(1 \times 10^2) + (1 \times 10) + 1$, i.e. $100 + 10 + 1$.

In the Mesopotamian system, by contrast, each place-notation is $60\times$ the previous one (rather than $10\times$). Thus, the configuration of cuneiform wedges (▼▼▼) could mean: $(1 \times 60^2) + (1 \times 60) + 1$, i.e. $3600 + 60 + 1$ $(3,661)$.[13] This system is evident in modern time reckoning, where 1 hour = 60 minutes = 3600 seconds.

One may conjecture, then, why the lengths of reign for the pre-flood monarchs involves multiples of 60: it idealizes and expresses perfection of leaders in a golden age, just after (as the text begins) "kingship descended from heaven." A similar concept apparently is at work in the assignment of dimensions to the boat of the Mesopotamian flood-hero, constructed at divine initiative: 120 (60×2) cubits per side, for a volume of ($60^3 \times 8$) units.

Base-60 is evident in certain of the ages of the pre-diluvians in Genesis 5: Enoch's 300 years is (60×5), Kenan's 840 is (60×14), Methuselah's 187 is (60×3) + 7, Sarah's 127 is (60×2) + 7, Isaac's 60 is self-evident, as is his 180 (60×3), Moses' 120 is (60×2), Enoch's and Sarah's 90 is $60 + 60/2$, and Shelah's 30 is $60/2$ (so also Peleg and Serug).

Turning to the dimensions of Noah's ark, note that it is 300 cubits long (60×5), 30 cubits high ($60/2$), and 50 cubits wide (Gen 6:15). Although the width does not conform, consideration has nonetheless been given to the resultant volume: 450,000 cubic cubits, or ($60^3 \times 2$) + ($60^2 \times 5$) units, or more simply ($60^2 \times 125$) units. Actual dimensions, or idealization? In any case, it is evident that the biblical authors were aware of computation in base-60, even if (for the ages of the pre-diluvians) the majority of the figures do not seem to "fit" (see, however, below).

The general relationship between the Mesopotamian lengths of reign and the biblical ages is that of reduction: from "unreality" (?) with a maximum of 72,000 years to "reality" (?) with a maximum of 969 years; from multiples of 60^2 to multiples of 60. Can such a principle of reduction be at work in the other ages of the pre-diluvians?

What is the mathematical common ground between the biblical ages which are divisible by 5, and the Mesopotamian reigns which are multiples of 60? It is the number 12 ($5 \times 12 = 60$), which is the number of months in a year. Otherwise put: periods of 5 years contain 60 months. Is it possible, then, that another means of biblical "reduction" is to reckon in months in base-60, but to express the total in years?[14] Thus perceived, the ages of the pre-diluvians in Genesis 5 take the form shown on Table No. 7.

That a sequence of ten historical generations might produce first-born at ages that are multiples of five years (multiples of sixty months) is quite unlikely. That their remaining years should fall within the same scheme, and this just "happen" to agree with a literary convention of the Ancient Near East, strains credulity to the breaking point. There is little doubt, then, that the entire list of ages has been crafted with the ideal (base-60) in mind. Their intent, their kind of "truth," lies in some realm other than biology and chronology in the modern sense of the terms.

The next question to be asked is far more difficult to answer: What has been the basis for assigning the individual ages? Is each of them a modification of one of the ages from the Sumerian King List? Have they been created freely, with no particular rationale for each? Were there other factors at work? At least the following possibilities should be noted.

1. Four of the patriarchal ages likely were influenced by the Egyptian

TABLE 7.   Ages of the Pre-Diluvians in Months (Multiples of 60)

name	age at time of first-born	remaining lifetime
Adam	60 x 26	$2(60^2) + (60 \times 40)$
Seth	60 x 21	$2(60^2) + (60 \times 40) + 7$ years
Enosh	60 x 18	$2(60^2) + (60 \times 43)$
Kenan	60 x 14	$2(60^2) + (60 \times 48)$
Mahalalel	60 x 13	$2(60^2) + (60 \times 46)$
Jared	(60 x 31) + 7 years)	$2(60^2) + (60 \times 40)$
Enoch	60 x 13	60^2
Methuselah	(60 x 36) + 7 years	$2(60^2) + (60 \times 35) + 7$ years
Lamech	(60 x 35) + 7 years	$(60^2) + (60 \times 59)$
Noah	60^2 x (60 x 40)	$(60^2) + (60 \times 30)$
	at flood: $2(60^2)$	

"ideal" ages of 110 and 120 (the latter expressed at Gen 6:3): Sarah (127), Joseph (110), Joshua (110), and Moses (120). Remember that 120 = (60 × 2). The intent of the age would be to suggest that these individuals enjoyed God's blessing to the full.

2. The lifespan of Enoch (365 years) has been the one figure that interpreters have traditionally solved. Is it a coincidence that this age is the same as the number of days in the solar year? Perhaps so. Nonetheless, it is interesting to compare what is said of him, the seventh generation of humankind, with what is said of his correspondent (seventh ruler, Enmenduranna) in the W-B 444 King List. A ritual text,[15] apparently concerned with the founding of a certain type of priesthood,[16] relates that Enmenduranna was summoned to the (heavenly) presence of the deities, presumably to teach him the divine mysteries of the priestly craft, following which he returned to the earthly realm of humans. Just so, it is uniquely said of Enoch that he ". . . walked

with God; and he was not, for God took him" (Gen 5:24). However this is to be understood in the context of the list of pre-diluvians (all of whom died at the end of the years specified), it may earlier have been understood to mean that he was absent from earth *temporarily* to learn the heavenly mysteries. Such a possibility of meaning is underscored by the Intertestamental Book of Enoch, wherein the description in Genesis gave rise to the idea that Enoch was indeed taken to heaven in order to learn the course of future human events.[17]

It is likewise important to note that, in Sumerian texts, Enmenduranna was the ruler of Sippar, a major center for the cult of the sun-god. The visible disc of that revered deity journeys in a circuit of 365 days' duration, precisely the age of Enoch. Has the yearly cycle of Enmenduranna's deity been transferred to the human Enoch, each tradition involving one who was the seventh generation from the "beginning"?

3. Enoch was 65 years old when his son Methuselah was born, and this was 687 since Adam's birth (total elapsed time in the genealogy). Methuselah then lived 969 years, to an elapsed time of 1656 years at the time of the flood. The compilers of the ages, then, meant to depict Methuselah as having died in that great catastrophe.

4. In the Ancient Near East, each letter of the alphabet might be assigned a numerical value as well as a phonetic one. This would correspond in English to saying: let "a" = 1, "b" = 2, "c" = 3, and so on. A fanciful number-game could then be played in which significance could be derived when the "value" of a word was totaled. Such a system came to be called *gematria,* related to the English word geometry.[18] (For details, see Appendix VIII.)

Could such values, applied to the names of the pre-diluvians in Genesis 5, be related to the ages listed for them? That possibility emerges only in the case of Methuselah and his son Lamech. The *gematria* of the word "Methuselah," the seventh successor of Adam, is 784, i.e. 777 + 7, surprisingly close to the figure given for his "remaining years," 782 (see Table No. 5). In the parallel geneaology[19] in Genesis 4, Lamech's father is Methushael,[20] the gematria of which is exactly 777. In that list, it is Lamech who is the seventh-born, and whose lifespan (in chapter 5) is 777 years! Thus Lamech, the mighty man who claims the right to 77-fold retribution, is depicted as a "perfect seven" in his age!

5. The Mesopotamian flood-hero (Ziusudra) reigned for 36,000 years (W-B text 62: see Table No. 6), that is $(60^2 \times 10)$. Noah, the biblical flood-hero, lived for 600 years prior to its onset, that is (60×10), or $2(60^2)$ months.

6. The lifespans of the pre-diluvians cluster around 900 years because of a desire to depict multiples of 60, specifically: $3(60^2)$ months = 900 years. Conversely, 900 years = 10,800 months, which coincides with the reign in years of Alalgar (Berossos' list).

7. It is possible that groups of ages within the pre-diluvian total may likewise be derived from Berossos' list of Sumerian kings. (See Appendix XVI for details.)

It is plausible to suppose that others (if not all) of the ages in the Genesis list have non-literal, mystic, symbolic significance. Keen, playful, creative minds apparently have been at work in the fashioning of this system, but much of the key to the result remains opaque to interpreters in the present.

2. The Primeval Ages in Non-Masoretic Texts

If any hope remains that the ages previously studied in Genesis 5 and 11 are actual biological lifespans, that the symbolic explanations are merely a remarkable series of coincidences, then one must face other clear and unimpeachable *biblical* evidence that such ages have been manipulated.

All the ages previously studied have been taken from one family of biblical manuscripts. That is, English Bibles use the Masoretic Text[21] as the basis of their translation. There are, however, two other basic families of manuscripts which translators consult for divergent readings (and there are thousands of such readings[22]). These families are: (1) the Greek Bible of the early church, which began with a translation commonly called the Septuagint (LXX) in the third to first centuries B.C.E., and is known to have been based upon an Egyptian family of Hebrew manuscripts, [23] and (2) the Samaritan Pentateuch (SP, Hebrew), thought to have descended from manuscripts in Palestine.[24] By contrast, the traditional (Masoretic) text is thought to have taken shape in Babylonia.

When these three families (traditions) are compared, the results are as shown in Table No. 8.

Concerning the lists of ages, at least the following observations can be made.

1. The LXX ages at time of first-born exceed those of MT in every case save for Mathuselah and Terah, the difference being 100 years (save for those two cases and Nahor). In the lifespan enumeration, LXX and MT agree save for Lamech. Whatever is at stake in the divergence, therefore, lies in the elapsed time between the creation of Adam and the coming of the flood at the time of Noah, or more extensively to some date beyond the birth of Terah's son (possibly the "call" of Abraham). Otherwise put: chronology depends upon the sums of ages at the time of first-born and not upon those of lifespan. A texual variation (for Methuselah at first-born) extends elapsed time to 2262 years and thus prevents Methuselah from outliving the flood.

2. The SP ages generally agree with those of MT in the lifespan column (slight divergences always producing a lesser age), but diverge widely in the

TABLE 8. Ages According to Textual Families

	Age at Time of First-Born			Lifespan			
	MT	LXX	SP	MT	LXX	SP	SP in Base-60
				The Pre-Diluvians			
Adam	130	230	130	930	930	930	(60 x 15) + 60/2
Seth	105	205	105	912	912	912	(60 x 15) + 60 months + 7 years
Enosh	90	190	90	905	905	905	(60 x 15) + 60 months
Kenan	70	170	70	910	910	910	(60 x 15) + 120 months
Mahalalel	65	165	65	895	895	895	
Jared	162	162	62	962	962	847	(60 x 14) + 7 years
Enoch	65	165	65	365	365	365	(60 x 6) + 60 months
Methuselah	187	167 (187)	67	969	969	720	(60 x 12)
Lamech	182	188	53	777	753	653	
Noah	500	500	500	950	950	950	(60 x 15) + 600 months
Shem	100	100	100	600	600	600	(60 x10)
(Shem's 100th year is the year of the flood)							
TOTALS	1656	2242 (2262)	1307	9175	9151	8687	
				The Post-Diluvians			
Arpachshad	35	135	135	438	565	438	
Cainan/Kenan	not listed	130	not listed	not listed	460	not listed	
Shelah	30	130	130	433	460	433	
Eber	34	134	134	464	504	404	
Peleg	30	130	130	239	339	239	
Reu	32	132	132	239	339	239	
Serug	30	130	130	230	330	230	
Nahor	29	79	79	148	208	148	
Terah	70	70	70	205	205	145	
TOTALS	290	1070	940	2396	3410	2276	

age at time of first-born for the post-diluvians. Generally, the divergence is 100 years. Once again, it is the total elapsed time that is the concern.

3. Despite the divergences, a concern for numbers that are divisible by five (i.e. base-60 in terms of months) is evident in all three lists of pre-diluvians. (Remember that an addition of the number 7 may apply, producing an ending in 2 or 7.) Lamech is the only exception (LXX and SP), when it is remembered that Methuselah's lifespan is otherwise explainable (see previously). Even the radical divergencies in the other figures for Methuselah adhere to the scheme (187 vs. 167, 969 vs. 720). The differences, then, are not random (as they should be for true ages of biological individuals), nor are they the result of accidents in the process of transmission of the text (errors), nor are they capricious. Rather, they have been carefully calculated to adhere to a numerical scheme.

For our purposes here, it does not matter whether one of these lists is "the original" and the two others modifications of it. Deliberate modification could only have happened prior to the time that the text became finalized ("fixed"), when elaborate safeguards were developed in order to protect it from adjustments (either by accident or design). This had not happened in the third to first centuries B.C.E., as can be demonstrated by comparison of the various scrolls from the Judean desert (primary the "Dead Sea Scrolls" from Qumran).[25] Thus, prior to that date of standardization (when the precursors of MT, LXX, and SP represented equally authoritative "families" of texts), the biblical traditions had an amount of fluidity sufficient to allow for the kind of divergences that we find for the ages of pre-diluvians and early post-diluvians. Informed scholars, therefore, have long since given up the concept of biblical "autographs" (*the* single, authoritative text, produced by the author; an *ur-text* from which all others descended).

Many interpreters, prior to modern (and technical!) understandings of the history of the text,[26] supposed that the MT list of ages (contained in English Bibles) must be "correct" (especially since that was the "family" of the medieval manuscripts behind such standard translations as KJV). It is now often supposed that the three lists may have developed independently, as ages were supplied to an earlier list of pre-diluvian generations. As a foremost interpreter has put it:

> Two things are certain: First, the numbers in Gen 5 do not belong originally to the names with which they stand. The series of names came down . . . without any life-span attached to them. The number scheme has an independent origin from the series of names.[27]

4. It is surprising that the total of elapsed years (from Adam to the flood) is not an exact multiple of 60. Contrast the reigns of the pre-diluvian mon-

archs from the Sumerian King List (Table No. 6). In fact, one of them (MT) does not even conform to the divisible-by-five scheme (base-60 in months), in contrast to the individual ages (Table No. 8). That is, whereas 2242 (LXX) is $[(60^2 \times 7) + (60 \times 27)]$ months + 7 years, and 1307 (SP) is $[(60^2 \times 4) + (60 \times 20)]$ months + 7 years, 1656 (MT) is an aberration. How can such non-conformity be, given the evidence of the base-60 scheme throughout the list? Has the addition simply worked out that way, and those who compiled the list ignored it? (Note that the sum of an age ending in 7 and one ending in 2 will give a non-conformist 9; add another ending in 7 and the result is a non-conformist 6.) Or has some external factor predetermined the total (i.e. it is the primary factor), and then the ages of the individuals were filled in subsequently with attention to base-60? Or is the total of elapsed time to the flood only of secondary importance, such that only a later total will be expressed in base-60? (If either of the last two possibilities has substance, then the first of them likely can be ruled out.)

a. *Has the elapsed time (to the flood) been determined by some external consideration?* A logical candidate, of course, would be the Sumerian King List, especially as reported by the W-B 62 text and Berossos with ten generations as in Genesis 5 (whereas W-B 444 has eight generations as in Genesis 4).[28]

The genealogy in Genesis 5 is guided by a concern for ages that are divisible by five, as pointed out previously. Such a concern is likewise attested among the Romans, who called such a period of time a *lustrum*. Were one to view Berossos' total from this perspective (as the compilers of Genesis might well have), then 432,000 years would yield 86,400 *lustra.*

The other basic consideration of Genesis, in the reckoning of time, is the week. Indeed, it is the fundamental time-unit, liturgically speaking, given the concern for sabbath observance. It might be relevant to ask, then, how many weeks are contained in the 1656 years from Adam to the flood? The answer would be: [(1656 years) × (365.25 days per year)] ÷ 7 days per week = 86,407 weeks. Another (and perhaps clearer) way to express this transformation is: Berosso' figure (432,000 years) is 72 × 6000 = 72 × 1,200 *lustra.* The MT figure (1656 years) is 72 × 1,200 weeks. Otherwise put: 6,000 years in the King List becomes 23 years in Genesis.[29]

One way, then, that the Israelite theologians may have reduced the fantastic ages of the Mesopotamian lists would be to convert *lustra* to weeks, and then the resultant figure into primeval (pre-diluvian) "years." The total of *lustra* involved would have multiple appeal for biblical reckoners, since, in base-60, each of its elements was a highly symbolic number: 86,407 = $(60^2 \times 24) + 7$, where 24 = (2 × 12).

Two considerations support this Mesopotamian origin of the 1656 year total. (1) The MT belongs to the Babylonian "family" of biblical manuscripts (i.e. scholars, in view of evidence in the Dead Sea Scrolls, assign that geographic origin to the text). This is, of course, the area that produced the Sumerian King List, so that the proposed connection would easily come to mind. (2) If those modern interpreters are right who assign the finalization of the Pentateuch (Gen.-Deut.) to the exilic and early post-exilic period (sixth to fifth centuries B.C.E.), then it is precisely the list of pre-diluvian monarchs as recorded by Berossos (third century B.C.E.) with which the biblical thinkers would most likely have been familiar.

It might be argued, of course, if one wanted to maintain the connection between Genesis 5 and Berossos and yet assert the historicity of the Genesis figure, that it was the reverse process that actually has taken place: the Mesopotamians derived their figure from the Bible. This would mean that they took the figure 1656, converted it to weeks, transferred that total into *lustra,* and obtained 432,000 years. Such a reverse process seems extremely unlikely, however, for the following reasons: (1) their mathematics does not show a concern for units of five; (2) the result, an ideal in base-60 ($60^2 \times [60 \times 2]$), would be an astonishing coincidence; and (3) the seven-day week was not for them a fundamental liturgical celebration.

It should be stressed that this proposed correspondence in elapsed time applies only to the total pre-diluvian figure: it has not been carried out for the individual ages within the genealogy in Genesis 5. (On groups within the total, however, see Appendix XVI.) That is, in order to determine the individual figures which would total 1656, other factors were invoked (on which see above).

The proposal that the MT total (1656 years) was derived from the King List would be greatly strengthened if the total from one of the other biblical traditions (LXX or SP) were similarly derived from an external source. Well, it turns out that the LXX total (2242 years) may be a modification of a chronology of the earliest rulers of Egypt (including gods and demi-gods) as reported by the Egyptian historian Manetho in the third century B.C.E. Since the LXX was translated (from Hebrew into Greek) in that very century, and belongs to the so-called Egyptian "family" of biblical manuscripts, perhaps this is only to be expected. (Since readers of the present volume may by now have grown tired of a series of calculations, it is well to spare the details and let those who desire to do so consult them in Appendix XII.)

Once the formulators of the LXX tradition determined their total of elapsed time, it then became necessary to adjust the individual ages at time of first-born so that the sum be 2242. *If* they had the MT list before them, the easiest way to achieve this would be to lengthen individual ages in units of 100 years, seeking a total change of 2242 − 1656 = 586 years. This apparently was done for the first five individuals in the genealogy (Adam, Seth, Enosh, Kenan, and Mahalalel: see Table No. 8). An additional adjustment of 86 years was then needed: Enoch, +100; Methuselah, −20; and Lamech, +6. Why those *particular* steps would have been taken is unclear.

b. *Is the elapsed time (to the flood) only a point on a much longer symbolic chronological scheme?* Is there a terminal point in such reckoning which extends far beyond the book of Genesis, such that the date of the flood is only of passing interest? If so, elapsed time from Adam to the flood might be a secondary calculation, even if derived from either the Sumerian King List (Berossos) or Manetho's history of Egypt. In that case, one might expect the grand total to be some conspicuous multiple in base-60 (say, $60 \times 60 =$ 3600 years).

Such a logical concluding point might be the founding of the second temple in 516 B.C.E. The first, or Solomonic temple, was destroyed by the invading Babylonians in 587 B.C.E., at the beginning of the Judean exile. It was the ultimately more important second temple that served as the nucleus for the emergence of Judaism and which will be familiar to readers of the New Testament and rabbinic literature. If modern critical scholars are right, it was during the early years of that temple that the Pentateuch (Gen.-Deut.) took its final (and present) shape, and thus its existence would be of momentous consequence for those who shaped the genealogies in Genesis 5 and 11. It would thus be nice symbolism if that temple could be said to have been founded in the year 3600 A.M. (*anno mundi,* "the year of the world," meaning "elapsed time since the creation of the world"). It would thus have been founded at a "perfect" time and with an auspicious beginning (60^2 years since creation). This may indeed have been the case, and those who desire to pursue the details may do so in Appendix XIII.

c. *Conclusions Concerning the Primeval Ages.* In view of the previous computations it is reasonable to conclude that:

1. Those who formulated the ages of the pre-diluvians and early post-diluvians did so with a preference for multiples of 60, in keeping with the Mesopotamian mathematical system which utilized base-60. This is reflected, in terms of months, in ages which are divisible by 5 (since 5 years equals 60 months). To such ages may be added a 7 (symbolic of completeness). An even higher ideal, apparently, is 120 years (60×2) or multiples thereof, as reflected in Egyptian thought.

2. Elapsed time from creation to the flood has been determined, not by multiples of 60, but by modification of other Ancient Near Eastern primeval chronologies: from Berossos' list of pre-flood rulers in the case of MT; from Manetho's list of pre-flood rulers in the case of LXX.

3. Elapsed time from creation to the founding of the second temple has been determined in MT by the idea of an ideal period of time: 3600 years, or 60^2.

4. Individual ages have been determined by a number of factors: mathematical ideals (e.g. 120 years), gematria (e.g. 777 years), the solar cycle (365 years), depiction of destruction in the flood (969 years), modification of a Babylonian age (600 years), and others yet to be understood. In all cases, the necessity to arrive at a total that was pre-determined must also have been a factor.

5. Individual ages vary from one manuscript tradition to another (MT, LXX, SP), and there is no reason to assume that one of them has remained unchanged while the others were modified.

This means that there is "hard" evidence in the Bible itself, in keeping with its own legitimate agenda and definition of "truth," that contradicts the opinion of "creationists" that

> The [chronological] record is perfectly natural and straightforward and is obviously intended to give . . . the only reliable chronological framework we have for the antediluvian period of history.[30]

> All in all, there is no reason whatever not to take this list in Genesis 5 as sober history in every way.[31]

To the contrary! Such a conclusion results from (1) a surface reading, rather than the detailed analysis which has been presented above (or at least such an analysis is not evident in "creationist" published works that I have seen), and (2) a prior assumption that the biblical text, as the word of God, is verbally inspired in matters of chronology *in the modern "creationist" definition of that term.* The possibility that the Bible might have a different chronological concern is not allowed.

There is a purpose, a truth, in the biblical lists of ages, even if it does not conform to modern ideas that the ages *ought to be* biologically and chronologically reliable. Nonetheless, in matter of interpretation, it is the agenda of the text that must be honored and not the agenda of the interpreter. The agenda of the primeval story, as regards time, is not compatible with that of modern "creationists" who would use its genealogies as part of a computation of the age of the earth.

The summary opinion of Claus Westermann is helpful:

> . . . the series of names with their astronomical numbers points to the extension of ancient time into an unimaginably distant past. . . . [The writer] wants to initiate with a genealogy the course of ordered, subdivided

time, the second part of which, the patriarchs, introduces God's dealing with his people. The genealogy sets in motion and puts into the length and breadth of human history the power of the blessing which God bestowed on his people.[32]

3. The Structure of Genealogies in Israel's Primeval Story

The format and composition of genealogies in the Bible, linked to the previous discussion of ages by the symbolic use of the number seven, further assists us in concluding what the agenda of the creation stories in Genesis is not.

That a genealogy ideally has seven generations or multiples thereof, or that a single generation ideally consists of seven siblings, or that the seventh born was deemed worthy of special comment,[33] is evident not merely from the abundance of such instances in the Bible but also is acknowledged in the accompanying description. This is quite clear when the evangelist Matthew, in the first chapter of his gospel, recites the genealogy of Jesus, beginning with Abraham (v. 2) and concluding with the one "who is called Christ" (v. 16). He then remarks:

> So all the generations from Abraham to David were fourteen generations, and from David to the deportation to Babylon fourteen generations, and from the deportation to Babylon to the Christ fourteen generations (v. 17).

Consequently, many recent versions of the Bible (e.g. RSV) have arranged the genealogy in three paragraphs of fourteen generations each.

It has long been observed that the number of generations in Matthew's structure is not in accordance with other biblical data.[34] For example, in the middle section (David to Jechoniah), although each monarch is said to have sired the next listed, the account in 1 Chronicles 3:10–16 contains four additional generations (Ahaziah, Jehoash/Joash, Amaziah, and the brothers Jehoahaz-Jehoiakim-Zedekiah). The correctness of this list in 1 Chronicles is attested by the longer narrative accounts in the books of Kings. The divergence is illustrated in Table 9 ("Genealogy from Abraham to Jesus").

The strange situation in the middle section of Matthew (Solomon to Jechoniah), where four generations from Chronicles are missing, has caused a modern interpreter to ask, whimsically, "Could Matthew count?"[35] Various modern "explanations" for the discrepancy are then reviewed, with the preferable solution being that (in the Greek manuscripts which Matthew apparently used) the four "extra" names were already missing because of similar spellings. That is, the eye of an earlier copyist may have skipped from

TABLE 9. Genealogy from Abraham to Jesus

Matthew	*Other Biblical Sources*
1:2–6a	1 Chr 1:34; 2:1—15
Abraham	Abraham
Isaac	Isaac
Jacob	Israel (Jacob)
Judah	Judah
Perez	Perez
Hezron	Hezron
Ram	Ram
Amminadab	Amminadab
Nahshon	Nahshon
Salmon	Salma (Salmon)
Boaz	Boaz
Obed	Obed
Jesse	Jesse
David	David
sub-total: 14	sub-total: 14
1:6b–11	1 Chr 3:10–16
Solomon	Solomon
Rehoboam	Rehoboam
Abijah	Abijah
Asa	Asa
Jehoshaphat	Jehoshaphat
Joram	Joram
Uzziah	*Ahaziah*
Jotham	*Joash*
Ahaz	*Amaziah*
Hezekiah	Azariah (Uzziah)
Manasseh	Jotham
Amos	Ahaz
Josiah	Hezekiah
Jechoniah	Manasseh
	Amon
sub-total: 14	Josiah
	Jehoiakim
	Jeconiah
	sub-total: 18
	("extras" in italics)

TABLE 9—*Continued*

Matthew	Other Biblical Sources
1:12–16	1 Chr 3:17–19
(Jechoniah)	(Jeconiah)
Shealtiel	Pedaiah
Zerubbabel	Zerubbabel
Abiud	(subsequent generations are
Eliakim	different from those of Matthew)
Azor	
Zadok	
Achim	
Eliud	
Eleazar	
Matthan	
Jacob	
Joseph	
Jesus	

sub-total: 13 (14 if Jechoniah
is counted for the 2nd time)

Ozeias (Ahaziah) to *Ozias* (Uzziah). Furthermore, since Jechoniah/Jeconiah is otherwise known as Jehoiakin, confusion with his father Jehoiakim would be common and might have led to the loss of the latter.[36] The result would thus be a reduction of the list from 18 names to 14, by accident rather than design, especially since "We know of no special symbolism attached to this number in terms of its being twice seven, the perfect number."[37]

This is not the entirety of the "arithmetic" problem in Matthew's genealogy, however. In the final section (from Shealtiel to Jesus), Jechoniah must be counted to arrive at a total of 14, even though he has been the concluding entry in the previous section.[38] Furthermore, from Zerubbabel downward, the line of Jesus deviates from that in Chronicles, and yet the total is the same as that of the other two sections. Is that a happy coincidence, or is there, after all, the desire to create a 14-generation scheme?[39]

In any case, the time-span covered by the total genealogy (about 1750 years) would seem to demand more generations than are listed here (about 83 years each, on the average). After all, the lifespan, as depicted by the Bible, drops radicaly in the post-diluvian age (chart above), and especially in the monarchical period. The average for the monarchs of Judah (none assassinated) is not quite 44 years![40] Even this figure may be unrealistic, since monarchs had better health care and may well have lived longer than the more ordinary folks in the final section of the genealogy! Abbreviation (omissions) in genealogies, ancient and modern, is well attested, and thus should not surprise us here. Consider the fact that, in 1 Chronicles 6:3–14, the number of generations of Aaron's descendants, to the time of the exile (587 B.C.E.) is given as 22. And yet Ezra, well into the exilic age, in tracing his lineage back to Aaron, lists himself as the 14th generation (7:1–5)!

At Genesis 11:14, we read of the birth of Eber. Apparently he is understood to be the ancestor of all "Hebrews" (since the two words are derived from the same verb), and hence he is a pivotal person in the genealogy. Curiously, he is the 14th generation since creation, and Abraham/Abram (11:26) is the 20th. However, in the Greek text (Septuagint), he is the 21st! It does not matter which of these is the "original" text, since the effort to create genealogies in clusters of 7 generations is evident.

The basic genealogy (7 generations) is evident in 1 Samuel 9:1, the line of King Saul. The Hebrew text makes him the 7th generation, reading ". . . Alphiah, the son of a Benjaminite." (English translations, however, considering the possibility of a textual corruption,[41] render " . . . Aphiah, a Benjaminite," and thus reduce the generations to 6.) An unambiguous example may be found in the 4th chapter of Genesis, where the line of Cain is traced from Adam through the siblings Jabal-Jubal-Tubal, they being the 7th generation of Adam's descendants (the 8th, however, of humanity). Again, the list of the tribes who came out of Egypt (Num 26) covers only the first one or two generations of descendants, save for the tribe of Joseph which continues through the 7th generation of descendants. Curiously, in this list of Jacob's sons, the order of which fluctuates from list to list, Joseph is listed in the 7th position. (See above, where Gad, the gematria of whose name is 7, is in the 7th position.)

It is plausible to conclude, then, if not compelling, that biblical genealogies were constructed in 7's and multiples of 7, even if deletions were necessary and if some entries were counted twice. Matthew's genealogy, then, conveys the idea: This Jesus is a triple of the ideal [3(2 × 7)], starting with Abraham! Even more symbolic would be the genealogy in Luke, which reckons from God to Jesus, assigning the latter to the 77th position (7 × 11). A "heavy dude," indeed!

It should also be noted that, in genealogies that total more than multiples of 7, the individual in the 7th position is often singled out for comment or is a person of unusual abilities/reputation. In Matthew's genealogy, those in this position are David (founder of the messianic line), Jeconiah (at whose exile the messianic line seemed eclipsed), and Jesus (the culmination of the messianic expectation). In the genealogies in Genesis (chapters 5, 10, 11), Enoch (who walked with God) is 7th; Eber (ancestor of the Hebrews) is 14th; Isaac is

20th (but 21st in the Greek text). In the genealogy at the conclusion of the book of Ruth (4:18–22), Boaz, the hero of the book, is the 7th generation listed. The list begins with Perez, apparently arbitrarily, since only in that way will Boaz be genealogically "proper." In the genealogy in Genesis 4, it is Lamech who is in the 7th position, he of the 77-fold retribution, who lives 777 years, and the name of whose father "means" (by gematria) 777!

Ray Brown is right, then, when he remarks: "The Matthean genealogy is 'artificial' rather than strictly 'historical' in its structure, although neither term is really precise if we consider that the primary purpose of a biblical genealogy is rarely involved with purely biological descent."[42] The same may be said for those in the primeval story.

The so-called "table of nations" (in Genesis 10) is related to our topic, although its point is the geographical distribution of Noah's descendants after the flood. Interpreters have long been puzzled by its classification (arrangement), once the various peoples are placed on a map of the Ancient Near East. It is not in accordance with race, language, or geographical proximity. Whatever its historical basis may be,[43] numerology is also a concern, as Table 10 reveals.

One of the more obvious things about this list is that it does not consistently refer to the same type of entity. Gomer, for example, is the name of a people (Ez 38:6; the Gimirrai of cuneiform sources and the Cimmerians of Greek sources, a name which may survive in the modern place name Crimea). While the word is singular, allowing identification as a personal name (just as the text suggests when he is listed as the son of Japheth), others are names of people in the plural (e.g. Kittim, where the -*im* ending denotes the grammatically plural). It cannot, therefore, have been construed as a personal name. Other names, rather than being that of a people, designate cities whose population seems not different from that of the surrounding country (e.g. Sidon). Yet others have the form of a gentilic: having a definite article and the -*i* ending which denotes "belonging to" (e.g. instead of Amor as a proper name, one finds "the Amorite," a singular with a collective meaning).

Note that such varying designations often are in clusters: the "descendants" of Cush are place-designations in the singular; the descendants of Egypt are plurals; those of Canaan are a mixture of gentilics (the "-ites") and non-gentilics.

This has plausibly been taken to suggest that the overall list of Noah's descendants is composite: it has been taken from a variety of sources (lists) that were available to the composers, among them commercial and diplomatic files. Especially instructive is the list of South Arabic entities ("descendants" of Joktam), with which Israel had contact only at limited and specific times. Thus Westermann concludes: "Because we know of commercial deal-

TABLE 10.   The Genealogy of Noah, According to Genesis 10

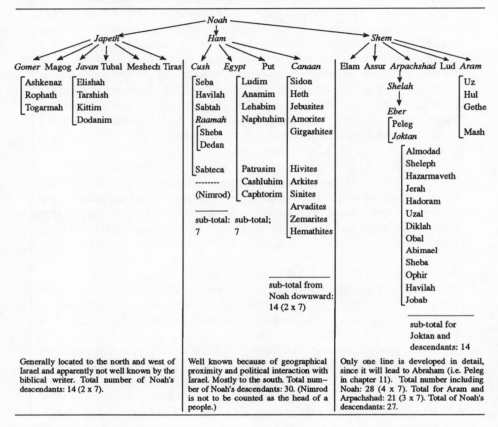

Japeth: Gomer, Magog, *Javan*, Tubal, Meshech, Tiras

Ham: *Cush*, Egypt, Put, *Canaan*

Shem: Elam, Assur, *Arpachshad*, Lud, *Aram*

Gomer	Magog	Cush	Egypt	Canaan	Arpachshad	Aram
Ashkenaz	Elishah	Seba	Ludim	Sidon	*Shelah*	Uz
Rophath	Tarshish	Havilah	Anamim	Heth		Hul
Togarmah	Kittim	Sabtah	Lehabim	Jebusites	*Eber*	Gethe
	Dodanim	*Raamah*	Naphtuhim	Amorites	Peleg	
		Sheba		Girgashites	*Joktan*	Mash
		Dedan				
		Sabteca	Patrusim	Hivites	Almodad	
		--------	Cashluhim	Arkites	Sheleph	
		(Nimrod)	Caphtorim	Sinites	Hazarmaveth	
				Arvadites	Jerah	
		sub-total:	sub-total;	Zemarites	Hadoram	
		7	7	Hemathites	Uzal	
					Diklah	
					Obal	
					Abimael	
					Sheba	
					Ophir	
				sub-total from	Havilah	
				Noah downward:	Jobab	
				14 (2 x 7)		

sub-total for Joktan and descendants: 14

Generally located to the north and west of Israel and apparently not well known by the biblical writer. Total number of Noah's descendants: 14 (2 x 7).	Well known because of geographical proximity and political interaction with Israel. Mostly to the south. Total num—ber of Noah's descendants: 30. (Nimrod is not to be counted as the head of a people.)	Only one line is developed in detail, since it will lead to Abraham (i.e. Peleg in chapter 11). Total number including Noah: 28 (4 x 7). Total for Aram and Arpachshad: 21 (3 x 7). Total of Noah's descendants: 27.

ings with Phoenician cities and with South Arabia from the time of Solo-mon, we presume that the basis of these enumerations are lists from the commercial chancery of the Jerusalem court" (*Genesis 1–11,* pp. 502–503).

It should furthermore be noted that the verb used to link the "genera-tions" together varies from place to place: "X" became the father of "Y" (vv. 8, 13, 15, 24, 26); "children were born" (vv. 21, 25); "the sons of X are . . ." (vv. 2, 6, 7, 22, 23). This has been taken, rightly or wrongly, to suggest that the list of Noah's descendants was not composed at a single sitting by a single author, but rather is composite and may have been supplemented from time to time.

In any case, from a multiplicity of possibilities, names have been (se-lected and?) arranged in several groups of seven: the line of Japheth totals fourteen (seven in the initial generation and seven in the next: 3 + 4); the line of Ham contains two lists of seven (with an extra generation at Raamah to bring about the "correct" total?) and may contain a larger list of fourteen; the line of Shem may contain a list of fourteen and a larger survey that has twenty eight (4 × 7). Nonetheless, there is an incongruity: the overall total is a multiple of seven only in the case of Japheth (14): it is 30 in the case of Ham and 27 in the case of Shem, for a grand total of 71. It would have been astonishing, and evidence of manipulation (or selectivity) of numbers, if the total had been 70, another of the Bible's "magic" (symbolic) numbers (10 × 7). Note may be made of seventy as the number of elders in the period of Israel's wandering in the wilderness (Ex 24:1; this becomes the model for a court during the early centuries of the Common Era ["A.D."]); the duration of a period of mourning (Gen 50:3); an amount of vengeance (Gen 5:24); a totality of princes (2 Kgs 10:1); duration of an exile (Is 23:15; Jer 25:11); totality of appointees by Jesus (Lk 10:1); and so on. In the case of the fanciful story of the translation of the Hebrew Bible (Genesis-Deuteronomy) into Greek, it occupied 72 translators for 72 days, which has been rounded-off to the symbolically appropriate 70 (hence its designation, the "Septuagint").[44] This total accidentally (?) coincides with the line of Noah, when Noah himself is included.

The closest parallel in number to Noah's descendants (71) may be the stated totality of the members of Jacob's household who went down to Egypt with him to be reunited with his son Joseph (Gen 46:27; Ex 1:5; Deut 10:22).[45] The total is given at 70. Were two sons who died in Canaan to be included (Er and Onan), the number would be 72 (as is the case in Genesis 10 when Noah is included).

In this case, the agreement between the two lists may not be accidental. The totality of Israel's ancestors, at the crucial moment of entry into Egypt, is the same auspicious (symbolic) number as the descendants of Noah after the universal flood. Thus a new beginning, at the time of Noah, prefigures the survival of the oppressed community at the time of Moses.

Perhaps, then, a theological statement is being made through the manipulation of numbers. The genealogy in Genesis 10 has an integrity and a "truth" of its own that transcends considerations of history ("Did this really happen"), biology ("Were these really individuals, and sons of Noah?"), and chronology ("Can we trust the list to help us date the age of the human race?"). If such numerology seems strange to us, and if it upsets our notions of what the Bible is all about, then that is our problem as interpreters and not grounds for denouncing the Bible as "unscientific" or for trying to make it appear to be "scientific."

Neither the individual ages (in the previous discussion), nor the number of generations in a genealogy, nor the groups included in the lists of peoples, was intended to be "literal." They do not intend chronology and geography in the modern sense of those terms, and thus the text itself argues against the use to which "creationists" have put it.

4. Genealogy and the Origins of Civilization

Ancient Near Eastern literature sometimes depicts the development of the arts and crafts by means of a genealogy of the discoverers. This may serve as another indication of what the agenda of the biblical creation stories is not.

It was plausible for ancient peoples to believe that the name of the group had been derived from a common ancestor's given name. Such ancestors (real or imaginary) are known to modern interpreters as eponymous ("name giving") ancestors. Consider the fact that, in the Bible, Israel (as a political and worshiping community) traced its beginnings to a Mr. Israel (Jacob). It was similarly assumed (rightly or wrongly) that all Egyptians had descended from a Mr. Egypt (Gen 10:6), that all "Hebrews" were descended from a Mr. Eber (Gen 10:25), all those who spoke a Semitic language from Mr. Semite (Shem, Gen 10:1, 21ff), and indeed all human beings from a Mr. Human Being (which is the meaning of the word Adam). This assumption is illustrated in the previous section (Table No. 10), where a mixture of group names, gentilics, and plurals is aligned as if all were derived from individuals in a genealogical scheme. Indeed, so thoroughgoing is this mentality that the creation of the world is described in terms of "the generations of the heavens and the earth" (Gen 2:4).

It was not geographical and political entities alone which the ancient mind arranged in such schemes, but professions as well. It was plausible to believe that, with the development of the human race, came new and creative endeavors which resulted in specialization of the labor force. Furthermore, since it was the gods who had fashioned the world and had placed human beings in it as laborers,[46] one might suppose that it was the deities who (in stages) had taught the civilizing arts to human beings. It was thus functional to treat the processes or parts of nature as persons (the name of a "thing" becoming the name of a person, human or divine) and to relate them one to the other by means of a genealogy.[47]

This is made clear in a sustained fashion in Philo of Byblos' *Phoenician History*. This learned writer, from the 1st century (C.E.), has recast a much older Phoenician account by the priest Sanchuniathon into Hellenistic (Greek) terminology. Therein, an account of cosmic beginnings is followed by that of "the discoverers."[48] A series of deities is depicted as mortal and their activities with respect to the origins of the civilizing arts are described as human discoveries, all within the framework of genealogy.

... from the wind *Kolpia* ⟨Thunder?⟩ and his wife *Baau* ⟨Chaos?⟩ ... there were born Aion ⟨World Order?⟩ and Protogonos ⟨First Born?⟩, mortal men called by these names. Aion discovered the food obtained from trees. The children born to them were called Genos and Genea and they settled Phoenicia. ... From Genos, the son of Aion and Protogonos, there again were born mortal children whose names were Phos ⟨Light⟩, Pyr ⟨Fire⟩, and Phlox ⟨Flame⟩. These (he says) by rubbing sticks together discovered fire, and they taught its use. And they begot sons ... whose names were given to the mountain ranges over which they ruled. ... From these were born Samemroumos ⟨High Heavens, a section of the city of Tyre⟩ who is also [called] Hypsouranios and Ousoos ⟨a section of the city of Tyre⟩. ... Hypsouranios settled Tyre and he invented huts made from reeds, and rushes and papyrus. And he quarreled with his brother Ousoos, who first contrived a covering for the body from skins of the animals he was able to capture ... (he) was the first to dare set out to sea. ... But many years later, from the family of Hypsouranios were born Agreus ⟨Hunter⟩ and Halieus ⟨Fisherman⟩ who discovered hunting and fishing. ... From them were born two brothers, the discoverers of iron and of the method of working it. One of these ... discovered the fishhook and bait and the fishing line and the raft, and was the first of all men to sail. ... Some say that his brothers discovered the use of bricks to make walls. Thereafter from their family two youths were born. ... They discovered the mixing of chaff with the clay of bricks ... roofs. From these were born other ... ⟨who⟩ thought of adding courtyards, enclosures and cellars to houses. They are the ancestors of [ordinary] hunters and those who use dogs in hunting. From them were born Amunos and Magos who introduced villages and flocks. From them were born Misor ⟨Right⟩ and Sydyk ⟨Justice⟩ ... who discovered the use of salt. From Misor came Taautos who devised the alphabetic writing, and whom the Egyptians called Thouth... Sydyk fathered the Dioskouroi ... the first to invent a ship. They gave birth to others who discovered herbs, a cure for venomous animal bites, and charms.

Philo's account seems parallel, both in concept and form, to the genealogy of the descendants of Cain in Gen. 4:17–22. Previously, Mr. Earth-creature ('*adam*)[49] and Ms. Life-giver (*ḥawwâ*, "Eve")[50] have produced children named Mr. Blacksmith (*qayin*, "Cain")[51] and Mr. Meadow (Shepherd? *hebel*, "Abel").[52] The names of the first children, then, seem to typify (if not be derived from) two basic life-styles in Canaan: agriculturalists who possessed iron technology (Canaanites?)[53] and pastoral semi-nomads who did not (Hebrews).

Cain, the first city builder, names his son after this technological accomplishment ("Enoch").[54]

Enoch's son is named Irad, which may be related to the development of reed-hut dwellings.[55]

The next generation, Mehujael, may be related to a type of priesthood, thus signaling the beginnings of cultic activity (or a particular cult).[56]

Three generations later come brothers who are the ancestors of tent dwellers (Jabal), musicians (Jubal), and metalurgists (Tubal-cain).[57]

The genealogy of the founders of the arts then comes to an end, not surprisingly comprising seven generations (for which see the previous section).

That this section of scripture (Gen 4:17–22) was once a self-contained independent story is shown not only by its form (a seven-generation genealogy) and parallels with other Ancient Near Eastern literature, but also by its tension with the larger context of the chapter:

1. This Cain (v. 27), the founder of urban dwelling, is quite unlike that of vv. 1–16, who wanders the face of the earth, fearful of "anyone who finds me."

2. Jabal seems hardly to be the first to have domesticated cattle (if that is what the text means by his being "the father of . . .") since that was already the occupation of Abel ("Abel was a keeper of sheep," 4:2).

3. Tubal-cain, as the "forger of all instruments of bronze and iron,"[58] is a curious repetition of Cain (whose name may mean Blacksmith).

While the genealogy of Cain means to depict human accomplishments in the civilizing arts, one may wonder at the resultant picture if it is taken to be a record of historical individuals. Can one really expect, within two generations, transition from the first couple with nothing other than their "fig leaf" underwear to city building? Did city dwelling precede nomadic shepherding? Could the smelting of metals have evolved in a mere "seven" generations?[59] Were bronze and iron simultaneously wrested from stone? After all, archaeological evidence assigns the so-called Bronze Age to 3000–1200 B.C.E., and the so-called Iron Age thereafter. The earliest evidence known of crude iron in the area is among the Hittites of Asia Minor, around 1500 B.C.E.[60]

The question may well be asked, if the previous analysis is correct: How did such material find its way into the Bible, and what did it mean for the community of faith? The answers necessitate a brief review of the editorial nature of the early chapters in Genesis.

The authors of biblical materials could rely upon their own observations when they analyzed and addressed the society of their time. The prophets, for example, will refer to events that are then taking place. The situation was a bit different, however, when they sought to use material from the past in order to express their point of view. Not always was there an established body of traditions to which they could appeal, but rather many kinds of literature, much of it in bits and pieces. It was then necessary to become a gatherer and editor as much as an author. This is especially true of Genesis 1–11, which refers to a time far prior to that of Moses (or whoever else the editor(s) may have been).[61]

The traditions in Genesis are not one unbroken narrative, stretching without literary transition from the "beginning" to the birth of Moses. Rather, there is abundant evidence of the joining of many short, complete, once independent units of material. The transition from one to the other is often marked by formula of introduction and conclusion. For example, the story of creation begins at 1:1, sounding as an opening might: "In the beginning . . ." (so RSV), and signal its completion as a conclusion should: "And that is how the universe was created" (so TEV). That there is here an ending, a transition in the literature, is indicated in NAB by an editorially inserted heavy-type heading: "Second Story of Creation" (so also NEB and JB). Otherwise put: the story in 1:1–2:4a is self-contained and complete, and contains no hint that other events will subsequently be related. Similarly, note how the 5th chapter begins: "This is the book of the generations of Adam" (RSV). It goes on to tell us about the creation of male and female, the divine blessing thereon, and so on. One does not get the sense of having begun in the middle as if this had ever and always been the fifth consecutive episode of a larger story. Rather, one could begin to read here and never suspect that there were chapters 1–4. Thus there is every reason to believe that there was a time when this chapter was in fact unconnected to the previous accounts.

Notice, furthermore, the use of the third person to describe the characters, meaning that it is not the characters themselves who have formulated and handed down the traditions: "Adam" is always spoken of as "he" (e.g. 4:1), as is Cain (4:17), Lamech (4:23), Noah (7:1), and all the other characters. Contrast Jeremiah when he speaks of his own experience: "Righteous art thou, O Lord, when I complain to thee" (12:1 and many other places), or St. Paul: "I am speaking the truth" (Rom 9:1 and many other places).

There were, then, many units of material which were already available to the person/persons who arranged Genesis 1–11 in its present form. Each unit had its own origin, its own creator(s), its own purpose, and its own history of transmission from its formation to its inclusion in the larger text of the Bible. The original purpose of each may not be the same as the purpose (message) for which it was included in the larger story, such that an originally secular piece can have been made to serve an overtly theological purpose.

There was thus undoubtedly a "truth" which those who formulated the genealogy of Cain wanted to depict: apparently the traditional Ancient Near Eastern way of relating the developments of civilization and its arts by means of a genealogy of personified activities. It may be doubted that its "truth" lay in the realms of what we would call chronology, biological parentage, or historical sequence of events. As the story now stands (within the framework of "In the beginning, God . . ."), the genealogy depicts the development of civilization under the sovereignty of God the creator upon whom all things depend (and later to be revealed as the one who elected Israel). Although the arts derive from human inventiveness (in contrast to being gifts of the gods, in Mesopotamian thought, giving them a sacral character), they stand under God's blessing and thus require accountability for their usage.

By contrast, if one assumes the genealogy to recite "mere facts," mere "happenedness," one may thereby not only misunderstand the text but also pervert it. It is just that approach, characteristic of "creationists," that *the text itself* suggests is unbiblical.

5. The Sequence of the Acts of Creation in Genesis 1

The placement of the creation of the heavenly luminaries may serve as an indication of what the agenda of the overall story is not.

Readers of Genesis 1 have long been struck by the curiosity that it is only on the fourth day that the stellar objects, including the sun and moon, were created (vv. 14–19). How, then, can there have been a preceding three days, each characterized by a period of darkness and a period of light and designated as "evening" and "morning"? Is it not the existence, the absence or presence, of the sun which ordinarily makes such days and nights possible?

Whatever the truth of the characterization of ancient societies as "pre-scientific" or even "pre-logical," it would seem to be rather extreme as an explanation for the problem under consideration. After all, the cause-effect relationship of sun to daylight, of the absence of the sun to darkness, is not one which requires great powers of observation or abstraction. By contrast, that persons in ancient Israel may not have understood condensation and evaporation or connected them to the process of rainfall, and thus conjectured instead the existence of a great reservoir above a hard dome of the sky, perhaps we can understand and designate as pre-scientific. (See Appendix XI.) It is quite a different matter, however, with the claim of light before the existence of the luminaries.

Is it possible that the biblical author(s) is here slavishly dependent upon other creation accounts in the Ancient Near East? That of the Babylonians, for example,[62] depicts the existence of light prior to the creation of a "firmament" (dome of the sky), dry land, and luminaries. However, while there are similarities between the two accounts (and no reason to doubt that the biblical author knew the Babylonian one), there are also significant differences.[63] Thus, what the Genesis account intends by this strange sequence of creative acts must be determined primarily by internal evidence.[64] This must be the case in view of the fact that the Genesis 1 account is unique in its arrangement of creation in a sequence of days (as will be discussed below).

Is it possible that the biblical author was advancing a polemic against the surrounding nations in whose thought the created objects were regarded as visible images of divine powers? Could it be that these "divine powers" are reduced, in the perception of Genesis 1, to mere "things" which the one true God has created? If one wanted to go beyond this general characterization to ask the meaning of the *sequence* of events, it might be that there has been an attempt so to "neuter" the "sun-god" that the solar object is merely made to assume a prior function of the generation of light. However, while such a point of view is well in keeping with Israel's denunciation of polytheism, and would be much needed in order to prevent the deterioration of the "true faith" in favor of that of the politically superior neighbors, it clearly is subordinated to a larger concern of the story which emerges only in 2:1–4a (as we shall see).

Alternatively, were the formulators of the Genesis account seeking to advance, not merely the chronology and sequence of creation as they understood it, but also "the way that it really was," so that the text (rather than being pre-scientific) is scientifically reliable by modern standards? Are "biblical creationism" and "scientific creationism" not only the same subject (as claimed by "Creationists"), but also a blueprint of reality? This is, of course, the question which we have been investigating all along.

The key to understanding the strange sequence of events in Gen. 1 (light prior to the luminaries) lies in the overall principle of organization of the account. Creation is uniquely set within the framework of a seven-day pattern: events take place within the boundaries of successive periods of evening and morning which total a week in duration. (For discussion of these days as being 24 hours in duration, see Appendix No. II.) So, if such days are to be the framework within which the creative activity takes place, then there must be, right from the first description or event, an alternation of light and darkness to set the boundaries. Thus, if "in the beginning . . . darkness was upon the face of the deep" (1:1–2), then the first order of business must be the production of light. Only then can it be said that "God separated the light from the darkness. God called the light Day, and the darkness he called Night. And there was evening and there was morning, one day" (1:4–5). Otherwise put, there must be designated and describable time units within which the acts of creation can take place. As one modern interpreter has put it: "And so those exegetes are correct who understand vv. 3–5 as a process which makes creation possible rather than a single work of creations" (Westermann, *Genesis 1–11,* p. 112). The point of the mention of "light" (v. 3) is not so much to relate the creation of a substance as it is to mark the framework of all things. One is mandated, by the day-week framework, to speak of light prior to the creation of substances. Otherwise put: Establishment of a temporal order is prior to any concern with material "things." Or, to put it another way: The basic concern is not to relate the sequence and relationship of substances, but to establish the week as the fundamental unit of time reckoning. God "puts the basis of the temporal order before the creation of the world of space" (Westermann, p. 112).

The text of Genesis 1, then, is not to be faulted (or excused) as "pre-scientific." Neither is it to be made into a "scientific" treatise by identifying its "light" with some sort of cosmic illumination prior to the creation of matter. The text must not be forced into the thought categories of modern interpreters who think that they know what it ought to say. Rather, it must be respected for what it is, with an openness toward its own agenda. Of that, more will be said later.

6. The Sequence of Human Emergence in Genesis 2:4b–25

The order in which animals and humans make their appearance in the sequence of creation, and especially that of the human female, may be yet another indication of what the agenda of the creation stories is not.

Modern translations of the Bible regularly ignore chapter divisions (and occasionally even versification) in order to indicate to the reader where the boundaries of a thought-unit are. Previously, we have noted such a transition such that Genesis 1:1–2:4a belong together, with 2:4b beginning a new story. NAB, for example, labels the former the "First Story of Creation" and the latter as the "Second Story of Creation." The transition is more than in topic (from the creation of the world to the creation of humans): it is one of literary form (a formal beginning) as well. That is, 2:4b opens as a once-independent account should:

> At the time when the Lord God made the earth and the heavens—while as yet there was no field shrub on earth and no grass of the field had sprouted . . . the Lord God formed man out of the clay of the ground . . . (NAB).

This suggests that the two stories are not in fact an account of sequential events by a single writer but rather are independent, alternative accounts of beginnings.[65] According to the former, it all began when the deity brought order out of watery chaos; according to the latter, it all began when the deity Yahweh ("the Lord God") created an oasis of life ("garden") amidst the barren semi-arid desert.[66] In that case, one should not be surprised to find diverging orders for the creation of things, as illustrated in Table No. 11.

TABLE 11. The Order of Creation

1:1–2:4a	*2:4b–25*
vegetation: plants and trees (1:11–12)	a single human male (2:7–8)
the luminaries (1:14–18)	vegetation (2:9; compare 2:5)
creatures of sea and sky (1:20–22)	animals of every sort (2:18–20)
beasts and creeping things (1:24–25)	a single human female (2:21–23)
humans: "male *and* female" (1:26–27)	

On the other hand, one should be surprised at the result if the two accounts are attributed to a single author who intended to describe sequential events of actual history. Attempts to resolve the tensions have ranged from the desperate to the humorous.[67] For the present purposes, it matters not which portrait of authorship is correct. Whatever the purpose of the author (or authors/editors) may have been, whether we have alternative accounts of beginnings or a sequence of events, it should be obvious that the intent was not to present a scientifically reliable biological and historical account. This conclusion arises from the reality of the text itself, rather than being imposed upon it by modern interpreters.

One may strive to make the accounts agree, and then say that "scientific creationism" agrees with the result. However, this is only an attempt to bring the text into line with "creationism" rather than to listen to the text itself.

Chapter IV   Notes

1. Which of these options is correct is of little consequence for the present discussion, although in other contexts it is an issue of heated debate. For a basic discussion, see Lloyd Bailey, 1981, Chapter One of Part III ("An Author? or Editors/Collectors"?).

2. The whole problem of translation is examined briefly in Lloyd Bailey, 1986, 266–277.

3. A brief overview of the documentary hypothesis (the common alternative to Mosaic authorship) may be found in any of the following sources: Preface to NAB ("The Pentateuch"); Preface to JB ("Introduction to the Pentateuch"); Preface to NEB ("The Pentateuch"); Preface to RSV ("Introduction to the Old Testament"); *The Jerome Biblical Commentary,* I, Chapter 1 ("Introduction to the Pentateuch");

The Interpreter's Bible, I, pp. 185–200 ("The Growth of the Hexateuch"); *The Interpreter's Dictionary of the Bible,* III (K-Q), pp. 711–727 ("Pentateuch"). Less compact and easier to read is Lloyd Bailey, 1981, Chapter I.

4. See Whitcomb and Morris, 1961; for a survey of a range of "vapor canopy" theories, see Lloyd Bailey, 1989, pp. 46–48.

5. For those factors which set Genesis 1–11 apart from the rest of Genesis, see Bailey, *ibid.* Chapter V.

6. Based upon evidence from the "historical books" of the Bible: see above.

7. Bruce Vawter, 1977, p. 108.

8. See V. Wessetzki, "Alter," 1972, pp. 154–156.

9. A good illustration is "Babylonian King List B," for which see *ANET,* p. 171 (with footnote 2).

10. W-B 62 and W-B 444 are cuneiform texts in the Weld-Blundell Collection of the Ashmolean Museum at Oxford University. For a detailed analysis, see Thorkild Jacobsen, 1939.

11. Berossos (Latin: Berossus) was a Babylonian priest who lived in the third century B.C.E. and wrote a history of his country. This work survives only in partial form, in extensive quotations by such early historians as Josephus and Eusebius (the latter getting them from Alexander Polyhistor and Appolodorus). See Paul Schnabel (1968) and Stanley M. Burstein (1978). The list given here is dependent upon Polyhistor: Aloros, 36,000; Alaparos, 10,800; Amelon, 46,800; Ammenon, 43,200; Amegalaros, 64,800; Doanos, 36,000; Evedorachos, 64,800; Amempsinos, 36,000; Otiartes, 28,800; Xisuthros, 64,800 (Total: 432,000 years). Other accounts vary somewhat. For example, the much later list by Michael the Syrian (12th century, C.E.) totals 324,000 years (i.e. $60^2 \times 90$).

12. The so-called "new math," popular in the public schools a decade ago, sought to deepen one's understanding of place-notation by teaching students to count in, say, base-8. Computers, on the other hand, reckon in base-2.

13. For general discussion, see Naugebauer and Sachs, 1962.

14. I came to this conclusion with some excitement of having at last solved the mystery of the ages, only to realize subsequently that Cassuto had previously done so (I, pp. 259–264).

15. K 2486 (from the Qouyunjik Collection in the British Museum), for which see, briefly, Jacobsen, 1939, p. 274, n. 28.

16. Heidel, 1963, p. 141.

17. See "Enoch, Book of," in *IDB,* II (E-J), pp. 103–105; *JBC,* Section 68.9–15.

18. A brief discussion may be found in the article "Wordplay in the OT," *IDBS,* pp. 968–970 (at section "1a"). A full discussion of various rabbinic applications may be found in Stephen J. Lieberman, 1987, pp. 157–225.

19. The relationship between the two genealogies is treated in the standard commentaries. See e.g. Westermann, 1984, pp. 348–351.

20. That the names are the same is suggested by the fact that both contain the name of an underworld deity. See the article "Shalah (God)," in *IDBS,* p. 820.

21. This is the traditional (or "received") text, the only one known prior to the discovery of the Dead Sea Scrolls in the 1940s. The term masoretic (also spelled massoretic) come from the Masoretes, a group of medieval scholars who "fixed" the

vowels and punctuation as a means of assuring (what to them was) the authentic interpretation. The term comes ultimately from the verb *masar,* "to hand down." See "Text, OT," in *IDB,* Vol. IV (R-Z), pp. 580–594; *JBC,* 69:36–42; "Text, Hebrew, History of," in *IDBS,* pp. 878–884.

22. See "Textual Criticism, OT," in *IDBS,* pp. 886–891.

23. See "Versions, Ancient," in *IDB,* Vol. IV (R-Z), pp. 749–760 (at section 2); "Greek Versions of the Old Testament," *JBC,* 68:52–79; "Septuagint," in IDBS, pp. 807–815.

24. *IDB,* Vol. IV, p. 190; *IDBS,* pp. 772–777; *JBC,* 69:33–34.

25. IDB, Vol. I (A-D), pp. 790–802; *JBC,* 68:66–104.

26. IDBS, pp. 580–594; *JBC,* 69:10–32.

27. Westerman, 1984, p. 352. The correctness of his claim (for which he does not offer justification) is supported by the apparent derivation of the MT total from the Sumerian King List (Berossos) and that of the LXX total from the works of Manetho. On these two calculations, see below.

28. Jules Oppert, 1903, p. 66. For a less convincing possibility, see the article by Bertheau, 1845, as cited in Franz Delitzsch, 1899, p. 207. Bertheau claims that the initial idea was that the pre-diluvians had lived an average of 160 years each, for a total of 1600 for the 10 generations through Noah. Then he claims that these were lunar years which, when converted to solar years, yields 1656. This seems to me unacceptable for the reasons that the ancient biblical years were not lunar (they had an annual adjustment to make them solar), and his mathematical calculation (reckoning a lunar month at 355 days) yields 1645 years rather than 1656. Delitzsch is also useful because of his listing of scholars who have defended the authenticity of LXX and SP ages as opposed to those in MT (pp. 205–214). In favor of LXX: "the Hellenistic Jews and the ancient Church," the Roman martyrology, L. Cappellus, I. Vossius, G. Rawlinson (in *Leisure Hour* magazine, 1876), T. Budd (1880). In favor of SP: Bertheau, 1845; Karl Budde, 1883; A. Dillmann, 1892. Budde's proposal for the origin of the MT total (1656) is that it was derived from elapsed time to the death of Noah in the SP tradition (1657 years: see below, Table No. 14). For a highly speculative possibility for the derivation of elapsed time, see Appendix VIII (Table 12-A and attendant discussion).

29. The simple formula for converting years from the King List to years in Genesis 5 is: (.0038333 × King List years) = Genesis 5 years.

30. Henry Morris, 1976, p. 154.

31. *Ibid.* p. 155.

32. 1984, p. 354.

33. For discussion of this particular aspect, see "Generation, Seventh," in *IDBS* (pp. 354–356).

34. For a full discussion, see Raymond E. Brown, 1979, pp. 74–95.

35. *Ibid.* p. 81.

36. *Ibid.* pp. 82–83.

37. *Ibid.* p. 75. Brown's conclusion is premature, as will appear below.

38. *Ibid.* pp. 83–84 for several modern solutions, none of them convincing, and some of them quite desperate in their attempt to "salvage Matthew's reputation as a mathematician."

39. Even in the first section, it is the choice of Abraham as the point of departure (rather than Jacob, who is called "Israel" and "our father" [Deut. 26:5]), which makes the total come to 14. This may, however, be related to God's "call" as the beginning of the community of faith (Gen 12:1–3).

40. Hans Walter Wolff, 1974, p. 79.

41. Specifically, the suspected error is a conflate text, for which see the Anchor Bible Commentary (Vol. 8, p. 168). On this type of textual problem in general, see the article "Conflate Readings (OT)," in *IDBS,* pp. 170–173.

42. 1979, p. 74.

43. For considerable detail, see the discussion by Westermann, 1984, pp. 501–530.

44. See the article "Septuagint" in *IDB,* IV (R-Z), at p. 273, where the suggestion is made that the original number of translators was 70, then expanded to 72 so that it would reflect 6 from each of the 12 tribes of Israel. That 72 has been rounded off is proposed in *The Jerome Biblical Commentary, p. 569.*

45. The list in Genesis 46 agrees with the stated total of 70 only with difficulty and shows evidence of manipulation. See the commentaries of Von Rad, Speiser, and Westermann.

46. Gen 2:15. Compare the Mesopotamian Epic of Atrahasis, wherein humans are created to relieve the minor gods of their duty of maintaining the creation (Tablet I, lines 189–339). See W.G. Lambert and A.R. Millard, 1969).

47. G.R. Castellino, 1957, 133–137.

48. So the designation of Albert I. Baumgarten, 1981, at Chapter 7. Excerpts from his translation are given below (from pp. 141, 142, 143). I have added an occasional rendering of his proper names into English (enclosed in brackets of the form $\langle\rangle$), in order that the reader may see how far removed they are from true human names. They are forces of nature, or human activities that have been personified.

49. The noun is derived from a verb meaning "to be red" (apparently in reference to blood), and is related to the noun *'adamah,* "soil, earth." Hence, the biblical pun: Call the first creature "Earthy/Earth-creature," since he was made from soil and to soil he returns (at burial). See Gen 2:7; 3:19. Since the noun is used with the definite article (hence Gen 3:20 RSV, "*the* man"), it would not have been understood by early hearers as a proper name of an historical, biological individual (any more than we would speak in English of "the Adam"), but rather as proto-human in primeval (non-chronological) time! English translators have needlessly introduced the name "Adam" (without the article) in Genesis 2–3.

50. The name is properly explained at Genesis 3:20.

51. The mark on his forehead was characteristic of blacksmiths, who wandered from place to place until recent times in the Near East. See Theodor H. Gaster, 1969, pp. 55–56.

52. This meaning, derived from Syriac, seems better to fit the context than the traditional "vapor, vanity" (referring to his short life). See Gaster, *ibid.* p. 51.

53. See 1 Sam 13:19–21 for the late acquisition of iron by the Hebrews.

54. The verb from which the name Enoch is derived (*ḥ-n-k*), with the meaning "to dedicate," is well attested. A cognate word, in Egyptian, denotes an offering at the laying of a foundation stone. Note that the resultant city is itself called "Enoch" at

Genesis 4:17b. Hence the name may mean something like "founder" (in the case of a person) and "foundation" (in the case of a city).

55. The cognate in Arabic (*ghardun*) means "reed hut," which is one of the discoveries in Philo's account.

56. The name has been compared with the Akkadian word *maḥḥu,* a class of ecstatic priests.

57. On these and other names discussed herein, one can easily consult the corresponding entries in *IDB.* The word *jabal* is otherwise used for watercourses and may be derived from a verb "to bring" (related to flocks of a tent dweller); herdsmen are often associated with music (compare the Greek shepherd god Pan as the inventor of an instrument), so that the nomadic shepherd and the musician make good brothers). The designation Tubal is reflected in other literature as an area of metallurgy (just as the name Cain suggests). Details may be found in the commentary of Westermann, 1984.

58. It has been argued that the word "Cain" in vv. 1–16 has a different meaning ("creature," from the verb *q-y-n,* "to form") from the word "Cain" in v. 17 ("metallurgist").

59. In the real (historical) world, likely not in six or eight generations (or one hundred, for that matter), but in the realm of the magic number seven all things are possible!

60. See the article "Iron" in *IDB,* II (E-J), pp. 725–726.

61. For our present purposes, the identity of the author/editor matters not. For the common alternative to the traditional Mosaic authorship, see the article "Pentateuch" in *IDB,* III (K-Q), pp. 711–727; *The Jerome Biblical Commentary,* pp. 1–6; Preface to the New American Bible ("The Pentateuch"). The proposal there is that Genesis-Deuteronomy has resulted from four stages of gathering and editing of traditional materials, the process stretching from the eleventh to the fifth centuries B.C.E. (the so-called Documentary Hypothesis).

62. Generally designated, from its opening words, *Enuma elish.* An English translation is available in James B. Pritchard, 1955, 2nd ed., pp. 60–72.

63. Parallels are outlined in Heidel, 1951, p. 129, with discussion of the relationship in pp. 128–140.

64. Thus also Westermann, 1984, p. 89.

65. So the NAB note to 2:4b–25; NEB note to 2:5–3:24.

66. Note that, according to 2:8, "the Lord God planted a garden *in Eden*" (i.e. Eden is not itself the garden but is a larger geographical area). On the two meanings of "Eden," see Westermann, 1984, pp. 208–211.

67. One modern interpreter, for example, proposes that Genesis 2:18–19 is not in tension with chapter 1 for the following reason: When it came time for the man to name the animals (already created according to 1:20–25), the deity opted to create specimens of each, on the spot, rather than round them up from wherever they might be at the time! (See Gleason Archer, 1974, p. 128.) God is free, I suppose, to do what God will do, but the reader might be surprised that the task of fetching the specimens was of such difficulty that a short-cut need be taken.

CHAPTER V

Indications of What the Biblical Agenda Is

PRIOR TO direct consideration of what the agenda of the biblical story of creation (Gen 1:1–2:4a) was, it may be helpful to consider the topic in larger perspective: What was God's agenda in the entirety of the pentateuchal materials (Genesis–Deuteronomy)? Does it center upon (or even include) the type of belief that is the essence of "creationism"? Do God's instructions and requirements as given at Mount Sinai emphasize the centrality of belief in an absolute beginning of time-space-matter, the chronology of creation, a "young" earth, genetic variation only within created "kinds," and in general the "tenets of biblical creationism"? If such "tenets" are central to the biblical faith, then one would not be surprised to find them in the material that is specifically put forward for adoption as part of the covenant faith at the very formation of the community.

1. The Revelation at Mount Sinai/Horeb

Following liberation from Egyptian bondage (Ex 1–12), the descendants of Jacob (a former resident of Canaan) set out for a sacred mountain at which they were to receive the guidelines ever thereafter to be foundational for their collective existence as the people of God. Upon their arrival, an extensive corpus of ethical and liturgical material was given to them, interwoven with narration of trips up and down the mountain (Ex 19:1–Num 10:32). Years of wandering finally brought them to the borders of the "promised land" (Num 10:33–36:13), during which other guidelines were given. Finally, on the border of that land, Moses summed up their past experience and gave directions for the future (Deut 1:1–33:29), died, and was succeeded by Joshua (Deut 34). Thereupon the people crossed the Jordan to begin the actualization of their destiny (Jos 1–3).

The true origin of some of the guidelines,[1] and the sequence by which they became a part of the larger story as it now stands,[2] have long been debated and need not concern us here. It is sufficient to observe that the totality is presented as divine revelation, mediated through Moses, and directed to the entirety of the community.

> And Moses went up [the mountain] to God, and the Lord called him . . . saying, ". . . tell the people of Israel: '. . . if you will obey my voice and keep my covenant, you shall be my own possession among all peoples . . .' " (Ex 19:3–5).

> . . . the Lord your God . . . keeps covenant and steadfast love with those who love him and keep his commandments, to a thousand generations. . . . You shall therefore be careful to do the commandments . . . (Deut 7:9–11).

When this vast corpus of material is surveyed in order to see what it is that God required of the faithful, one will see that its concerns are: (1) worship (where, how, when, and by whom); (2) ethics (not merely in a wide range of socio-economic matters, but also in such family matters as incest); and (3) regimentation of diet and dress, whereby one's mind and heart are disciplined and one's identity is maintained in the face of pressures to conform to the values of neighboring states or conquerors. All of this is set within the context of God's gracious initiatives, the memory and recitation of which was intended to move the hearer to willing obedience: "I am the Lord your God, who brought you out of the land of Egypt, out of the house of bondage. [Therefore] you shall (do so-and-so) . . . you shall not (do so-and-so)," according to Exodus 20:1–17.[3]

It was quite in keeping with the focus of this material, then, when Jesus was asked to summarize it and he replied (Mt 22:34–40): "You shall love the Lord your God" [as Deut 6:4 had commanded as the ethical basis of action] and "You shall love your neighbor" [as Lev 19:18 requires].

It is important to notice, in all this vast body of material which was to define the life of the people of God, what is conspicuous by its absence: No regulation, or even a hint of a suggestion, is to be found concerning what one is to believe about the origin of the world, its age, the origin of species, and so on. (This is not to state whether Israel did, or did not, have beliefs about such matters. It *is* to state that such ideas were not put forth as central to the identity of and membership in the community! Such ideas certainly have a theological dimension, and they may be pressing issues to certain groups in the present, but that is no concern of the Sinaitic guidelines.)

It may be observed, of course, that the Sinaitic materials are not the totality of the pentateuchal guidelines, and certainly do not include the pri-

meval story (Gen 1–11) which contains the account of creation. It is necessary, therefore, to review the *totality* of God's expectations of humans as
expressed in these early chapters.

1. "Be fruitful and multiply and fill the earth and subdue it; and have
dominion . . ." (1:28).

2. "I have given you every plant-yielding seed . . . and every tree with
seed in its fruit; you shall have them for food" (1:29).

3. "You may freely eat of every tree of the garden; but of the tree of
knowledge of good and evil you shall not eat . . ." (2:16–17).

4. "So . . . the Lord God formed every beast . . . and every bird . . . and
brought them to the man to see what he would call them" (2:19).

5. ". . . pain in childbirth . . . desire for your husband" (3:16).

6. ". . . in toil you shall eat . . . till you return to the ground" (3:17–19).

7. "If you do well, will thou not be accepted? . . . sin is couching . . . but
you must master it" (4:7).

8. ". . . you shall be a fugitive and a wanderer. . . . If anyone slays Cain,
vengeance shall be taken upon him sevenfold" (4:12–15).

9. "My spirit shall not abide in man for ever . . ." (6:3).

10. "The Lord saw that the wickedness of man was great . . . and it
grieved him to his heart . . ." (6:5–6).

11. "I will never again curse the ground. . . . I set my bow in the cloud,
and it shall be a sign of the covenant . . ." (8:21; 9:13).

12. "Every moving thing . . . shall be food for you. . . . Only you shall
not eat flesh with its life . . ." (9:3–4).

13. "For your lifeblood I will surely require a reckoning . . ." (9:5–6).

14. ". . . 'this is only the beginning of what they will do!' . . . so the Lord
scattered them . . ." (11:6–8).

And there you have it: the totality of God's requirements and concerns
as expressed in the primeval story. Only numbers 1, 2, 12, and 13 express
perpetual direction for human response, and the concern of each of them
falls within the range of concerns of the Sinaitic regulations expressed above.
One finds, then, nothing commanded concerning cosmogeny, astronomy,
geology, biology, or chronology. While the text touches upon those matters,
it does not do so in the context of directives for either belief or action.

2. The Shape of Thought Units in the Primeval Story

As stated previously, the materials in Genesis 1–11 (and much else in the
Pentateuch for that matter) began as independent, complete units which
were later gathered and arranged in their present sequence. Not only do they
have formal beginnings and endings, but also they seem to move (as do many

narratives ancient and modern) toward a conclusion wherein the thrust of the whole is expressed. They are not, by contrast, legal materials wherein each statute may be appropriated in an independent, self-standing way. Similarly, they are not proverbs, each of which may be detached from its context as regards to meaning. Rather, an entire thought unit in the primeval story has an overall purpose which is larger than its constituent parts (verses).

The account which begins at 2:4b reaches its conclusion (the point originally scored) at 2:24, when the woman is fashioned in order to bring human creation to its completion. The text then states: "*Therefore,* a man leaves his father and his mother and cleaves to his wife, and they become one flesh." It has thus been argued, and plausibly so, that the major idea of the account (that which it "means") is to explain or encourage or sanction monogamous marriage. This is precisely the way that it was understood when cited by Jesus (Mt 19:1–5; Mk 10:7). Thus, considerations such as historicity (Did it happen?) or chronology (When was this?) are of no concern to the text and should not be made central by the modern interpreter. Otherwise put: "Stick to the point" would seem to be good advice.

The account of the expulsion from the garden (beginning at Genesis 3:1) reaches a conclusion at v. 23 with the word "*Therefore.*" The point would seem to be that humans are mortal and justifiably so. They cannot attain the deathlessness which they so desperately desire. Any conjectures concerning such secondary matters as "Can a serpent really talk?" would be entirely beside the point as far as the agenda of the text is concerned.

The account of the flood (likely beginning at 6:5) is enclosed in a formal literary "envelope" which seems to single out the major idea of the entire episode. The preface part of the "envelope" reads:

> The Lord saw that the wickedness of man was great on the earth, and that every imagination of the thoughts of his heart was only evil continually. And the Lord was sorry that he had made man on the earth . . . (6:5–6).

The concluding part of the "envelope" reads:

> . . . the Lord said in his heart, "I will never again curse the ground because of man, for the imagination of man's heart is evil from his youth . . ." (8:21).

God's promise of the continuity of existence, in opposition to the prior intent to destroy (save for Noah's family), would seem to be the "point," which is then strengthened by the account of the covenant (9:1–17). If modern interpreters want to descend from that (the text's own) agenda, and ponder whether a universal flood is possible (e.g. "Where did all that water come from, where did it go, and is there geological evidence?"), they are certainly free to do so. Nothing essential to the text is learned thereby, however. Arguments about such matters are divisive at best and harmful at worst, and arguably are non-biblical (if by "biblical" one means the "burden of the text").

By viewing materials from this perspective I do not mean to imply, absolutely, that such stories may not have *secondary* meanings. Nonetheless, the stories seem to have a "thrust" toward which the whole is directed, an emphasis above all else, and this must not be dislodged from the center of one's search for "meaning." Anytime that the interpreter moves from that which is central to that which is subordinate (or even incidental), the probability of misunderstanding is enhanced.

The conclusion thus reached now directs us to ask the relevant question concerning the creation story itself.

3. Genesis 1:1–2:4a as a Complete Thought Unit

The creation story has both a formal beginning and a formal conclusion. We know, from its opening words, that we have not missed any previous descriptions. The account then moves smoothly, day after day, until we begin to hear such language as "finished," "rested," "had done," and "blessed." Ordinarily, such language signals the end of an account, and this is confirmed by the summary retrospective view at 2:4a: "Such were the origins of heaven and earth when they were created" (JB); "And that is how the universe was created" (TEV).

Even without such formal indications of a self-contained thought unit, an interpreter might expect things to be finished on the seventh day. After all, that is the "perfect" total, the ideal, as is clear elsewhere from genealogies, tables of nations, and so on (see above).

That such thought units are no mere topical transitions by a single author is clear from transitions in vocabulary and grammar as well. Thus, throughout 1:1–2:4a the deity is referred to as "God" (Hebrew: *'elohim*) without exception. This is a general designation which could be used to refer to the deities of surrounding cultures as well as to the sole deity in whom Israel believed. That there is a radical transition at 2:4b is clear, furthermore, from the shift in the way by which the deity is designated. Hereafter (through the end of chapter 3), the deity is referred to by a proper name: Yahweh the deity (Hebrew: *Yahweh 'elohim,* usually translated as "the Lord God"). The only exception is when the serpent speaks (3:1, 5), as if it were inappropriate for the beguiling creature to utter the divine name.

It is plausible to conclude, then, and indeed many interpreters do so, that the creation story (1:1–2:4a) and the story of the couple in the garden (2:4b–3:24) have a separate origin, each with a history and authorship of its own, and that they were placed back-to-back at a later date than the origin of either. This would help to account for certain differences between them, including the "problem" of the order of creation: all the animals, then the humans ("male and female") in 1:1–2:4a, but the human male, then the animals, then the human female in 2:4b–25. That tensions remained, unresolved, when the two accounts were joined, indicates that such biological sequencing was not the concern of those persons who finalized the text as it now stands. The sequence may be a problem for "creationists," but it is the text instead which is the final authority in indicating what its focus was intended to be.

4. The Construction and Goal of the Creation Story

The account of creation is a finely wrought schematic presentation, featuring a genealogical format with poetic sensitivity. There is a unity, a central focus, as the account moves relentlessly through formal stages and drives toward an overall "point": God's rest on the seventh day. Whatever else may be stated in transit, the account drives toward that end, with all else but a preparation for it. In recognition of this goal, the chapter divisions in the English Bible (following those of the older Latin Bible) sever the seventh day from the previous six, thereby making quite clear the climactic nature of the former. Even the creation of human beings, often regarded as the climactic act, is only one stage among others as the account moves toward the central revelation (divine concern).

The account relates eight individual creative acts. Each is introduced by the divine command, "Let (so-and-so) happen": light (v. 3), a "firmament" or dome (v. 6), a gathering of waters (v. 9), vegetation (v. 11), the luminaries (v. 14), sea creatures and birds (v. 20), land creatures (v. 24), and humans (v. 26). Rather than assign each of them to a day, however, they have been compressed into a six-day work week, resulting in two such creative acts on the third and sixth days. The "day of rest" is thus deliberately made to fall on the seventh day by those who put the text in its present form (rather than, as it might, on the ninth day). Such a chronology of creation is unique in the Ancient Near East, but it is hardly surprising in view of the symbolic significance which biblical literature attributes to the number seven. This is but another indication of the overall goal of the account, of the "point" toward which the entirety is oriented.

Furthermore, individual sentences within the account, rather than being spontaneously composed, have been carefully thought out and refined by the author(s). Concern for the number seven is evident even at this level of composition, as the following examples serve to illustrate.[4] The first verse contains seven words.[5] The second verse contains twice that number of words. The concluding section of the unit (2:2–4, concerning the seventh day) contains thirty-five words (5 × 7), with three of its clauses containing seven each. The entire account, then, is "enveloped" by constructions of seven words, thereby giving it an aura of perfection and sanctity as its authors sought an appropriate way by which to express their inspired perception of the implications of creation. Thereby, once again, the focus of the hearer/reader is directed toward the goal of the story, its religious significance, i.e. what happened on the seventh day.

Even the key words of the first verse occur in the entire unit in multiples of seven: "God" is found thirty-five times; "heaven" and "earth" are found twenty-one times each.[6] The sections concerning the division and gathering of the "waters" (vv. 6–8, 9–10) contain seven instances of that word. The section concerning the creation of animals (vv. 20–23, 24–30) contain seven instances of a word (*ḥayyâ*) that is translated as either "living creatures" or "beasts."

That observance of the sabbath is the goal of the story, that which the account intends to teach the reader, is suggested by more than the form of the unit. Of all the aspects of the account, it is only concerning God's "rest" that the Bible itself subsequently commands belief and observance by those who have identified with Israel. The ten commandments (Ex 20:8–11) require that the community imitate God's weekly rest. To conclude, therefore, that this is the focus of the creation story, that alone which is important for the life of synagogue and church, is merely to follow the Bible's own lead. To suggest that the teaching of the story is "Keep the sabbath" (rather than to accept the "tenets of creationism") is thus not a modern, rationalistic, subjective "interpretation." Rather, it is only when one departs from the Bible's own focus (in order to secure unintended answers to such questions as "When, and in what sequence, did creation take place?") that one should be wary of subjective "interpretation."

The sabbath was of such importance for the communal life of Israel that the author(s) of Genesis could illustrate it by speaking of God's having "rested" as the pinnacle of the creation of all things. That is, unless there is a regular, frequently observed day set aside for reflection upon the history and purpose of the community, other agendas will crowd out the agenda of the deity. Consequently, Israel as a religious community will be assimilated to the faiths of the surrounding and predominant cultures. This was no hypothetical danger, given the ancient and revered values of the indigenous Ca-

naanite population of "the promised land," and given the successive con-
quests of the area by foreigners (Assyrians, Egyptians, Babylonians, Persians,
Greeks, and Romans).

To be sure, there were some moments in Israel's history when the problems of "forgetting" and assimilation were more pressing than at others. It
may well be that one especially pressing moment led to the finalization of the
creation story as we now find it in the Bible. To judge from the speeches of
several biblical figures (the authors of Isaiah 40–55, and of the so-called
Deuteronomic history [Joshua–2 Kings] among them), such a moment was
that of exile to Babylonia (587–539 B.C.E.) and its aftermath under the
Persians. Thus, the majority of modern critical scholars place a major and
final stage in the formation of the Pentateuch during this period. Scripture,
formerly having begun at Genesis 2:4b, was now prefaced with 1:1–2:4a.[7]

The possibility of secondary emphases in a biblical unit cannot be ruled
out in some cases, as has been mentioned above. In the case of the creation
account, such an emphasis may involve a polemic against alleged divine
forces, the worship of which made sabbath observance a necessity in the first
place (see Chapter IV, at n. 33). This possibility must now be discussed.

Canaan ("the promised land"), as a land-bridge between empires and
continents, was a melting pot of populations and ideas. This is attested in the
Bible itself, where the deity identifies it as ". . . a good and broad land . . . the
place of the Canaanites, the Hittites, the Amorites, the Perizzites, the Hivites,
and the Jesusites" (Ex 3:8). So substantial was the Hittite population of
Syro-Palestine (whose empire was in Asia Minor) that the Assyrians sometimes designated it as "the hatti land." Similarly numerous was a Hurrian
population element (whose empire was in northwest Mesopotamia), sufficient to cause the Egyptians sometimes to refer to Canaan as "ḫr." Often
during the second millennium (B.C.E.), the area was under political and
cultural influence from Egypt, and during the first millennium under the
domination of Assyria, Babylonia, Persia, Greece, and Rome.

There is little doubt that the Israelites were well aware of the sacred
literature of the neighboring cultures. In fact, fragments of the Babylonian
creation epic (*Enuma elish*), written in cuneiform script, have been found in
Palestine. Orthodox worshipers of the God Yahweh (English Bible: "the
Lord"), hearing neighboring accounts of creation, might well be struck by
the significant departures in their own account. In addition to the unique-
ness of schedule (a seven day period), the following emphases would have
stood out: Who was the creator? How did creation take place? What was it
that was created? (It will now be helpful to comment upon each of these,
in turn.)

Who Was the Creator?

The answer to this question will have varied from society to society, of course, since the lordship of a given deity was seldom accepted by the neighboring populations. For the ancient Sumerians of lower Mesopotamia, it was the wind god (Enlil) who separated heaven from earth and set the stage for the creation of animals, plants, and humans. For the Babylonians, it was the god Marduk (whose visible image was the planet Jupiter) who slew the chaos monster and fashioned heaven and earth from the body parts. Among the Canaanites, El (itself the word "god," even in the Bible), a remote, aged figure, was designated the creator of all things. Each such deity was part of a pantheon, a family or governing board of divine figures, who regulated daily life.

By contrast, Israel's orthodox religious leaders not only attributed creation to a deity named Yahweh but also denied the existence of other deities (i.e. they were monotheists[8]). This (sole) deity was intimately connected with their formative historical events, such as the deliverance from Egyptian bondage, guidance in the wilderness of Sinai, issuance of torah (guidelines) at the sacred mountain, and the gift of the land of Canaan. By prefacing the history of Israel (which begins with the call of Abraham in Genesis 12) with the primeval story, Israel's teachers linked their saving deity with the creator of all things. Consequently, creation was not a self-standing event to be lauded in isolation, but was a preamble to the life of the "chosen" community. Israel's liturgical life, later to be spelled out in great detail (e.g. in the book of Leviticus), was thus grounded in creation itself, beginning with sabbath observance. At the same time, one thus realized that the formulator of Israel's particular (and peculiar) cult was the Lord of the whole of humanity as well.

How Did Creation Take Place?

Here also the divergence of Genesis 1 from the creation accounts of neighboring cultures is conspicuous. For example, according to the Babylonian account (*Enuma elish*), creation resulted from the resolution of divine conflict. The god Marduk slew the dragon of primordial chaos, Tiamat (a personification of the stormy, raging *tiamtu,* "sea"). He then sliced her body in half ("like a shellfish"), and fashioned heaven and earth between the two parts (the "upper sea" and the "lower sea," for which see Appendix XI). Annually thereafter, it was believed that the power of chaos sought to reassert (reunite) itself in the heavy rains of the winter season. Liturgical reenactment of Marduk's victory was the means whereby order was maintained for the coming year.

Echoes of this conflict, adapted to Yahwism, may be found in fragments of ancient tradition in a few places in the Bible:[9]

> With his strong arm he (Yahweh) cleft the sea-monster,
> and struck down the Rahab by his skill.
> At his breath the skies are clear,[10]
> and his hand breaks the twisting sea-serpent (Job 26:12–13, NEB).

> By thy power thou didst cleave the sea-monster in two
> and break the sea-serpent's heads above the waters;
> Thou didst crush Leviathan's many heads
> and throw him to the sharks for food (Ps 74:13–14, NEB).

The account in Genesis 1, by contrast, has suppressed the conflict theme to the faintest possible hint: "And God . . . separated the waters which were under the firmament from the waters which were above the firmament" (v. 7). Instead, one finds a series of divine commands ("Let there be . . ."), followed laconically by a report of accomplishment ("And it was so"). Emphasis is upon the actor (creator) and upon the ease of the action, rather than upon the specific content, chronology, or relationship to the next action. (That is, it is not upon matters of modern scientific interest such as "creationists" desire.)

It is instructive to note, elsewhere in scripture, the content of recitations of God's creative activity. Illustrations include the "cosmological doxologies" in the book of Amos (4:13; 5:8–9; 9:5–6). Focus is upon the "Who?" of creation, expressed in liturgical form (poetry), and not upon "When?" and "How long?" Plausibly, therefore, in Genesis the intended response should be the same and to the same emphases. The purpose of the account is not to tell us the "how" of creation and thus incite us to scientific inquiry, but to inform us of the "who" of creation and thus incite us to praise.

What Was It That Was Created?

Yahwistic monotheism, wherein creation results from the effortless utterance of divine commands (as opposed to divine conflict), produces only inanimate objects. This is in contrast to the polytheistic perceptions of the surrounding cultures in which a multitude of divine wills is manifest in the processes of nature. Those processes, construed as deity, then both allure and make demands upon human beings. For example, the fertilizing rains and the destructive drought could be seen as forces in opposition to each other, as manifestations of divine wills that have opposing agendas. Or the moon as an object of beauty which makes travel possible during the cool of the desert night is obscured by the clouds of the storm which brings destructive floods, as if the moon-god had evil enemies who sought to obscure his face (presence) and ravage his domain. Or the chaotic sea beats relentlessly against the shore as if it were an ancient force that had been bounded by the land, forever seeking to break its bonds and destroy the domain of its captor. Thus, such "natural forces" (as we would call them) were easily perceived to be divine wills, projected back to the formation of the world (or beyond) and described in dramatic mythological language. Remnants of such thought, deprived of their polytheistic environment, survive in biblical references to Leviathan, Rehab, and the sea-monster (on which see above).

One should not be surprised, then, to find in Genesis 1 a sustained although subtle attack upon polytheism.[11] The mythology of surrounding cultures is brushed aside as their divine forces are reduced to mere physical processes. The following illustrations should clarify the intent and accomplishment of the text.

In Sumerian creation stories, it is the wind-god (Enlil, "Lord Wind") who brings order out of chaos. This was done, in part, by carrying and depositing fertile soil from afar and thus counteracting the sterile and hostile desert. Even in the Babylonian creation account (*Enuma elish*), it is the wind-gods (seven in number!) who assist Marduk in slaying the chaos monster (Tiamat, the raging sea). In Genesis 1, however, the wind is reduced to an impersonal "thing" which does the bidding of the sole divine power. We are merely told that a mighty wind was stirring the surface of the sea.[12]

In the Babylonian account, Marduk slays the chaos monster and fashions the world between parts of its body. In Genesis 1, there is but the faintest echo of this idea. The chaos monster has become the impersonal "deep" (*tehom*, a possible variation on the name of the chaos monster, Tiamat). It is the sole deity (Yahweh, although the name is not used) who separates the "waters from the waters" and places the earth in between. One reads only of impersonal matter which is shaped without a cosmic struggle by the deity who was sovereign from the beginning. The older Babylonian story has been depolytheized, de-Mardukized, de-Mesopotamianized; it has been thoroughly monotheized, Yahwized, and Israelitized. No longer are the sea, wind, and darkness manifestations of an eternal, self-generating, willful, destructive power; they have been reduced to impersonal matter as part of a "good" creation (1:31).

Light, considered by the Persians to be an eternal manifestation of the deity Ahura Mazda, is, according to the Genesis account, created by Yahweh who then separates light from darkness. These opposites are only physical realities of the world, and not the manifestations of twin, dualistic deities.[13]

The earth is commanded, in the Genesis account of creation, to produce vegetation. It is a mere object which the sole deity has brought into being. It is not the body of an ancient goddess who must be worshiped in order to bestow her blessings upon humankind. The Canaanites, who have temples and priests dedicated to the worship of such powers of fertility, are deluding themselves.

The sun, the moon, and the stars likewise are nothing other than inanimate matter. They are not the images of powerful gods, each with myth and ritual of its own, contrary to the deeply ingrained belief and practice of Mesopotamians and Syro-Palestinians. For example, so revered was the sungod (called "Shamash") that his name became a synonym for the word "god."[14] In the Genesis account, the sun is not even allowed to be the initial source of light, and thus can only assume that function on the fourth day of creation.

Finally, one reads of the formation of animals, many of which, for Israel's neighbors, symbolized a divine power. The lion, for example, was sacred to the goddess Ishtar (Venus), since it was thought to embody her gracefulness, courage, and power. The bull was thought to be the sacred animal upon which the weather-god (called "Baal" by the Canaanites) rode across the sky, since its bellow sounded like thunder and since its virility resembled that of this fertility deity. In Genesis, however, all the animals are merely Yahweh's creatures. At the bidding of this deity alone do they all "multiply and fill the earth."

In sum, then, Genesis 1 likely was heard (and intended) to suggest that Israel's neighbors, and even some of her own people, have been attributing deity to mere things, "to birdies, beasties, and fishes."[15] Neighbors, hearing this creation account, would have been acutely aware of what it implied for their own faith, since it refused to see nature as alive with forces to which humans should subject themselves. It would thus have seemed that the text proclaimed the rankest of "atheistic propaganda."[16]

What the text seeks to proclaim is advanced by the author of Isaiah 40–55 in much more direct terms.[17] Here are specimens of such rhetoric, laying out the issue very clearly:

> Before me no god was formed,
>   nor shall there be any after me.
>
> . . . .
>
> I am God, and also henceforth I am he;
>   there is none who can deliver out of my hand (43:10–13).
>
> Thus says the Lord, the King of Israel
>   and his Redeemer, the Lord of hosts:
> "I am the first and I am the last;
>   beside me there is no god (44:6).

> I am the Lord, and there is no other.
>   I form light and create darkness,
> I make weal and create woe,
>   I am the Lord, who does all these things (45:6–7).

The great problem for the audience of the time was: How do I remember and embody this proclamation, in view of the historical reverses which seem to call it into question? How do I counteract the influence of those persons who make proclamation to the contrary? What is to be done, according to Genesis 1, is to imitate the action of God at the conclusion of creation: a day of rest and remembrance, a day of reflection upon Israel's history and purpose, a day when the agenda of ordinary life is set aside.

Thus it is that the secondary emphases of the creation story (How? What?) are not only related to each other but also reinforce the primary one toward which the story itself leads. This serves as a check on the accuracy and perception of what the agenda of the text was, and makes it even clearer what that agenda was not. Something far more profound than the agenda of "creationism" was at work, and the need for such an agenda has not diminished in the passing centuries since the time of the text. Indeed, in today's secular world, in which work on the sabbath is sometimes demanded by one's employer, the issue is even more pressing for church and synagogue. This conclusion has been adequately expressed by Conrad Hyers:

> Even a cursory reading of the context in which and to which Genesis 1 was written would indicate that the alternative to its "creation model" was obviously not some burgeoning theory of evolution. . . . one senses immediately that the modern debate over creation and evolution would have seemed very strange, if not unintelligible, to the writers and readers of Genesis. . . . what pressed on Jewish faith from all sides and even from within were the religious problems of idolatry and syncretism.[18]

Chapter V   Notes

1. Some of them seem to presuppose settled life in the land of Canaan, and perhaps were added to the biblical tradition in the post-Sinaitic period. For a brief treatment, see the article "Law in the OT" in *IDB,* Vol. III (K-G), pp. 77–89. For more detail, see Dale Patrick, 1985.

2. *Ibid.*

3. For this understanding of the commandments, see the article "Covenant" in *IDB,* Vol. I (A-D), pp. 714–723.

4. For these and other examples, see Umberto Cassuto, 1961, pp. 14–15.

5. This is the Hebrew word count, and not that of English translations.

6. It is perhaps accidental that the words "heaven" and "earth" contain (in Hebrew) seven consonants, just as the word for "world" is written in cuneiform sources with seven wedges (to represent the word *an-ki,* "heaven-earth").

7. See the prefaces to such established translations as NEB, NAB, and JB; discussions of the Pentateuch in *JBC, IO-VCB,* and *IB;* the article "Pentateuch" in *IDB* and "Priestly Writers" in *IDBS.* A detailed treatment of the theology of the Priestly writers may be found in Lloyd Bailey, 1987.

8. For a discussion of this issue, see the article "God, OT View of," in *IDB,* Vol. II (E-J), pp. 417–430, at section D.6.

9. See the following articles in *IDB:* "Leviathan," "Rahab," "Dragon" and "Cosmology" (especially section A.2.D, "The myth of primordial combat"). The Phoenicians have a different perspective (according to Sanchuniathon, as reported by Philo of Byblos): a primordial slime evolved from the chaotic waters, "And from this [putrification] was born every seed of creation and [the] origin of all [things]." See Baumgarten, 1981, p. 97.

10. More in keeping with the context, and resulting from an allowable redivision of consonants, is the AB translation of this line: "By his wind he bagged the Sea," referring to the seven wind-gods who assisted Marduk.

11. See David Neiman, 1973, pp. 47–63.

12. Genesis 1:2 is difficult, and allows a translation option: "the Spirit of God" (RSV, JB, KJV, cf, TEV) vs. "a mighty wind" (NAB, NEB, RSV footnote). The latter is in accordance with Ancient Near Eastern parallels.

13. Briefly, see the article "Persia, History and Religion of," in *IDB,* Vol. III (K-Q), pp. 739–747.

14. For example, the personal name of a famous Assyrian monarch was Shamshi-Adad, "My Shamash is Adad" (meaning: "My deity is the god Adad"). Such biblical place-names as Beth-Shemesh and such personal names as Samson similarly reflect worship of the solar deity.

15. I owe this memorable characterization to James A. Sanders.

16. So Harvey Cox, p. 23.

17. Interestingly, many modern interpreters think that the creation story in Genesis 1 took its present form at approximately the same time as the proclamations of the author of Isaiah 40–55: during and shortly after the exile of Judah to Babylonia (587–539 B.C.E.).

18. Hyers, 1984, p. 43.

CHAPTER VI

Does the Text Describe "Creation out of Nothing"?

ANY DISCUSSION of what a passage in the Bible intends should presuppose clarity of what the author (or at least the surviving text) says, that is, it should begin with accuracy and clarity of translation. It is precisely at this point that the story of creation, at Genesis 1:1, presents us with uncertainty. Consider the following options.

1. An absolute beginning of all things. This has two articulations. (a) "In the beginning, God created the heavens and the earth" (KJV, RSV, JB). That seems to be clear enough: There was a time prior to which "the heavens and the earth" (an idiom for "all things") did not exist, such that one can speak (in classical terms) of *creatio ex nihilo* ("creation out of nothing").

Such a translation presupposes that what is now called 1:1 is (and was intended to be) a complete sentence. This is in agreement with the punctuation of the Masoretic text (the traditional Hebrew Bible of the synagogue, which was vocalized and punctuated around 900–1000 C.E.).[1]

A slight syntactical variation (b) is represented by NAB: "In the beginning, when God created the heavens and the earth, the earth was a formless waste, and darkness covered the abyss, while a mighty wind swept over the waters" (so also NEB, TEV). The meaning is unchanged, but the story begins with the temporal word "when," necessitating that the sentence continue at least as far as the end of verse 2. Such a translation correctly recognizes that the present versification (endings) in the "received" Hebrew text is secondary (added at a later time) and thus that the true (intended) endings might come elsewhere.

There is a difference in meaning only for a small segment of Protestant interpreters, who have proposed that there was an indefinite (but substantial) period of time between the present v. 1 and the present v. 2: the earth of v. 1 fell into moral decay (reflected in the chaos of v. 2) and a new beginning was then necessary (the "present" earth in v. 3). Thus, the KJV-type translation would be regarded as correct and the NAB-type rejected. For details, see Appendix I.

2. Creation as the ordering of previously chaotic matter. The AB reads: "When God set about to create heaven and earth—the world being then a formless waste, with darkness over the seas and only an awesome wind sweeping over the water—God said, 'Let there be light.' And there was light." This possibility is recognized in a footnote in RSV: "When God began to create." See also NJV. Now, the main thought consists of v. 1 and v. 3, with v. 2 reduced to a circumstantial clause which describes the conditions at the time when the creative activity began. Rather than an assertion of "creation out of nothing," the reader may suppose that the following things were already in existence at the time when the biblical story opens: formless matter, darkness, chaotic oceans, and violent winds. The initial divine act, as related, would be the following: "When God began to create heaven and earth . . . God said, 'Let there be light.' " That is, the creative activity consisted in bringing form from formlessness, light from darkness, order from chaos, meaning from meaninglessness.

As one tries to decide, from these options, what the text intends, it is important to realize that the differing translations have not arisen from the incompetence or bias of translators. Rather, the problem resides in the imprecision of the Hebrew text itself. Each option is defensible from the point of view of biblical syntax and lexicography. It should also be realized that perception of the problem is not of recent origin, such that the AB-option could be dismissed as "modernism." As early as Emperor Julian (fourth century C.E.) it was observed:

> . . . Moses does not say that the deep was created by God, or the darkness or the waters. . . . he says not a word to imply that they were not already existing. . . . God is . . . only the disposer of matter that already existed. . . . he [Moses] regards the wet and dry substances as the original matter and . . . introduces God as the disposer of this matter.[2]

These differing translations are sometimes used in the "Bible vs. science" controversy. (1) If one asserts that the KJV/NAB-type translation is correct, and if one believes that the Bible is authoritative (infallible?) in matters of modern science, then those scientists who assert that the cosmos is "all that is or ever was or ever will be"[3] must be in error. (2) If one proposes that the AB-type translation is correct, then the Bible may be said to agree with scientists about the eternality of matter. It is into the former camp that "creationists" place themselves. It is perhaps in order, then, to investigate the translation problem further (leaving more technical details for Appendix X).

1. The Meaning of the First Word of the Bible

The word translated "beginning" (RSV) or "set about to" (AB) is derived from the noun "head (of a human being)," "top," "leader," and is in no wise exclusively used for divine activity. Within itself, it does not imply creation, either out of formless matter or "out of nothing."

The meaning of Genesis 1:1 hinges in part upon the absence or presence of the preposition "of." If we say, "In the beginning . . ." as does the KJV, an absolute creation would be implied and the sentence should end at v. 1. However, if we say, "In the beginning *of* (God's creating)," we must continue either into v. 2 (NAB) or into v. 3 (AB). Thus a crucial question is: Is the word "of" there or not?

Hebrew ordinarily does not use a separate word corresponding to the English word "of," but rather implies it in certain syntactic constructions (that is, the English translator must supply it). Thus, if one wanted to say in Hebrew, "The son of the king," the word "son" would be modified by a change of spelling (vowel: from *bēn to ben*) which would signal the possessive ("of") relationship between "son" and "king." Unfortunately for the present case, the word "beginning" is a noun-type which does not use such internal modification. Within itself, as always spelled, it can mean either "beginning" or "beginning of." The ambiguity is to be resolved (one ordinarily hopes) by other grammatical indicators (the context).

Prefixed to this noun is a preposition which can mean "in," "at," or "when." The definite article ("the"), in such constructions, may or may not be used, and is signaled only by the nature of the vowel which follows the preposition. (That is, the article does not consist of a separate word.) If there is a long "a"-class vowel, the reading would be *bā* and the meaning would be "In the beginning." On the other hand, if the preposition has a short "e"-class vowel, the reading would be *bᵉ* and the meaning would *usually* be "In the beginning *of* " (but it could still mean "In the beginning"). Now, what does one actually find in the text? The traditional (Masoretic) Hebrew Bible has *bᵉ,* which (as just stated) is ambiguous but usually would mean "In the beginning of." Some ancient manuscripts, however, have *bā,* "In the beginning."

In conclusion: The meaning of the first word of the Bible, with or without a prefixed preposition, is ambiguous. Various translations (KJV, NAB, AB) are allowable.

2. The Punctuation of the First Word of the Bible

Hebrew has marks which guide the reader in grouping words together into meaningful units (corresponding to the English comma, semicolon, and period). One such mark, corresponding to a comma, occurs at the end of the first word in Genesis. This might suggest that the word is to be set apart in meaning from the rest of the verse. It would thus be a clause unto itself, exactly as in the KJV-type translation: "In the beginning, . . ." Thereby, the supposed "of" relationship with that which follows would be ruled out and the NAB-type (also AB-type) translation would not be possible.

However, the punctuation of the Hebrew Bible is not exactly like that of English prose. It is intended, instead, to aid the reader in chanting the text as part of the service of worship. The Bible was intended to be sung rather than read. The punctuation, therefore, is more like that of an English hymn than of English prose. Thus, note the dashes in the following well-known verse, corresponding to pauses: "Ho-ly, ho-ly, ho-ly! Lord God Al-mighty!" In the Hebrew Bible, such musical "pauses" can even occur in the middle of an "of"-relationship clause. Despite its presence at the first word of the Bible, the correct translation still *might* be: "In the beginning—of God's creating" (that is, "When God began . . .").

In conclusion: The presence of the "pausal" punctuation mark does not demand that the translation of the verse favor one side or the other in the argument at hand.

3. The Syntax of the First Verse of the Bible

If there is an implied "of" relationship in a Hebrew sentence, it usually occurs when two nouns are linked in a possessive relationship: "The son of the king" (that is, "The king's son"). Presumably, then, if this is the syntax of the first word of Genesis, the next word should be a noun (gerund): "In the beginning of God's *creating* . . ." However, this is not the case in the Masoretic text. The next word, instead, is a verb (past tense, 3rd masculine singular): "(he) created." An "of" relationship would then produce the translation: "In the beginning of he created," and seem quite unlikely. Consequently, the KJV-type translation would seem to be mandated: "In the beginning, he (God) created . . ."

Unfortunately, things are not quite so simple. Hebrew syntax is very flexible and allows options in some constructions. There are numerous examples of such "of" clauses which are indeed followed by a verb of the type found here at Genesis 1:1 and which thus must be translated as if they were nouns. Thus, a rendering of the AB-type ("When God set about to create . . ."—literally, "At the beginning of God's creating . . .") is still quite possible.

In conclusion: The ambiguity in the first sentence of the Bible continues from the first word to the second.

4. The Syntax of the First Three Verses of the Bible

The question now must be asked: Are there indicators beyond v. 1 about where the initial sentence terminates? If the sentence ends at v. 1, then a translation of the KJV-type is mandated. If it does not, then the question becomes: Does one continue to the end of v. 2 (NAB-type), or v. 3 (AB-type)?

Ordinarily, if the sentence ended with v. 1, then the next sentence (v. 2), changing the subject as it does from "God" to "earth," would begin with the noun. This wording is in fact the case, as is reflected in most English versions: "The earth was . . ." Some modern interpreters see this as the only decisive indicator for the proper location of the end of the first sentence. Thus the KJV-type would be correct.[4] By contrast, were the sentence to continue into v. 2 or v. 3, the Hebrew word order would *ordinarily* begin v. 2 with a verb (literally: "And was the earth . . .").

However, one is speaking here only of probabilities, of that which authors do in most (but by no means all) cases. Thus able scholars have used the nature of the transition from v. 1 to v. 2 to argue to the opposite conclusion of the one just outlined (that is, to argue for the AB-type translation).[5]

In conclusion: Nothing in the vocabulary or syntax of vv. 1–3 settles the issue which here concerns us.

5. Parallels with Other Creation Accounts

If the ambiguity of Genesis 1:1–3 cannot be settled by internal evidence, then perhaps appeal may be made to literature outside the Bible. It is not unreasonable to suppose that the biblical account would begin in a way similar to other creation stories in the Ancient Near East.

The most famous potential parallel is that of the Babylonians. *Enuma elish* (which has been mentioned previously) relates (the god) Marduk's conquest of the chaos-monster (Tiamat). It begins, in part:

> *When* heaven above had not yet been named,
> Earth below had not yet been given a name,
>
> . . . .
>
> No reed-dwelling had been constructed,
> Not even a reed marsh could be found,
>
> . . . .
>
> *Then* it was that the gods were formed . . .
> (Tablet I, lines 1–2, 6, 9)

Here one finds a three step development: (1) When . . . , (2) at which time certain conditions prevailed, (3) then, so-and-so happened. Just such a structure and sequence is attested by the Bible itself, in the so-called "Second Story of Creation" (as NAB and JB designate Genesis 2:4b–25):

> 4bAt the time when the Lord God made the earth and the heavens—
> 5–6While as yet there was no field shrub . . .
>   no man to till the soil, . . .—
> 7the Lord God formed man out of the clay . . . (NAB).

Since this is, then, a widely attested form, included in the Bible itself, some scholars have argued that the same pattern occurs at 1:1–3,

> 1When God set about to create heaven and earth—
> 2the world being then a formless waste . . .—
> 3God said, "Let there be light." And there was light (AB).

Other interpreters have stressed the divergences of Genesis 1 from the Babylonian account or suggested that there is no compelling reason why the biblical account should follow the common pattern.[6]

In conclusion: While the "common pattern" does not rule out the KJV-pattern or the NAB-pattern, it strongly favors the AB-pattern.

6. The Meaning of the Hebrew Verb "To Create" in Genesis 1

Here, one might hope, one can finally "cut the Gordian knot" and get to the heart of the matter. Regardless of the ambiguities of vocabulary, punctuation, and syntax, or of the parallel (or lack thereof) with other creation stories, does the verb in Genesis 1 (*bārā'*) mean "to create (out of nothing)," or does it not? About this there has been a long history of debate.[7]

In cognate (similar) languages, the verb can mean "to shape (materials that already exist)." For example, in Old South Arabic, it means "to build"; in Punic, it is used in association with acts of sculpting and engraving. If it has those same associations in Hebrew, the AB-type translation would be mandated, since God's shaping of pre-existent matter would be indicated.

In the Bible, the verb is only used with the deity as subject. It describes either (1) God's initial act (as in Gen 1), or (2) subsequent divine initiatives in history. (Curiously, the latter descriptions are largely concentrated in Isaiah 40–55, which some modern interpreters think date from about the same time as the present formulation of Genesis 1.) Examples of the second type include the following instances, wherein the prophet anticipates God's impending deliverance of the Judean exiles from captivity in Babylonia.

> I will open rivers on the bare heights . . . that men may see and know . . . (that) the Holy One of Israel has *created* it (41:18–20).

> I make you hear new things . . . They are *created* now, not long ago . . . (48:6–7).

Clearly, in these and other texts, the divine action is within history and involves actions performed upon existing matter.

When used in connection with God's initial act, there is no intrinsic reason to believe that "creation out of nothing" is intended. Indeed, an able scholar who believes that such creation is implied in Genesis 1 realizes that it cannot be deduced from the meaning of the verb: "There is no conclusive evidence in the entire Old Testament that the verb itself ever expresses the idea of a creation out of nothing."[8] Nonetheless, the verb does imply something that is new and extraordinary and which only the deity can accomplish.

In conclusion of all the previous analyses: The intention of Genesis 1:1–3 with respect to "creation out of nothing" remains debatable. Criteria numbers 1–4 are ambiguous; criterion 6 does not support it; criterion 5 tends to oppose it. Thus, if such an idea were the intention of the author(s), they have clearly failed to convey it. On the other hand, there is no reason to believe that the doctrine is overtly being denied by the text of Genesis. Otherwise put: It may be doubted that the issue of "creation out of nothing" was a living one in the Ancient Near East during the time of the Hebrew Bible. In fact, even a translation of the KJV-type need not be taken to advance that doctrine: "In the beginning [of creative activity], God fashioned heaven and earth [from material at hand]."

Finally, it may be relevant to inquire as to when belief in "creation out of nothing" became a topic of conversation in the area (to judge from unambiguous testimony of surviving records, at least). The answer, apparently, is during the intertestamental period (second century B.C.E.–first century C.E.). Thus, the historian Diodorus Siculus (first century B.C.E.) reports that the Babylonians say that "the world is by its nature eternal, and neither had a first beginning or will at a later time suffer destruction . . ."[9] Conversely, it is in Jewish literature of this same period that we begin to find explicit assertion to the contrary: ". . . look at the heavens and the earth . . . and recognize that God did not make them out of things that existed" (2 Mac 7:28; see also Heb 11:3 and Rom 4:17).

The solid conclusion, then, and a biblical one, is expressed by Claus Westermann:

What is peculiar to biblical talk about the creation of the world is that it looks wholly and solely to the creator: God has created the world; and so everything has been said that one can say. If one wants to know more, one must move outside this [the biblical] framework. The sentence, "God created the world out of nothing," does not say more but rather less than the sentence, "God created the world." The question, "Is it *creatio ex nihilo* or not?" is not relevant to the text.[10]

Chapter VI   Notes

1. Briefly, see the article "Masoretic Accents" in *IDB,* Vol. III (K–Q), pp. 295–299.

2. *The Works of the Emperor Julian,* III, 1923, pp. 331–333.

3. Carl Sagan, 1980, p. 4.

4. So Umberto Cassuto, 1961, p. 19.

5. So E.A. Speiser, 1964, p. 5.

6. So Heidel, 1951, pp. 95–96; Westermann, 1984, pp. 96–97.

7. Full discussion may be found in *TDOT,* II, pp. 242–249. Less adequate, although more readily available, is the article "Creation" in *IDB,* Vol. I (A–D), pp. 725–732, especially Section 2.

8. Heidel, 1951, p. 89.

9. Loeb Classical Library Edition, I, p. 449.

10. 1984, p. 109. However, for the assertion that *creatio ex nihilo* is intended, arising not from grammatical considerations but from its close connection "with the important concern of the priestly conception of history," see Eichrodt, 1984, p. 72.

CHAPTER VII

An Immense Journey: From "Star-Stuff" to "Child of God"

A sermon preached in
Duke University Chapel
by
The Reverend Dr. Lloyd R. Bailey
Associate Professor of Old Testament
The Divinity School
April 29, 1984

Scriptures:
OLD TESTAMENT LESSON: GENESIS 12:1–3
NEW TESTAMENT LESSON: REVELATION 21:1–4

WHAT ARE WE to make of the Bible in a scientific age? What is there about it that can engage us in a significant way, since it comes to us from an age that is radically different from our own?

Here is an illustration of the problem. The authors of the Bible do not seem to realize the inter-connectedness of events in the physical world. Each "happening" in the realm of nature may thus be independent of any other. It arises, not from natural law, not because something "went before," but from the will of a divine being. Thus, one could not have said, as do we: "It is raining," as if one knew about evaporation and condensation. One could only have said, "God is causing it to rain!" There is thus no sense of that closed inter-connectedness, which the Greeks denoted by the term "cosmos."

What, then, are we to make of its message in an age of science? Or, more to the point: What is its message?

Shall we, on the one hand, reject it as a mere datum of history, an interesting statement of how things once were but which we modern persons, come of age, can no longer accept? That is the point of view of secular humanism.

Shall we, at the other extreme, try to accommodate science to the Bible and thus try to salvage the Bible in its totality? Shall we, for example, search for evidence that the earth is only a few thousand years old and that humans did not evolve from other creatures? That is the point of view of modern creationism.

This dilemma is especially interesting and demanding for me. This is because of my particular history. Before I "got into" this theology business, I was trained as a physicist, here at Duke University. Consequently I have tried to live responsibly in both realms of thought. It may not surprise you, then, that I will suggest a point of view that is between the two extremes that I have mentioned.

For some of you, this may be an unusual sermon. It will quote with approval both the astronomer Carl Sagan and the author of the book of Genesis. That is foreshadowed in the sermon's title: "AN IMMENSE JOURNEY: From 'Star-Stuff' to 'Child of God.' " It will attempt not merely to reflect upon the problem, but to exhort you to live in accordance with the Bible's agenda.

We began by hearing two formative texts from scripture: one from Genesis, one from Revelation; one a projection, and the other a conclusion. Thus, the sermon will attempt to put forth the center of the Bible's agenda, as we would say in the mountains where I grew up, "from kiver to kiver."

We are participants, all of us, in a vast experiment. We will not live to see how that experiment "turns out." But we have bet our lives on what the outcome will be. I conclude this from the fact that you are here, this morning, when you could have chosen to be somewhere else.

The pre-conditions of this experiment were a long time in the making. The beginning was some fifteen billion years ago, as the astronomer Sagan would say: "bill-yuns and bill-yuns of years ago." It began in a universe that contained huge clouds of formless matter. Much of the universe is still like that, with vast clouds of hydrogen gas: matter in its simplest natural state.

Then some of the clouds began to collapse, to "thicken" under their own weight.

Particles in the clouds were crushed closer together;

tremendous pressures and heat were generated;
heavier elements were forged into being;
light was emitted . . . and the stars began to "turn on."

In a modest sized star, such as our own "sun," there is just enough power to convert hydrogen into simple helium. But, in massive stars, there is enough power to press carbon, and even iron, into being.

Then, some of the massive stars exploded. We can still see them through telescopes, and we call them "super-novae." The result was that the heavier elements were spewed across space and thus became available for reassembly in the bodies of smaller, second generation stars.

Our sun, and its planets, congealed from such prior "star-stuff" about five billion years ago. Thus, they now contained all of the basic materials that would be necessary for the creation of life.

That, in simplified form, is the way that astronomers explain it. Their basic questions are: "How long did it take?" "Under what prior conditions did it happen?" "By what processes did matter evolve, so that things can be explained as we now find them?"

The book of Genesis, needless to say, has quite a different perspective. The questions of the astronomer are of little concern, and thus it should not be taken to contradict them. Rather, its central concern is with "meaning" and with the source of "meaning." Genesis proposes that the events of creation were not random, not accidental, and this is so because a single purpose was at work: a purpose which the text calls "God."

This theological perspective is not concerned with how long the process took or even with whether there was an absolute beginning. It merely reports that there was formless matter ("chaos") and that the deity began to act upon it. Thus, the first three verses may be rendered as follows:

> When God began to create the heavens and the earth—the earth being unformed and void, with darkness over the surface of the deep, and a wind from God sweeping over the water—God said, "Let there be light"; and there was light (NJV).

"Meaning" results because God is at work. Otherwise, there is only "meaninglessness," chaos, formlessness.

The stage is not yet set for our experiment, but almost! Here is what happens next, according to the chemist and the biologist.

We now have an earth that has congealed from previous generations of "star-stuff";

> it is bathed in the light of the sun;
> its atmosphere is stimulated by violent electrical storms.

Such activity aids in the formation of molecules, as can be demonstrated in the laboratory. The molecules can be torn apart and recombined in new ways.

About four billion years ago, the carbon-based molecule had learned to reproduce itself and an elementary form of "life" had begun. A billion years later, and the first cellular organisms were on the scene. Another billion years pass, and the organisms had learned "the joys of sex." (I suppose it had to happen, sooner or later, but it was the slowest adolescence on record, something parents pray for!)

Such activity allowed for the exchange, the intermingling, of genetic information, and thus life-forms became more complex. Another billion years pass, a mere billion years ago now, and the earth begins to "green-up." Algae are now the most advanced life-forms, and they fill the seas and supply oxygen for an atmosphere as we now know it. Suddenly there is an explosion of life:[1] first in the seas, then on the land, and finally in the skies. Fish are succeeded by amphibians, then reptiles, then mammals, and birds, and, finally, primates.

There has been some debate, in recent days, about the specific mechanisms for change and especially about its pace. Nonetheless, there you have it, in simplistic form.

About all these activities, the Bible has very little to say. It seems content to say that it was God who arranged for the seas and earth to become populated with "living creatures." It was not a meaningless, accidental, sequence of events, contrary to what some modern persons think!

And it was not the result of a multitude of divine forces: gods of sky, and earth, and sea, contrary to what some ancient persons thought! Rather: it was the working-out of a single divine will.

Now the pace of biological development quickens. Only a few million years ago, human creatures emerged on the earth. Ultimately, the molecules in their bodies had been bred in the interior of stars. To quote the astronomer Sagan, we are all "made of star-stuff" (*Cosmos,* p. 233).

Again, Genesis has a different, though not contradictory, perspective. It is not a matter of Genesis vs. geology, but Genesis beyond geology! Our scripture is not primarily concerned with our molecular development, but with our moral responsibility. God's life-force had animated all the creatures, as well as the human one, but of us alone does the deity have expectations and require accountability. This creature, says the text, mysteriously, is "created in the image of God."

At last we come to what will make the experiment necessary: and that is the maladjustment of the human creature to its environment. We humans are haunted by our finitude; we are hostile to the other creatures and to each other; and in fact we seem bent on self-destruction. The human creature is torn by warfare between its brain and its heart: between emotion and reason, between "feeling" and "knowing." Even if we know what we should do, we often find ourselves unable, unwilling, to do it. If we are indeed made from "star-stuff," then our performance has been far from stellar. On that, scientist and theologian will agree. "Why were human beings created?" some joker has asked? His answer: "To provide a bad example for the other creatures!"

Why humans are like this, and what is to be done about it, is a pressing problem. It is literally a matter of life-and-death for millions, if not for the race itself. For some biologists, the fault lies in the evolution of the brain. Evolution, so to speak, has left us with a "loose screw." Rather than developing uniformly, the brain seems to have developed in layers as new abilities were needed.

There is the oldest part: the brain-stem, which is buried deep inside the skull. It controls respiration and heartbeat: those involuntary actions that are vital to life.

Above that is an area that expanded during the age of reptiles:[2] its values are aggression, territorial possessiveness, and the drive toward procreation. It treasures those things that a reptile treasures, and urges us to act in the same way that they do.

Above that is an area that did not expand until millions of years later, during the age of mammals.[3] Its forte is not the blind urges of the reptile, but feelings, emotions, social hierarchies, and care for the young.

These two parts together were once called the "visceral brain," [4] because they directed us through the viscera. They control courage, which we call "guts"; they translate fear into sweat, and also affect our kidneys and bowels; they convert loss of a loved-one into a "broken heart."

Lying above these areas is a region that expanded only in higher primates: it is the cerebral cortex, or "new brain." It gives us the power of self-awareness, as the poet Robert Burns put it: "the power to see ourselves as others see us." It makes use of reason and of language. It is this portion of the brain that gives us the potential to rise above animal concerns and nature. But it must do so in competition with the other parts, and thus it may fall under their power. Thus the "new brain" may rationalize and justify the base behavior to which the lower brain is already urging us. Then, as the prophet Isaiah puts it: We will call evil "good," and we will twist goodness into something evil.

No wonder, then, that we may be torn between what we know to be "right," on the one hand, and what we "want" to do, on the other. It is a misfortune of our biological development that we can say, "My head tells me one thing and my heart another!" As a modern researcher in this area has put it:[5] When a psychiatrist tries to bring us to self-understanding, it is like asking a crocodile, and a horse, and a higher primate to stretch out together on the couch and to converse with each other. The three parts of the brain have different values.

The Bible's view of the human predicament is pretty much the same. Genesis depicts the human creatures as ego-centered, vindictive, and torn by inner conflicts. It attributes this not to human biology, as if we were innocent victims of evolution, but to the human will, and thus it makes us guilty. Just how the creature got this way, the text does not speculate.

What is to be done about this lamentable state of affairs, this maladjusted creature that has the audacity to call itself "homo sapiens," ("wise man"), and which desires to become, in the words of Genesis, "like God"? At last we come to the experiment to which I alluded in the beginning.

The answer, of course, depends upon whom you ask. One suggestion is that an appeal must be made to the creature's "lower brain," through threats of punishment. Key words to this approach are "swift justice," "strict law enforcement," and "teach them a lesson they won't forget." The book of Genesis had already rejected that as the ultimate solution before the story even got started: the flood, meant to remove an entire generation and to provide for a new beginning, did not turn out to be a cure-all. Humans would remain rebellious, but God would never again resort to massive punishment in order to deal with them.

For others, the correct approach is through the creature's "new brain." Key words in this solution to the problem include: act from "enlightened self-interest," and "be reasonable." This means of salvation is to be found in the public school system. But, as someone has said, "We are a mentally sick race, and as such, we are deaf to logical persuasion." [6]

For yet others, including biologists, the only possible solution lies in pharmacology. We need to understand the chemistry and functions of the brain. With the use of the proper drugs, perhaps we can bring the parts of the mind into balance so that we can be unified human beings.

A different approach is found in Genesis. It has passed very quickly over creation, and over the arrival of humans on the scene of history. You might say that it displays very little interest in what Charles Darwin called "the origin of species." Instead, it quickly grasps the problem created by the rebellious human. Then it cites a number of ways through which their potential for evil can be limited. The length of life-span is reduced to a minimum: it is unfitting that such creatures should live forever (says Genesis 6), and they are separated from each other at the tower of Babel (in Chapter 11).

The Bible then turns to its real agenda: What is to be done with, or for, this creature that has rejected its bounds? The response is found in the first of our scripture lessons. God now appeals to Abraham and Sarah to set out on an immense journey to a foreign land. They are to be found a community there and to "be a blessing to all the families of the earth." It is an immense journey that will lead through ancient Israel to the synagogue and the church in the present. It is the beginning of an experiment that will not be completed in Abraham's lifetime: it is to involve not only his generation, but an untold number of those who would arise after him. It is an experiment that is still in process, and one whose success is not yet certain.

The basis for this new community's appeal, how it would be a blessing to others, is not stated in this initial text. We are merely told that Abraham set out, that he obeyed, and that God considered it a meritorious act. We are also told that God preserved this undertaking, even when Abraham betrayed it, when, for example, he gave away his wife to Pharaoh. Whatever the goal of this community is, the deity seems firmly committed to it and strives passionately to preserve it for the task ahead.

It is only at the time of Moses and Joshua, some five hundred years later, that the nature and purpose of the experiment become clear. It is a sociological answer to the human problem: We see the formation of a radical alternative to society as humans have structured it. There is to be a haven from the tyranny of human political power, from economic abuse, and from social stratification. We hear an appeal for the actualization of life to the full, to life as it could be and as the deity had intended for it to be. What was offered was not merely an ideal, but a structure by which it could come into being. The "message" came with its own "delivery system." It was an appeal to experience: one ought to have learned from the past, from life as it naturally is, and thus be able to see the merits of a different approach. Thus, "Israel" was a word of freedom to the slave, security to the landless, acceptance to the alienated and the stranger, justice for the wronged, and protection for the powerless (such as the orphan and the widow). It was a religion whose sociology was, in some respect, unique in the ANE. "Yahweh was such a different God," one modern scholar has said, "because Yahweh was the God of such a different people" (N. Gottwald).

The response to this experiment has been mixed, from its beginnings to the present day. On the social level, it has been opposed by those who saw it as a threat to existing structures. For the Pharaoh, it meant the loss of a free labor-force; for the city-state rulers in Canaan, it implied an upheaval of the traditional socio-economic order; for the kings of Israel, it provided the potential for rebellion if they failed to honor the ancient ideals. To the successive empires which ruled the Near East, it meant a group of non-conformists which refused to accept the values of the dominant culture. The Bible thus has fueled a persistent dissatisfaction with the status quo, a longing for the world as it could be, because it remembered the world as it once was.

And thus it was that the prophets painted an alternative to present reality:

> And they shall beat their swords into plowshares,
> and their spears into pruning hooks;

nation shall not lift up sword against nation,
neither shall they learn war any more (Is 2:4).

Let justice roll down like waters,
and righteousness like an ever-flowing stream (Am 5:24).

Then I saw a new heaven and a new earth; for the first heaven and the first earth had passed away, and the sea was no more. And I saw the holy city, new Jerusalem, coming down out of heaven . . . for the former things have passed away (Rev 21:1–4).

The world, then, is a testing ground for two competing value-systems: that of Israel vs. that of Canaan; that of the Judean exiles vs. that of their Babylonian captors; that of the early church vs. that of the Roman empire. That competition still rages, both in the remotest settlements on earth and on the streets of the "urban jungle." The battle is being waged, not merely by the bishops and the pastors of the largest congregations, but by modest congregations and solitary individuals.

The response to this experiment, to this alternative value system, has not been uniformly positive on the individual level, either. It poses a challenge to the values of the "lower brain." It urges restraint, rather than aggression; it limits our power to possess and to keep; and it extols selflessness, rather than dominion. It is the nemesis of the human ego; it tells us that we are creatures, and not God; that death was willed for us, and properly so; that we are "dust, and to dust we must return."

It is a risky experiment because it relies, to some extent, upon the very creatures which it has been designed to transform. Thus, there were moments when its success hung precariously in the balance. But "star-stuff" can become a "child of God," and can rise to the occasion. God can use it, even when it is unaware. Thus, the community began insignificantly, when Abraham was but a single individual; it depended upon a foreigner, the Pharaoh, when Abraham gave his wife away; it depended upon a little girl, Miriam, as she watched over her baby brother as he floated in the Nile; it rested with an Egyptian princess, as she decided what to do with an outlawed child; it was held in abeyance, as the former slaves "wandered in the wilderness" for forty years and an entire generation passed away; it risked oblivion when it went into exile to Babylon; and much of its future rested on a helpless child in a manger in Bethlehem.

In this struggle, one is not able to know, at a given moment, the ultimate importance of our seemingly insignificant actions. Who could have imagined, when Joseph was sold into Egypt, that it would become the occasion for the salvation of his brothers and thus of the entire experiment? He says to his brothers, "As for you, you meant evil against me; but God meant it for good, to bring it about that many people should be kept alive, as they are today" (Gen 50:20). Who could have imagined, when Samson was out merely to "have a wild night on the town," that God was at work for the liberation of the people? The narrator says, "His father and mother did not know that it was from the Lord; for God was seeking an occasion against the Philistines" (Jgs 14:4). Who could have imagined, when the maiden Esther became the wife of Xerxes, king of Persia, that it would help ensure the survival of the people of God? Her uncle advised her to accept this status, since "Who knows whether you have not come to the kingdom for just such a time as this?" (Est 4:14).

So, we do not know what role we shall play in the resolution of this conflict but we may be sure that our modest contribution can affect the remote future. Hear what Paul had to say to the ordinary citizens at Corinth:

> . . . not many of you were wise according to worldly standards; not many were powerful, not many were of noble birth; but God chose what is foolish in the world to shame the strong; God chose what is low and despised in the world, mere nothings to overthrow the existing order (1 Cor. 1:26–29, RSV & NEB).

What we do know is that, sooner or later, one side or the other will win the struggle. Ultimately, either the kingdom of God must prevail, or hell will prevail and we will destroy ourselves. And I have bet my life, and so have you, on who the winner will be.

May God bless you, brothers and sisters: "star-stuff" changed into children of God, and may the kingdom come, and in your lifetime, speedily, and very soon.

Chapter VII   Notes

1. The so-called "Cambrian explosion."
2. The archicortex.
3. The mesocortex.
4. Now called the limbic cortex.
5. Arthur Koestler, 1968, pp. 34–43, at p. 37.
6. *Ibid.* p. 43.

APPENDIX I

The "Gap Theory": A Chronological Gap Between Genesis 1:1 and 1:2?

A BIBLICALLY based chronology for the age of the earth can be computed by determining a fixed absolute date (such as that of the founding of the Solomonic temple) and then work backward using biblical data. For example, 1 Kings 6:1 tells us that Solomon began the project 480 years after the exodus from Egypt, and Exodus 12:40 tells us that the duration of Israel's bondage there was 430 years. The age of Jacob, at the descent to Egypt, was 130 years, according to Genesis 47:7–8, and one can then compute backward using the common refrain, "Mr. X was so many years old when son Mr. Y was born." Using such reckoning, the date of creation was set at 4004 B.C.E. by John Lightfoot and Archbishop James Ussher (both of whom lived in the seventeenth century C.E.). Lightfoot was the more specific, suggesting the month, day, and hour as well. Other interpreters, using ambiguous points in the data in differing ways, have arrived at different dates. Modern scientific estimates, on the other hand, are in the billions of years.

The extreme resolutions of this conflict would be to maintain that one approach is correct and that the other is in error. An ardent biblical literalist, therefore, might reject the opinions of the scientists outright. Conversely, someone who was convinced of the correctness of the scientific estimates might either reject the Bible or see it as concerned with a non-scientific realm of reality at this point. Sometimes, however, an accommodation of one approach to the other has been preferred. One form of accommodation of the Bible to science, by "old earth" creationists, is the proposal that periods of time are missing from the chronological data in Genesis 1–11. One of them is the so-called "gap theory" ("hypothesis of restitution" or "ruin-reconstruction theory"), whereby there is an immense chronological expanse between Genesis 1:1 and 1:2.[1]

This proposal not only provides for the scientific age of the earth within a biblical framework, but also defines the time span within which an otherwise troublesome biblical happening could have taken place. Ezekiel 28 has seemed, to some interpreters, to speak of an angelic being whose pride and iniquity led to expulsion from "the mountain of God." [2] By linking this figure with another, similarly described in Isaiah 14, one could conclude that the angelic being was named "Lucifer" (so KJV, following the Latin Vulgate version of the Bible).[3] The expulsion could then be identified with that of "the devil and Satan" as described in Revelation 12:7–12, elsewhere called "the dragon, that ancient serpent" (Rev 20:1–3). "Serpent," of course, reminded interpreters ancient and modern of the tempter in the garden of Eden, which (in early Christian tradition) had come to be identified with the Satan, a fallen angel.[4]

Thus could be derived the idea of an ancient satanic rebellion which led to expulsion from heaven to earth, the consequence of which for humans was (among other things) the disobedience of the first couple and the subsequent sentence of death (Gen 3). Such a rebellion, then, must have taken place prior to the events which Genesis 3:1 begins to narrate.[5] But when? Would an event of such magnitude and consequence find no chronological anchor in scripture? Enter advocates of the "gap theory," who proposed that there is a faint reference to it in the way that Genesis 1:2 begins (as they propose that it be translated, at least): "The earth *became* without form, and darkness was upon the face of the deep." Thus understood, what the earth was not formerly it now became: a chaotic, rebellious state. This came about within history, at some undetermined time, perhaps millions or even billions of years after the completed creation of "heaven and earth" in v. 1. By the end of v. 2, that "world," perverted by satanic influence, has been cleansed in a catastrophic fashion and the deity has begun anew by v. 3: "Let there be light." The world as we know it then emerged as a consequence of divine activity during the familiar six days.

This system of thought, popularized in the early 1800s, found wide readership through the notes in the Scofield Reference Bible (1909). Formerly attached to the text of the KJV, the notes are now available (in modified form) with modern versions under the title the New Scofield Reference Bible. Although the notes are now less explicit about the "gap theory," at least the following instances occur.

Note to Genesis 1:2. "Two main interpretations have been advanced. . . . The first, which may be called the Original Chaos interpretation, regards these words as a description of an original formless matter in the first stage of the creation of the universe. The second, which may be called the Divine Judgment interpretation, sees in these words a description of the earth only [that is, not the entire universe], and that in a condition subsequent to its creation, not as it was originally (see Isa. 45:18, *note;* cp. also *notes* at Isa. 14:12; Ezek. 28:12)."

Note to Isaiah 45:18. " 'He created it not in vain [*tohu*].' This is one of the Scripture passages that suggests the Divine Judgment interpretation of Gen. 1:1–2 (see Gen. 1:2, *note*). This interpretation views the earth as having been created perfect. After an indefinite period of time, possibly in connection with Satan's sin of rebellion against the Most High (see *notes* at Isa. 14:12 and Ezek. 28:12), judgment fell upon the earth and 'it was [became] without form and void.' Another indefinite interval elapsed after which 'the Spirit of God moved upon the face of the waters' (Gen. 1:2) in a re-creation of the earth. Some of the arguments for this viewpoint are . . ."

In this view, the "gap" between v. 1 and v. 2 would account for scientific estimates of the age of the earth, locate the time of the fossil record of prehistoric plants and animals, and establish a relative chronology for the proposed satanic rebellion and expulsion.

"Creationists," of course, virulently reject this interpretation, not merely because it opposes their "young earth" position, but also because it allows accommodation of the Bible to the sciences. By contrast, "creationists" want to establish the independent congruency of the Bible and science (asserting that this is not an accommodation of science to the Bible).[6] As for the creation of the angelic beings, a "creationist" has suggested that it probably took place on the first day (Gen 1:1–5) rather than prior to it.[7] Soon thereafter came Satan's rebellion, involving "possibly a third of them" [the angels],[8] so that Satan (in the guise of the serpent) was available to tempt the human couple in the garden of Eden. It is not likely, however, that Satan was waiting when they arrived on the scene on the sixth day, since the deity pronounced the creation to be "good" even at that late date. Likely, then, say "creationists," Satan was not yet on earth at that time. Thus his heavenly rebellion and expulsion, leading to his appearance in the garden, likely occurred sometime between Genesis 1:31 and 3:1.[9] That is, a "gap theory" is required to account for the chronology of the rebellion in heaven.

What may one say about the proposed translation that allows the "gap theory" at Genesis 1:2 ("The earth *became* without form. . .")? Is it a defensible translation which has engendered the theory, or has the prior necessity for the "gap" led to the translation? The Hebrew verb used there (*hāyâ*) ordinarily means "to be," with the addition of a following preposition (*lᵉ*, "to") being necessary to give the meaning "to become." In fact, in the KJV, every instance where this verb is translated "to become" involves the preposition, and the preposition is not found at Genesis 1:2. The major modern versions of the Bible in English (be they Jewish, Protestant, or Catholic; be they prepared by "conservatives" or by "liberals") do not render the verb here in any other sense than the familiar one from KJV: "And the earth *was* without form . . ." Furthermore, in creation stories elsewhere in the Ancient Near East, a condition of chaos exists from the beginning rather than reflecting a deterioration of creation. In short, it was only the need by some interpreters to find a time for an angelic rebellion and expulsion from heaven (based upon a misunderstanding of texts in Ezekiel 28 and Isaiah 14) that led to a forced and inaccurate translation ("became") at Genesis 1:2.

Appendix I   Notes

1. For a full discussion of the history and form of this idea, see Tom McIver, 1988, pp. 1–24.

2. Usually, this figure is understood to be the king of Tyre (as the text itself says plainly at v. 2), described in images of the creation of the first human. See the notes in NAB, RSV, NEB, JB.

3. Usually this figure is understood to be the king of Babylon (as the text itself says plainly at v. 4). See the notes in NAB, RSV, NEB, JB. On "Lucifer" (RSV: "Day Star") as a title borrowed from Canaanite mythology, see the article "Day Star" in *IDB,* Vol. I (A.-D), p. 785.

4. Such a traditional interpretation, without evidence in the text of Genesis itself, is carefully avoided even in the note in NAB (but not so JB); so also RSV, NEB.

5. Although, curiously enough, the references in Revelation clearly refer to events in the present and future of the writer, who lives in the first century C.E.

6. See e.g. Morris, 1970, pp. 62–65.

7. Morris, 1976, p. 57.

8. *Ibid.* p. 108.

9. Morris, 1970, p. 63.

APPENDIX II

The "Day-Age Theory": How Long Is a "Day" in Genesis 1?

THE WORD "day" in the Hebrew language may have several meanings, just as does the word in English. We use this word for (1) the alternation of light and darkness ("day" as opposed to "night"); (2) a period of twenty-four hours' duration, including both light and darkness; (3) an indefinite period of time (as in the expression, "Every dog has its day!"); (4) a portion of a twenty-four hour period (as in the expression, "I work an eight-hour day"); (5) a specific period of time (as in the expression, "at that day and time"). Just so, in Hebrew, the word "day" (*yôm*) can mean "daylight" (Gen 8:22), or a period of twenty-four hours (Job 3:6), or a future period of indefinite length (as in the expression, "the day of the Lord" at Amos 5:18 and elsewhere).

Such flexibility of usage has given rise to speculation about the meaning of the word "day" in the creation story: What is the chronological duration of the individual creative acts, eight in number, organized into six periods of time each of which is called a *yôm?* Are they each of twenty-four hours' duration? Are they longer, but identical periods of time? Are they irregular periods, none necessarily the same as the other, corresponding to the modern geological ages? Do they designate periods of "God's time," which cannot be specified in terms of human chronology? Do they provide a clue as to the age of the earth?

The rise of modern science, with its idea that the earth was of great age (millions or even billions of years), was initially perceived by many to challenge the biblical account of creation which seemed to move from an absolute beginning to the emergence of human beings within a single week which was made up of twenty-four-hour days. The flexibility of the word "day" provided a means of easing the tension through an accommodation of the Bible to science, commonly known as "the day-age theory." On the one hand, "conservatives" (mostly "old earth" creationists) noted that, according to 2 Peter 3:8, ". . . with the Lord one day is as a thousand years." On the other hand, "liberals" noted that the eras proposed by modern geologists were seven in number, perhaps corresponding to the "days" of Genesis: Azoic, Archeozoic, Proterozoic, Paleozoic, Mesozoic, Cenozoic, and Modern. Furthermore, the latter group noted the scientifically correct sequence of creation in Genesis (first plants, then animals, then humans) and that life had emerged from the seas ("Let the waters bring forth swarms of living creatures . . ."—1:20). Thus the "conservative" group could maintain belief in "special creation" (non-evolution), over a vast time scale, accommodating to astronomy and geology but not to biology. The "liberal" group could propose "theistic evolution," thus accommodating to biology as well. By contrast, modern (young earth) "creationists" virulently reject the entire "day-age theory," holding instead to creation within six days of twenty-four hours' duration each, in congruence with independently derived "true" science.[1]

In seeking to evaluate the "day-age theory," the following particulars should be kept in mind.

1. Each "day" consists of an alternation of light and darkness, called "evening" and "morning." Consistency of interpretation in the "day-age theory" would demand a long period of light and darkness during each of the ages. This would quickly be fatal both to plant and animal life. (It could be argued, of course, that such consistency of interpretation is not necessary!)

2. The text of 2 Peter (3:8) has been misused by those who would bring it to bear upon the word "day" in Genesis 1 such that one gets the "biblical" mathematical equivalent "one day equals one thousand years" (or make it a million, while one is at it). Rather, the purpose of that text is to point out that "The Lord is not slow about his promise [to establish justice in the world] . . . but is forbearing . . . not wishing that any should perish . . ." (3:9; cf. v. 4). That is, God is not subject to time in the sense that human beings are (". . . as some count slowness," v. 9). The intent, then, is to make a statement about God's fidelity to promises, and not to define the meaning of the word "day" as it is used in Genesis 1.

3. After six such "days," the text in Genesis relates that God "rested." Although the text does not say so explicitly, this is an allusion to the sabbath, especially since the noun "sabbath" and the verb "to rest" are ultimately the same word (involving the same consonants, *sh-b-t*). This is then explicitly recognized in the ten commandments: "Remember the sabbath day. . . . Six days you shall labor . . . but the seventh day is a sabbath to the Lord your

God . . . for in six days the Lord made heaven and earth, the sea, and all that is in them and rested on the seventh day . . . ." (Ex 20:8–11).

If the "days" were actually long ages, presumably we would then be commanded to observe the sabbath only every thousand years or so, rather than weekly.

The fact that the creation is set within this week-long framework, that the goal of the entire story is that regular period of rest, and that the seventh day is the goal of creation as cited in the commandment, points the reader in the correct direction for understanding the whole story. What is important is sabbath observance, and not particulars of chronology, sequence, or the nature of creation (in contrast to "creationism").

Thus one must agree with "creationists" in the rejection of the "day-age theory," but that in no wise enhances the accuracy of their own understanding of the text in Genesis 1.

Addendum 1. Attempts to depict that creation, as presented in Genesis 1, did not involve days of twenty-four hours' duration have included appeal to the use of the word "day" in the opening words of the so-called "Second Story of Creation." Genesis 2:4b reads, "In the day that the Lord God made the earth and the heavens . . ." (RSV, KJV). Concerning this, a detractor from "creationism" has written:

> Furthermore, whereas the first chapter treats the whole work of creation as occupying six separate *yōmīm* [*sic!* properly *yāmîm*], the second chapter refers to a single *yōm* [properly *yôm*] in which the Lord God created the earth and the heavens (Gen. 2:4). Clearly, the Hebrew word *yōm* cannot here be calibrated into a specific chronological measure as creation-science presupposes: it must be understood, not as an inflexible twenty-four unit, but as a time of flexible and uncertain duration, within the overall symbolic context of biblical parable.[2]

In actuality, the literary unit 2:4b–25 uses the word "day" in a different sense than does 1:1–24a. In fact, proper English translation of 2:4b would not have even produced the word "day" such that the alleged ambiguity could arise. The verse opens with a temporal clause (*bᵉyôm ᵃsôt*) which, if rendered word-for-word ("on the day of making"), is misleading and inaccurate. This is a well-known idiom, consisting of *bᵉyôm* ("on the day of") followed by an infinitive (in this case, "making"), which is to be rendered as "*When* (the Lord God) made." This is clearly recognized by NAB ("At the time when . . ."), NEB ("When . . ."), TEV ("When . . ."), JB ("At the time when . . ."). Thus, KJV and RSV ("In the *day* that . . .") have created an unnecessary problem for the interpreter.

Addendum 2. The idea that the length of a "day" in Genesis 1 is an extended period of time receives support, in the opinion of a few modern interpreters, from the use of the term "sabbath rest" in Hebrews 4:1–11.[3] Since the text thereby refers both to the week of creation and to the unfinished work of God at the emergence of Christianity (unfulfilled rest that has been promised to all Israel), the promised "sabbath" lies yet in the future even though it may have begun at Genesis 2:2. "Scripture does not at all teach that Yahweh rested only one twenty-four-hour day at the conclusion of His creative work. No closing formula occurs at the close of the seventh day, referred to in Genesis 2:2. And, in fact, the New Testament teaches (Hebrews 4:11) that seventh day, that 'Sabbath rest,' in a very definite sense, has continued on right into the church age."[4] If, then, the seventh day could be thought of as still in progress, perhaps the previous six were of similarly undetermined and indeterminate length.

Appendix II   Notes

1. See Richard Niessen, 1980.
2. Roland Mushat Frye, 1983, p. 13.
3. This idea is examined and rightly rejected by Stambaugh, 1989.
4. Gleason Archer, *Encyclopedia of Bible Difficulties* (1982), p. 62 (*nv*), as quoted in *ibid.* p. iii.

APPENDIX III

The "Genealogical Gap Theory": Are There Generations Missing in the Biblical Genealogies?

ATTEMPTS TO harmonize the Bible's seeming assertion of a recent creation with the vast ages proposed by physical sciences have generally concentrated upon the idea of "gaps." The idea is that certain periods of time have been compressed in biblical chronology and thus not overtly mentioned. By "reading between the lines" (or verses, as the case may be), it is proposed that one may recover such lost time.

The "gap theory" (Appendix I) and the "day-age theory" (Appendix II) provide for "missing" time *prior* to the appearance of humans. Thereby, an accommodation is made both with astronomers (who put the age of the universe at twenty to ten billion years) and geologists (who date the age of the earth to about five billion years). That, however, leaves a "problem" with biologists (who assert that human-like remains may be traced backward for several million years). If that evidence is not to be discounted, then similar "gaps" must have occurred in biblical chronology *after* the account of human beginnings. The location of such compressed data would likely be in the genealogies of Genesis chapters 5, 10, and 11.

There is ample evidence of "missing" generations in biblical lists (whether by accident or design need not concern us here). Instances of this have been presented in the main text (above). For example, there is the fact that Kenan is among the post-diluvians in the LXX list but not in those in MT and SP (Gen 11:12–13). Again, there is the fact that four generations in the chronicler's genealogy of Solomon (1 Chr 3:10–16) are missing in

Matthew's review (1:6b–11). Furthermore, there is the fact that the Hebrew word ordinarily translated "son" (*bēn*) can also mean "grandson" (Gen 31:43; RSV, "children") or even "descendant" (as when Jesus is described as the "son of David" at Matthew 9:27). Conversely, the word ordinarily translated "father" (*'āb*) may also mean "ancestor" (for example, at Is 51:2).

The "old earth" creationists are willing to allow a number of such gaps and of sufficient magnitude to bring about an agreement between biologists and the Bible concerning the age of the human race. (Such creationists would not thereby necessarily subscribe to the idea of evolution of the human species, however.) "Young earth" advocates ("creationists") propose only a minimum necessity for such "gaps," perhaps amounting to no more than a thousand years.[1]

Appendix III   Note

1. Morris, 1976, pp. 308–310; 1970, pp. 66–68. He rejects the "old earth" approach in the following way: If the minimum age for humans on earth is set at a million years ("now generally accepted by evolutionary anthropologists"), that figure can only be brought within the chronological span from Adam to Abraham (about 2,000 years according to the MT), twenty generations, by an average gap of 50,000 years between each pair of names. Such vast gaps, however, were not objectionable to such a respected and famous "conservative" as B.B. Warfield who wrote:

> There is no reason inherent in the nature of the Scriptural genealogies why a genealogy of ten recorded links, as each of those in Genesis v. and xi. is, may not represent an actual descent of a hundred or a thousand or ten thousand links. The point . . . is not that these are all the links . . . but that this is the line of descent. . . .

Warfield's overall argument is that the genealogies are "trustworthy for the purposes for which they were recorded," and that the purpose had nothing to do with chronology. That they "lend themselves ill to employment for chronological calculations has been repeatedly shown very fully" (1932, pp. 237, 238). He goes on to cite with appreciation an article by William Henry Green in *Bibliotheca Sacra* for April 1890.

APPENDIX IV

"Creationist" Principles of Interpretation

THERE IS NO comprehensive list of such principles, either in general or for individual interpreters. Occasionally, however, partial lists may be found.[1] The following, by no means intended to represent a wide survey, are either explicitly stated or implied in the writings of Henry Morris.

1. *The Bible, "as the divinely-inspired revelation of the creator," is inspired in a verbal fashion which guarantees that it is infallible ("free from error of any sort") even in scientific and historical matters.*[2]

Such a point of view, of course, is not limited to "creationists." It is held by some interpreters in a wide spectrum of "conservative" Protestant groups. Indeed, it is an issue which has recently caused heated debate and vitriolic denunciation within the Southern Baptist Convention.

Those who care to ponder such a principle should be made aware that its parts do not inevitably follow one from the other. That is, to state that the Bible is "inspired" or is "revelation" is, within itself, a statement which theistic evolutionists (the nemesis of "creationists") might also affirm. It does not necessarily follow that such inspiration is "verbal" (i.e. the very words), or that it guarantees infallibility (and least of all in "scientific and historical matters").

In deciding matters such as this, it might be well to let the Bible speak for itself. It does use the term "inspired" in connection with itself (2 Tim 3:16, likely having only the Old Testament in mind) and claims that its contents are "revealed" (Deut 29:29; Rev 1:1). However, the concept of infallibility does not appear within its pages, and its stated agenda does not include matters of science.[3] In fact, such assertions are nothing more than prior (subjective) assumptions which "creationists" (and others) have brought *to* the text,[4] rather than having arisen *from* it. Neither do such claims find expression in the great creeds of the church.

131

In actual practice, it sometimes appears that it is their interpretations that "creationists" think are infallible, and not the text of the Bible itself. From many examples that could be chosen, consider Henry Morris' understanding of how Noah's boat was made watertight.[5] According to the text in Genesis (6:14) it was to be caulked with "pitch" (RSV, NEB, NAB, JB, KJV). Morris passes deftly over the problem: "Whatever the exact nature of this 'pitch' may have been (probably a resinous substance of some kind, rather than a bitumenous material), it sufficed as a perfect covering. . . ." The unstated reason for this definition, presumably, is that bitumen is a natural substance formed from organic matter which has been subjected to great periods of decay after having been buried beneath the earth. To evolutionists, such deposits (bitumen, petroleum, gas, coal) require the passage of millions of years. To "creationists," however, they resulted from the waters of the flood[6] and thus presumably could not have existed in the pre-diluvian world of Noah. Thus, if the "pitch" which Noah used was bitumen (petroleum tar) rather than resin (pine tar), "creationism" is in serious trouble!

What, then, does the word "pitch" (*koper*) signify? Unfortunately, this is its only use in the Bible, and thus its context does not help us define it. The verb from which it is derived (apparently meaning "to cover") would allow for a number substances and that is why translators chose the more neutral term "pitch." Nonetheless, the word is widely used in other documents (that is, outside the Bible) where its meaning is quite clear and unambiguous. Let us note, first, that it is with the same substance that the Mesopotamian flood-hero caulked his boat (*kupru*).[7] That the substance is in fact bitumen is shown from texts where it is said to "come up from the depths [of the earth]," and in which mention is made of "the bitumen spring."[8] A photograph of just such a spring, flowing profusely in Iraq, may be found in *Everyday Life in Bible Times* (published in 1967 by the National Geographic Society, at p. 60). In Canaan, masses of the stuff rose to the surface of the Dead Sea, where it was gathered and used in building projects. In Mesopotamia, it was used likewise: "I bonded large limestone (blocks) with bitumen." Remnants of buildings indicate that this was in fact the practice.

On the one hand, it may be that Morris was unaware of the meaning of the word *koper,* relied entirely upon his English Bible, and took advantage of the ambiguity of the word "pitch" in order to salvage the "creationist" position from ruin. In that case, he should have investigated the matter in order to reach a more reliable position rather than blithely reading the English text through the eyes of "creationist" presuppositions.

On the other hand, Morris may have been aware of the abundant extra-biblical evidence for the meaning of the word *koper.* In that case, he would have placed the infallibility of "creationism" above that of scripture and have given the word *koper* a "verbal oil change" in order to make it conform to "creationism."

2. *Any statement in scripture may, in theory, be used to interpret any other, since the totality ultimately has a single author (God) who infallibly inspired each human speaker or writer.*

While I did not find this principle explicitly stated, it does seem to underlie much of Morris' interpretation. Consider the case of Genesis 5:24 and its fantastic interpretation.[9] The text reads: "Enoch . . . was not; for God took him." This means that Enoch was taken to heaven, says Morris, "in actual physical flesh," and hence he did not experience death (as expressed at Hebrews 11:5). How can this be, in view of the explicit statement of scripture that "it is appointed unto men *once* to die" (Heb 9:27; emphasis Morris')? This statement would seem to be contradicted also in the case of Elijah who was taken alive to heaven (2 Kings 2:11–12). However, he is scheduled to return to earth at some future date in order to preach to the generations then present (Mal 4:5–6; Mt 17:11). This episode will then provide the opportunity for Elijah to die, in keeping with the mandate of the author of Hebrews. Just so, Enoch must also return, although scripture does not say so explicitly: ". . . it does seem probable that Enoch . . . will yet finish his ministry of witness to a godless generation . . ."

Morris makes even more of the word "once" at Hebrews 9:27. According to Revelation 11:1–12, two witnesses to God's truth will be slain but then brought to life again. The language used brings to mind (says Morris) the "two anointed ones" of Zechariah 4:14, who (at the time of the author) "stand by the Lord." Since this seemingly refers to heaven, it denotes persons who departed the earthly scene prior to Zechariah's time but who cannot have done so by means of death since they are to die at the time of the fulfillment of Revelation 11:1–2. Otherwise, they would have died *twice,* and thus only Elijah and Enoch can qualify.

Even a fleeting glance at Hebrews will show how far afield Morris' principle of interpretation has taken him. The author speaks of the superiority of Jesus' priesthood over that of the levitical system (7:1–28), then specifically of Jesus' ministry as high priest (8:1–10:18). Whereas the levitical priests approach God daily in order to affect reconciliation, Jesus (as priest) has affected it once-for-all. An analogy is then offered: Just as humans do not die repeatedly, neither does Christ offer himself as sacrifice for human sin repeatedly. "And just as it is appointed for men to die once . . . so Christ, having been offered once to bear the sins of many . . ."

As for the "two witnesses" of Revelation 11:3, they are described in the language of Zechariah 4. There one reads of "two olive trees" on either side of the lampstand in the temple. The text then identifies one of them as the prince Zerubbabel, and the other apparently is the priest Joshua.[10] They are called "the anointed ones," which is precisely the status of prince and priest (having oil poured over their heads as part of a consecration service).[11] There is not the slightest reason why Enoch or Elijah should come to mind when this passage is read, or any reason why they should qualify as "anointed ones" who function in the temple which was built after the return from exile (sixth century B.C.E.).

3. *To know what a text in the Bible says is to know what it means.*

This principle of interpretation is illustrated in a cartoon which appeared in an ICR publication.[12] In the first of two drawings, Dr. Brown informs his class: "It's not what Genesis says that's important—it's only what it means!" In the second drawing, Brown cowers in alarm as one of his students drives him through a stop-sign at high speed, with a collision just ahead. The student says, "I know what it [the stop-sign] says, Dr. Brown, but what does it mean?" Presumably, then, the Bible (with all its diversity of literature and translational difficulties) is as clear as to meaning as is a traffic signal and is to be taken just as literally.

One might be inclined to regard the cartoon as a mild attempt at humor, expressing gross overstatement on the part of the artist. This is apparently not intended to be the case, however, since the cartoon is part of an article on how congregations should closely question prospective pastors concerning the literal historicity of the book of Genesis, lest they escape detection as "evolutionists" by stressing what the book "means" rather than what it "says." Congregations which fail to do this are then compared with the lukewarm Laodicean church of whom Christ would "spew thee out of my mouth" (Rev 3:15–16). Further comparison is made with those for whom "it were better for him that a millstone were hanged about his neck, and that he were drowned in the depth of the sea" (Mt 18:6).

One would have thought that "creationists" would want to honor the traditional distinction between "letter" and "spirit," wherein what a text literally "says" may not be the same as what it "means" (its intent, "spirit"). For example, while the "letter" of Deuteronomy 15:1–3 is to cancel loans at the beginning of every seventh year, its "spirit" is to prevent deprivation of the poor. However, the effect of the law was the opposite of its intent when lenders refused credit as the seventh year approached. Consequently, a way was found to remedy the situation.[13] Or, consider a clearer example: The "letter" of 1 Kings 1:40 is clear enough when it reports that the volume of the music at Solomon's coronation "split" the earth. The signs of that worldwide crack are nowhere in evidence today, and one would be surprised if "creationists" were to launch a search for it. Rather, they might well recognize that the intent of the text is, by means of hyperbole (exaggeration), to report the splendor and importance of that ancient liturgical occasion. Nor would "creationists" propose, I suspect, that Abraham's descendants have literally been as numerous as the stars of heaven or as the sands of the seas (Gen 22:17). Not even the entire population of the earth, throughout its entire history, would approach even a fraction of such enumeration! There is in these examples (and others that could be listed at great length) a clear distinction between what the text "says" and what it "means." "Creationists" are *not necessarily* the authentic interpreters of the creation story, therefore, just because they say that they are "taking it literally."

It is surprising to find a multitude of places where the "plain" meaning of the text is not acceptable to "creationists." For example, consider the tension between the creation account in Gen. 1:1–2:4a and the remainder of chapter 2. In the former, the order of creation is: plants, animals, humans (male and female together); in the latter, the order is: a human male, plants, animals, and a human female.[14] Note the sequence (RSV): ". . . when no plant of the field was yet on earth (2:5) . . . the Lord God formed man of dust (v. 7) . . . the Lord God planted a garden . . . made to grow every tree (vv. 8–9) . . . the Lord God formed every beast . . . and brought them to the man (v. 19) . . . the rib . . . he made into a woman (v. 22)." This is the plain sequence in all major translations as readers may determine for themselves, but "creationists" seemingly cannot allow it to stand. Thus, a new understanding must be proposed, and we are told that "a perfectly plausible translation [for v. 5] would be . . ."[15] Furthermore, "it would be quite legitimate to translate verse 19 as follows . . . ,"[16] with the result that the "problem" with the two accounts disappears! It might strike some readers as curious that Morris' suggested wordings (not reproduced here) have eluded generations of professional translators, persons of great learning in the biblical languages, ranging from "conservative" to "liberal," from Jewish to Roman Catholic to Protestant. And this from a person who is described in the preface to his book (*The Genesis Record*) as having "not received formal theological training." (In fact, Morris is an engineer, specializing in hydraulics.) His "perfectly plausible" and "quite legitimate" suggestions seemingly have arisen, not from minute linguistic analysis of the Bible in its original languages, but from the needs of a pre-conceived scheme called "creationism."

4. *When a "creationist" interpretation leaves questions in the mind of readers, it is legitimate to supply historical details which the text lacks.*

This principle of interpretation is not formally stated but is abundantly evident in "creationist" literature. The "details," rather than being presented as speculative, are often asserted with confidence. A few illustrations follow.[17]

a. How was it possible for the animals, presumably scattered across the face of the earth and each "kind" in its own habitat, to have been gathered to Noah's ark on such short notice (within a period of *seven* days,[18] according to Genesis 7:4, 10)?

Morris offers two observations which would have facilitated the procedure. (a) It would have been easy for the various animals to arrive, since "the seas, hills, and other geographical features were more or less uniformly distributed over the globe."[19] In actuality, however, the text tells us nothing of the geography of the pre-flood world. (b) The animals arrived, apart from any time consuming search on Noah's part, because God had planted within a few couples of each "kind" (either one couple or seven couples, according to Genesis 7:2–3) special genes "which were programmed to impart such migratory instincts."[20] That is, at a pre-determined time, the genes would switch-on and direct the animals to wherever it was that Noah was building his boat! As a matter of fact, however, the text says nothing of the animals migrating to Noah on their own, by instinct or otherwise. Indeed, Noah is commanded to "bring" them in (6:19). The statement that the animals "shall come unto thee, to keep them alive" (v. 20 KJV) is part of Noah's obligation, not a statement of animal instinct. Morris may have been misled by KJV's "unto thee," as opposed to the more correct "come in to you" (RSV). The verb used here (*bô'*) means "to enter" (here, the ark). Note JB: "must go with you"; NAB: "shall come into the ark with you."

b. The story of Noah's drunkenness (Gen 9:20–27) prompts a series of assertions by Morris for which there is no shred of evidence in the text. The text reads (RSV):

> Noah was the first tiller of the soil. He planted a vineyard; and he drank of the wine, and became drunk, and lay uncovered in his tent. And Ham, the father of Canaan, saw the nakedness of his father, and told his two brothers outside. Then Shem and Japheth took a garment, laid it upon both their shoulders, and walked backward and covered the nakedness of their father; their faces were turned away, and they did not see their father's nakedness. When Noah awoke from his wine and knew what his youngest son had done to him, he said,

> "Cursed be Canaan;
>   a slave of slaves shall he be to his brothers."

> He also said,
> "Blessed by the Lord my God be Shem;
>   and let Canaan be his slave.
> God enlarge Japheth,
>   and let him dwell in the tents of Shem;
>   and let Canaan be his slave."

Morris supplies the following additional details: (1) Noah's sons each lived at some distance from him; (2) Noah had not expected any visits from his sons that day and hence was careless about his appearance; (3) son Ham went visiting at the instigation of Satan so as to catch Noah in his disreputable state; (4) Ham was surprised at what he saw; (5) Ham "gazed at" his father, "evidently with satisfaction" [concerning the suggestion of some interpreters that Ham's look was lustful, Morris remarks that "The passage does not say this . . ."—advice that Morris might well heed!]; (6) the other brothers "rushed" to Noah's tent; (7) Canaan was cursed because he had "inherited the carnal and materialistic nature" of father Ham; (8) Canaan's status as a "slave of slaves" may designate worldwide "service" and "may be prophetic of Christ"; (9) the term "slave" likely designates a "steward," of which, in God's service, there are three fundamental types: spiritual, intellectual, and physical; Noah recognized that his three sons had "characteristics representing these three emphases": Shem = spiritual, Japheth = intellectual, and Ham = physical. That is, the Hamites (Egyptians, Sumerian, Phoenicians, Hittites, Canaanites, Africans, Mongols, Chinese, Japanese, American Indians, South Sea Islanders, etc.) "have been largely unconcerned with either science, philosophy, or theology, and have been occupied largely with material pursuits" (i.e. great inventors and technologists, hard laborers and fighters).

In relation to the process of filling in "historical" details, one might (with no more or no less textual support) have proposed the following alternatives to those of Morris: Noah and his sons lived in the same structure; Noah's sons had gone fishing and came back early; Ham came visiting on his own initiative; Ham was repulsed by what he saw; Ham resolved never to be caught in a situation similar to his father's; the brothers came reluctantly and slowly; why Canaan was cursed remains a mystery; the term "slave" or "servant" means exactly what it says; and so on. In short, Morris has indulged in wholesale subjectivism and then concluded with a series of cultural characterizations that boggle the mind.

In other places, Morris' "additions" to the text go beyond anything that "creationism" might mandate (as far as I can tell). A few brief illustrations will suffice.

a. Speaking of Eve's conversation with the serpent (Gen 3): ". . . there may really be no reason why we should not assume that, in the original creation, the serpent was a beautiful, upright animal with the ability to speak and to converse with human beings. . . . It is at least possible (*as well as the most natural reading*) that the higher animals could originally communicate with man . . ." (emphasis added).[21]

b. Speaking of Adam's "deep sleep" during which a part of his body was taken with which to fashion the woman: "Since this sleep was not necessary to prevent pain (as yet, there was no knowledge of pain or suffering in the world), there must have been some profound spiritual picture in the action."[22] What? No rock upon which to stub one's toe? No limb upon which to bump one's head? No stomach ache from too many green apples? No sunburn on one's naked hide? (How in the world does Morris know these amazing things?)

c. On the fact that the ordinary word for "God" in Hebrew (e.g. at Gen 1:1) is grammatically a plural (hence meaning either "God" or "gods" according to the context): ". . . a 'uni-plural' noun, thereby suggesting the uni-plurality of the Godhead. God is one, yet more than one" (i.e. an allusion to the Trinity).[23]

This idea, as old as some of the Greek fathers of the church, is devoid of a shred of evidence, especially in the light of what one knows of the Hebrew language. One might as well point to the fact that the ordinary word for "face" in Hebrew is a plural by form (used for both humans and deity), and thereby argue that God is "two-faced" or that humans were created in the image of the Roman deity Janus.

The same line of interpretation is continued by Morris for the entirety of Genesis 1:1: The fact that the product of God's creativity was a "tri-universe" supports the idea of a Trinity here, since that creativity involved a unity of time, space, and matter.[24]

Encountering such surprising insights, devoid of textual basis, might remind one of the rabbinic story of Moses who was allowed to return to earth, centuries after his death. He arrived at a synagogue where a famous rabbi was expounding the text of the Bible according to the conventions of the day, which far exceeded its literal meaning. Astonished at what he heard, Moses (unrecognized) inquired as to the source of such derivations. He was informed that it was nothing other than the teachings of Moses, revealed long ago at Mount Sinai. At that point, Moses, astonished at all that he apparently had implied (but had not perceived at the time), went to the back of the class and sat with the "beginners" in order to learn the full meaning of the text! (Verily, "creationist" interpretations of the text of Genesis abound with insights that only they have discovered and which, I suspect, would send Moses to the back of the class in order to learn to understand himself.)

Morris' seeming innocence of all this is charmingly stated in the following way: "Therefore, the only proper way to interpret Genesis 1 is not to 'interpret' it at all. That is, we accept the fact that it was meant to say exactly what it says."[25]

Appendix IV   Notes

1. Henry Morris, 1976, pp. 30–32.
2. From the "Tenets of Creationism," for which see above, Chapter II.

3. For the agenda of the biblical text, see above, Chapter V. Also see the article "Inspiration and Revelation" in *IDB*, Vol. II (E-J), pp. 713–724; "Inspiration and Inerrancy" in *JBC*, Chapter 66.

4. See, briefly, Hyers, 1984, pp. 27–28.

5. Henry Morris, 1976, p. 182.

6. Whitcomb and Morris, 1961, pp. 277–278, 434–436.

7. Tablet XI, line 65 (*ANET*, p. 93). The Akkadian word *kupru* would become *koper* in biblical Hebrew, just as we find it.

8. *CAD*, Vol. 8 (K), pp. 553–555.

9. Henry Morris, 1976, pp. 156–159.

10. In addition to the standard commentaries, see the annotations in NAB, NEB, JB.

11. See the articles "Anoint" and "Anointed, The" in *IDB*, Vol. I (A-D), pp. 138–139, 139–140.

12. Ham, 1989.

13. For a brief discussion and sources, see George Foot Moore, 1927, I, pp. 259–260.

14. This has been discussed above, at Chapter III.

15. Henry Morris, 1976, p. 84.

16. *Ibid.*, p. 97, suggesting that the verbal tenses be rendered as past perfects ("had formed," "had brought"), referring to events prior to vv. 18–19.

17. A series of difficult questions for those who would read the flood story literally is posed by Stanley Rice, 1988.

18. Should not the use of the number seven alert the reader to the possibility of a non-literal intention in the text? See Appendix VII.

19. Henry Morris, 1976, pp. 185–186.

20. *Ibid.* p. 186.

21. *Ibid.* p. 109.

22. *Ibid.* p. 99.

23. *Ibid.* p. 39.

24. *Ibid.* p. 41.

25. *Ibid.* p. 54.

APPENDIX V

Ecclesiastical Statements Concerning "Creationism"

CHAPTER II of the present volume presents statements by "creationists" which indicate a belief that their interpretation of the biblical creation story alone is accurate, that other positions by Christians lack personal integrity, and that theistic evolution is an "anti-God conspiracy of Satan himself." Such points of view are repeated many times over in "creationist" writings.

Be those charges valid or not, it is important for readers of the present volume to gain an understanding of who at least a part of the "creationists' " enemy is. I speak not of individual interpreters (be they secular or theistic), but of entire denominations of the Christian church; not of the private opinions of a few leaders, but of official pronouncements by the duly elected representatives of laity and clergy.

1. *Minutes of the General Assembly of the United Presbyterian Church in the United States of America,* Part I, Journal of the One Hundred and Ninety-Fourth General assembly, Seventh Series, Volume XVI, 1982, pp. 410–414.

14. The Program Agency Board *recommends* to the 194th General Assembly (1982) that the following Resolution on Evolution and Creationism be adopted, and that the Stated Clerk be instructed to disseminate the entire document, preferably by direct mailing, to all congregations of The United Presbyterian Church in the United States of America.

EVOLUTION AND CREATIONISM

I. Resolution

Whereas The Program Agency of The United Presbyterian Church in the United States of America notes with concern a concerted effort to introduce legislation and other means for the adoption of a public school curriculum variously known as "Creationism" or "Creation-Science"; and

Whereas over several years, certain groups resourced by the Creation Science Research Center and an Institute for Creation Research have prepared legislation for a number of states calling for "balanced treatment" for "creation-science" and "evolution-science," requiring that wherever one is taught the other must be granted a comparable presentation in the classroom; and

Whereas while this issue represents a new situation, there are General Assembly policies on church and state and public education that guide us to assert once again that the state cannot legislate the establishment of religion in the public domain; and

Whereas the dispute is not really over biology or faith, but is essentially about biblical interpretation, particularly over two viewpoints regarding the characteristics of biblical literature and the nature of biblical authority;

Therefore, the Program Agency *recommends* to the 194th General Assembly (1982) the adoption of the following affirmation:

The 194th General Assembly (1982):

1. Affirms that despite efforts to establish "creationism" or "creation-science" as a valid science, it is teaching based upon a particular religious dogma as agreed by the court (McLean *vs.* Arkansas Board of Education);

2. Affirms that the imposition of a literalist viewpoint about the interpretation of biblical literature—where every word is taken with uniform literalness and becomes an absolute authority on all matters, whether moral, religious, political, historical, or scientific—is in conflict with the perspective on biblical interpretation characteristically maintained by biblical scholars and theological schools in the mainstream of Protestantism, Roman Catholicism, and Judaism. Such scholars and, we believe, most Presbyterians find that the scientific theory of evolution does not conflict with their interpretation of the origins of life found in biblical literature.

3. Affirms that academic freedom of both teachers and students is being further limited not only by the impositions of the campaign, most notably in the modification of textbooks, which limits the teaching about evolution, but also by the threats to the professional authority and freedom of teachers to teach and students to learn;

4. Affirms that required teaching of such a view constitutes an estab-

lishment of religion and a violation of the separation of church and state, as provided in the First Amendment to the Constitution and laws of the United States;

5. **Affirms that exposure to the Genesis account is best sought through the teaching about religion, history, social studies, and literature, provinces other than the discipline of natural science; and**

6. **Calls upon Presbyterians, legislators, and school board members to resist all efforts to establish any requirements upon teachers and schools to teach "creationism" or "creation-science."**

II. Supporting Information

A. *Current Climate and "Creationism"*

"Creationism"—more often called "creation-science" by proponents who seek to gain a place for this concept in public school teaching—is a theory based largely on the first 11 chapters of Genesis. It maintains that the universe and the earth are 6,000 to 10,000 years old and that all current and extinct forms of life were created in six days, as stated in the Bible.

However, by denying that their theory is based on religion, creationists attempt to circumvent the prohibition of religious instruction in public schools. They ask that their "creation-science" be accepted as comparable to "evolution-science" and be given comparable time and presentation when evolution is taught.

Attempts have been, and continue to be, made to induce legislation that will mandate the teaching of "creationism" in public elementary and secondary schools. Such efforts have been made with state legislatures in more than twenty states, including Iowa, Georgia, Arkansas, Kentucky, Florida, and Louisiana, and with school boards in several major cities.

The first state to pass a "creation-science" bill was Arkansas, in March 1981. The Creationism Act (Act 590 of 1981, Acts of Arkansas— "Balanced Treatment for Creation-Science and Evolution-Science Act"— March 18, 1981) defines two subjects it labels "creation-science" and "evolution-science." The act does not require that either be taught but does provide that if either is taught, there must be balanced treatment of the other in all public secondary and elementary schools.

The model bill for this legislation was drafted by members of creationism organizations who subscribe to religious beliefs that the universe, energy, and life were all created suddenly by a Creator, as described in Genesis.

With the participation of major church leadership in Arkansas as plaintiffs (including Rev. William S. McLean, General Presbyter, Arkansas Union Presbytery, Rev. George W. Gunn, Minister of the Pulaski Heights Presbyterian Church in Little Rock, and Rev. Richard B. Hardie, a Presbyterian minister), a suit was entered May 27, 1981, seeking to have Act 590 declared unconstitutional in violation of the First and Fourteenth Amendments to the Constitution of the United States. In the trial conducted December 7–18, 1981, expert witnesses in religion, science, and education made very clear that Act 590 was neither good education nor good religion.

On January 5, 1982, Federal Judge William R. Overton rendered a decision for the plaintiffs and entered a permanent injunction prohibiting enforcement of Act 590. In his decision, Judge Overton said that the creationists themselves had admitted that the law "is a religious crusade coupled with a desire to conceal this fact." Judge Overton held that the Arkansas law failed all three of the "establishment" of religion tests. The law (1) had a religious purpose, (2) had the effect of advancing religion, and (3) would excessively entangle government with religion.

In the testimony provided in the Arkansas case several characteristics of the contest between "evolution-science" and "creation-science" became evident:

• "Creationists" have played upon public tendencies to ascribe mistakenly to "science" an authority for total wisdom. Science thrives on alternative explanations that must be subject to observational and experimental testing. Science is involved in the comparing of alternative ideas about what the cosmos is, how it works, and how it came to be. Some ideas are better than others. However, they continue to be tested and are not accepted as closed authoritarian systems.

• The proponents of "creation-science" do not recognize the distinctive roles of science, religion, and philosophy as major efforts to explore the origins and purposes of life. These are proper subjects for exploration in classes in literature, history, social studies and in the teaching about religions in the schools. The separation of church and state is not violated by the examination of these various claims to truth in human understanding. Teaching for commitment in belief and in faith is the function of church and home.

• The argument for "balanced treatment" calls forth a deep-seated American commitment to "fair play." However, it tends to prejudge the basic question of whether "creation-science" is really a "science," and adds confusion about the basic principles of science as these are being imparted through schooling.

• The imposition of a literalist viewpoint about the interpretation of biblical literature—where every word is taken with uniform literalness and becomes an absolute authority on all matters, whether moral, religious, political, historical, or scientific—also distorts the perspective on biblical interpretation as characteristically maintained by biblical scholars and theological schools in the mainstream of Protestanism, Roman Catholicism, and Judaism. Such scholars find that scientific study of evolution does not limit their study of the origins of life. (*Note:* The report of the Advisory Council on Discipleship and Worship, Part Two, Section C, "Biblical Authority and Interpretation," cites the history of the inerrantist viewpoint on Scripture and may be a useful document for reference and study.) [See page 316.]

• The threats to teachers and schools from the ten years of campaigning for inclusion by "creation-science" advocates have already led to significant modification of textbooks, most notably by the sharp reduction in the treatment of evolution in biology and other texts.

B. *Presbyterian Precepts*

United Presbyterians have a long-standing record in support of the separation of church and state, as well as the freedom for pursuit of truth in schools and colleges. Presbyterians are equally clear about their faith and their understanding of the important creative and creating work of God. The following passages from the church's confessions, and from actions approved by the General Assembly, clearly establish such a record:

(1) *The Confession of 1967*

> God has created the world of space and time to be the sphere of his dealings with men. In its beauty and vastness, sublimity and awfulness, order and disorder, the world reflects to the eye of faith the majesty and mystery of its Creator. (9.16.)
>
> God has created man in a personal relation with himself that man may respond to the love of the Creator. He has created male and female and given them a life which proceeds from birth to death in a succession of generations and in a wide complex of social relations. He has endowed man with capacities to make the world serve his needs and to enjoy its good things. Life is a gift to be received with gratitude and a task to be pursued with courage. Man is free to seek his life within the purpose of God: to develop and protect the resources of nature for the common welfare, to work for justice and peace in society, and in other ways to use his creative powers for the fulfillment of human life. (9.17.)
>
> . . . The church is called to bring all men to receive and uphold one another as persons in all relationships of life: in employment, housing, education, leisure, marriage, family, church, and the exercise of political rights. (9.44.)

(2) *175th General Assembly—Relations Between Church and State— May 1963*

> American Presbyterians believe in religious liberty. They do not believe that the state should exercise control over the church. . . .
>
> While American Presbyterians share John Calvin's passion for the relating of faith to life, we have no desire to emulate the pattern of Calvin's Geneva, where civil authority was largely controlled by churches . . .

The General Assembly redeclares its conviction that church and state must be organically separate. . . .

Public schools are creations of the whole society operating through civil authority and justify their existence solely in terms of their usefulness to the society. Their role is to nurture the cultural, social, and material advancement of all citizens by a special system of instruction through intellectual and social disciplines and to stimulate a free search for truth within this discipline.

In the fulfillment of this role, public schools should not ignore the personal beliefs in God which are a part of the life of its pupils, but should recognize and respect such beliefs. Public schools should neither be hostile to religious beliefs nor act in any manner which tends to favor one religion over another . . .

Churches recognize the administration of religious training and observance as the domain of church and family. (*Minutes,* 1963, Part I, pp. 182–186.)

(3) *The Church and Public Education*

(Position Paper of the Program Agency, October 29, 1979, published in *Church and Society* magazine, Nov.-Dec. 1979, Vol. LXX, No. 2, pp. 11–13, 59–60.)

Persons are called "to glorify God and to enjoy Him forever." Within the Reformed tradition, this calling is God's act of grace. On the Christian's side the act of grace is affirmed through commitment. But commitment is not simply the acceptance of the truth of certain doctrinal statements. It is much more the embodiment of the lifestyle of Jesus. This embodiment takes place in the everyday struggle to make decisions about the common life of God's creatures. Decision-making implies the freedom of self-determination. It calls for consciousness of alternatives and their consequences. Growth in self-determination is thus best achieved in a setting where alternate loyalties are experienced and reflected upon and where the freedom to create new alternatives is not only permitted but encouraged. Pluralism comprises such a setting, and the public school is the context of pluralism which provides an appropriate atmosphere for growth and development toward the maturity of decision-making and commitment.

In addition, Christian love and respect for persons demand that all persons be free to search for the truth wherever they may find it. This free search for truth which is essential to maturity calls for an appreciation and respect for all human efforts toward justice and love. When public education is not restricted by theological positions or secular ideologies, it provides such an arena for free inquiry and appreciation of all efforts toward humanization.

The Reformed tradition seeks, therefore, to sustain and support all efforts toward the removal of ignorance and bigotry and toward the establishment of free institutions as a source of a high degree of social stability. Public education can be such a free institution where ignorance and bigotry are challenged.

Finally, the Reformed tradition holds that privatism, which implies refusal to participate in a creative way in the social milieu, is incompatible with God's intention for our lives. It affirms that growth toward self-determining, responsible, committed persons, concerned for the freedom and stability of their society, is best fostered in the pluralistic and ideologically open setting of public education.

Committed to share in the maintenance of public schools and in the renewal of public education. The United Presbyterian Church in the United States of America will

—Support programs and measures which continue to provide as the right of all children and youth integrated education of high quality. Such education must avoid discrimination on the basis of class, race, religion, sex, place of national origin, or of physical, mental and emotional capacities.

—Enable parents to understand, accept and fulfill their responsibilities for the education of their children. These responsibilities include the relationship of parents to teachers and school administrators, their participation in community decisions which bear upon schooling, and upon other learning opportunities for children and youth.

—Help teachers, parents and others to reinforce, both in and out of schools, the development of basic skills by children and youth.

—Support programs and measures which enable teachers and school administrators to work together with parents and other community persons in the defining and developing of opportunities for education outside the school.

—Support programs and measures which provide for cultural education in public schools about the history, literature and symbols of varied religious traditions. Church and other religious communities should be encouraged to provide for quality instruction in the experience of religious faith and practice.

III. Urgency of the Issue

Because "Creationism" has found political favor in a number of circles, including a public endorsement by Ronald Reagan while a candidate for the presidency, "creation-science" has become a symbol of attack upon the academic freedom of educational institutions and the science disciplines of academic life. It has also signaled attack upon long-standing principles of separation of church and state and the freedom from any imposition of particular religious concepts through public institutions. It is generally agreed that the proponents of "creation-science" will continue their efforts despite the decision in Arkansas. Many believe increased efforts will be made to force the teaching through local school boards.

The ever-widening attention to the campaign of persons for the cause of "Creationism" also affords Presbyterians opportunity to witness to the confidence that is of faith. "Creation Faith," as found in the first eleven chapters of Genesis, rather than "Creation-Science," affirms confidently the creating work of God, is not anti-intellectual, is always open to the search for truth in new and renewing forms. It seeks the insight from experience, from science, and from new technologies that extend our capacities to relate information and to know.

To counter such a campaign, these suggestions for action are prepared for Presbyterians:

(1) Study the issues:

(a) Alternative ways of interpreting the Bible and the consequences when applied to the creation stories found in Genesis.

(b) The claims of advocates of "creation-science" to be "science" rather than religion.

(c) Papers on "essentials of science" as prepared by teachers and persons in science who have been confronted with creationism's claims to be a "science."

(d) Essentials of church-state relationships as they apply to public education.

Note: Resource materials on these subjects are included in the bibliography.

(2) Affirm legislators who vote against ill-advised "creationist" bills. Where legislation has been passed, join the community forces that seek, through the courts, to have the legislation declared unconstitutional, in violation of the First and Fourteenth Amendments to the Constitution.

(3) Provide literature on the issues for circulation to other concerned persons in the community.

(4) Monitor school board meetings for any attempts at imposing "creation-science" in the classrooms.

(5) Find ways to tell school board members, school superintendents, and teachers where you stand on the efforts for "balanced treatment" of "evolution-science" and "creation-science."

(6) Make clear to school personnel and to the public that the desire for programs to impose religious teaching in the classroom is a view not shared by most church members.

(7) Ask your pastor to preach on "creation-faith" ways of interpreting the first eleven chapters of Genesis and other related Scripture passages.

(8) Provide a reference library shelf of books and articles on creation and "creation-science" for use of church members and public persons who may be concerned.

(9) Provide for Presbyterians a list of, or copies of, the relevant statements on the subject found in the church confessions and actions.

(10) Examine textbooks now being utilized in science classes for their adequacy in treatment of evolution as a science and for their handling of "creation-science."

(11) Encourage teachers and administrators to be sensitive to the religious perspectives of all persons without capitulating to teaching "creationism" as a science with equal claims upon teaching time and presentation.

IV. Printed Resources

Eldridge, Niles, "Creationism Isn't Science," reprinted from the April 4, 1981, issue of *The New Republic.*

Harris, C. Leon, Associate Professor of Biological Sciences, State University of New York at Plattsburgh, *Evolution—Genesis and Revelations—1981.* (Order from State University of New York Press, University Plaza, Albany, NY 12246, 265 pages, plus footnotes and extensive bibliography, paperback, $9.95.) Describes major contributions to the theory of evolutionism—with attention to general cultural influences and philosophical-religious bases.

Judgment Day for Creationism, reprinted from February 1982 issue of *Discover,* pp. 16–18.

Description of Little Rock Trial—McLean *vs.* Arkansas Board of Education.

Brief filed by Plaintiffs in McLean *vs.* Arkansas, Board of Education.

Opinion and Decision of Judge William R. Overton—McLean *vs.* Arkansas Board of Education.

Mayer, William, Chairperson of NABT Committee for Education in Evolutionary Biology, "The Fallacious Nature of Creation-Science," a paper written for the Biological Science Curriculum Study, Boulder, CO, November 1981.

Murray, N. Patrick, and Buffaloe, Neal D. *Creationism and Evolution—the Real Issues.* (Order from the Bookmark, Inc., P.O. Box 7266, Little Rock, AR 72217, $1.75 single copy postpaid, $1.50 for 100 or more postpaid. Write for large quantity rates.) A pamphlet that focuses on the issues and consequences in "creationism-evolution" perspectives when one uses alternative ways of reading and interpreting the Bible.

The Creationists, reprinted from December 1981 issue of *Science '81,* pp. 53, 55, 56, 57, 58, 59, 60, 81.

REFERENCE X-136
[See page 82.]

2. *Journal of the General Convention of the Protestant Episcopal Church in the United States of America . . . 1982,* pp. C-161, D-110.

Creationism

House of Deputies

On the eighth day, the Chairman of the Committee on Education presented Report #18 on Resolution D-90S (Creationism) and moved adoption of a substitute resolution.

Motion carried
Substitute Resolution adopted

Communicated to the House of Bishops in HD Message #157.

House of Bishops

On the ninth day, the Secretary read:
HD Message #157—D-90S, Creationism.

[D-90S]

Resolved, the House of Bishops concurring, **That this 67th General Convention affirm its belief in the glorious ability of God to create in any manner, and in this affirmation reject the rigid dogmatism of the "Creationist" movement; and be it further**

Resolved, **That we affirm our support of the scientists, educators, and theologians in the search for truth in this creation that God has given and entrusted to us.**

The House concurred
HB Message #249

Education

The Chairman of the Committee on Education presented Report #18 on Resolution D-90S (Creationism) and moved adoption of the substitute resolution.

(The text of Resolution D-90S is on page C-161)

Motion carried
Substitute resolution adopted

Communicated to the House of Bishops in HD Message #156.

3. An "Address to Scientists and Members of the Pontifical Academy of Sciences, by Pope John Paul II," as printed in *Origins,* Vol. 11, No. 18 (October 15, 1981), pp. 277, 279–280. Only the first three points are relevant for the current topic and thus the remainder is not reproduced here.

"The Bible itself speaks to us of the origin of the universe and its makeup, not in order to provide us with a scientific treatise, but in order to state the correct relationships of man with God and with the universe," Pope John Paul II told a group of 150 scientists who met with him Oct. 3 at Castelgandolfo. The group included 50 members of the Pontifical Academy of Sciences. Others in the group were participating in a study week preceding the academy's plenary assembly. The Bible, the pope said, "does not wish to teach how heaven was made but how one goes to heaven." At the same time, he noted, hypotheses regarding the first moment of the universe leave open the problem that science of itself cannot solve: the question for which one needs not just physics and astrophysics, but metaphysics. The pope described scientific work to eradicate parasitic diseases in Third World nations as part of the work of development. And he praised scientists for their discussions of the health of humanity in the event of a nuclear conflict. Such discussions, he said, cannot fail to be a reminder to heads of state of their tremendous responsibility to work for peace. A Vatican Press Office translation of the pope's address follows.

1. The program of work which your president has presented, and which I was already acquainted with before this meeting, demonstrates the great vitality of your academy, its interest in the most acute problems of modern science and its interest in the service of humanity. On the occasion of a previous solemn session I have already had the opportunity to tell you how highly the church esteems pure science: It is "a good, worthy of being

loved, for it is knowledge and therefore perfection of man in his intelligence . . . It must be honored for its own sake, as an integral part of culture" (Address to the Pontifical Academy of Sciences, Nov. 10, 1979).

Before speaking of the questions which you have already discussed during these days and those which you now propose to study, permit me to express my warm thanks to your illustrious president, Professor Carlos Chagas, for the congratulations which he kindly expressed in the name of your whole assembly for my having regained my physical strength, thanks to the merciful providence of God and the skill of the doctors who have cared for me. And I am pleased to avail myself of the occasion to express my particular gratitude to the members of the academy who from all parts of the world have sent me their good wishes and assured me of their prayers.

2. During this study week you are dealing with the subject of "cosmology and fundamental physics," with the participation of scholars from the whole world, from as far apart as North and South America and Europe and China. This subject is linked to themes already dealt with by the Pontifical Academy of Sciences in the course of its prestigious history. Here I wish to speak of the sessions on microseisms, stellar clusters, cosmic radiation and galactic nuclei, sessions which have taken place under the presidency of Father Gemelli, Msgr. Lemaitre and also Father O'Connell, to whom I address my most fervent good wishes and whom I pray the Lord to assist in his infirmity.

Cosmogony and cosmology have always aroused great interest among peoples and religions. The Bible itself speaks to us of the origin of the universe and its makeup, not in order to provide us with a scientific treatise, but in order to state the correct relationships of man with God and with the universe. Sacred scripture wishes simply to declare that the world was created by God, and in order to teach this truth it expresses itself in the terms of the cosmology in use at the time of the writer. The sacred book likewise wishes to tell man that the world was not created as the seat of the gods, as was taught by other cosmogonies and cosmologies, but was rather created for the service of man and the glory of God. Any other teaching about the origin and makeup of the universe is alien to the intentions of the Bible, which does not wish to teach how heaven was made but how one goes to heaven.

Any scientific hypothesis on the origin of the world, such as the hypothesis of a primitive atom from which derived the whole of the physical universe, leaves open the problem concerning the universe's beginning. Science cannot of itself solve this question: There is needed that human knowledge that rises above physics and astrophysics and which is called metaphysics; there is needed above all the knowledge that comes from

God's revelation. Thirty years ago, on Nov. 22, 1951, my predecessor Pope Pius XII, speaking about the problem of the origin of the universe at the study week on the subject of microseisms organized by the Pontifical Academy of Sciences, expressed himself as follows:

"In vain would one expect a reply from the sciences of nature, which on the contrary frankly declare that they find themselves faced by an insoluble enigma. It is equally certain that the human mind versed in philosophical meditation penetrates the problem more deeply. One cannot deny that a mind which is enlightened and enriched by modern scientific knowledge and which calmly considers this problem is led to break the circle of matter which is totally independent and autonomous—as being either uncreated or having created itself—and to rise to a creating mind. With the same clear and critical gaze with which it examines and judges the acts, it discerns and recognizes there the work of creative omnipotence, whose strength raised up by the powerful fiat uttered milliards of years ago by the creating mind, has spread through the universe, calling into existence, in a gesture of generous love, matter teeming with energy."

3. Members of the academy, I am very pleased with the theme that you have chosen for your plenary session beginning this very day: "The impact of molecular biology on society." I realize the advantages that result—and can still result—from the study and applications of molecular biology, supplemented by other disciplines such as genetics and its technological application in agriculture and industry, and also as is envisaged for the treatment of various illnesses, some of a hereditary character.

I have firm confidence in the world scientific community, and in a very special way in the Pontifical Academy of Sciences, and I am certain that thanks to them biological progress and research, as also all other forms of scientific research and its technological application, will be carried out in full respect for the norms of morality, safeguarding human dignity, freedom and equality. It is necessary that science should always be accompanied and controlled by the wisdom that belongs to the permanent spiritual heritage of humanity and that takes its inspiration from the design of God implanted in creation before being subsequently proclaimed by his word.

Reflection that is inspired by science and by the wisdom of the world scientific community must enlighten humanity regarding the consequences—good and bad—of scientific research and especially of that research which concerns man, so that on the one hand there will be no fixation on anticultural positions that retard the progress of humanity, and that on the other hand there will be no attack on man's most precious possession: the dignity of his person, destined to true progress in the unity of his physical, intellectual and spiritual well-being.

APPENDIX VI

Radiometric Dating Techniques[1]

THE NAME "radiometric" derives from the measuring ("metric") of compounds that are radioactive (where the term "radio" indicates emission of radiation). The method is based upon the fact that certain elements in nature spontaneously decay (that is, are radioactive). The rate of decay is regular, can be measured in the laboratory (for example, a Geiger counter is a form of such measurement), and is different for each element. Here, for example, is a diagram of what happens when a form of uranium decays into a form of thorium:

$$^{238}U \rightarrow {}^{234}Th + \alpha$$

That is, an atom of uranium (U) with an atomic mass (total number of particles in its nucleus) of 238 disintegrates into an atom of thorium (Th) with an atomic mass of 234 plus an *alpha*-particle.

The nucleus of an atom consists of (1) a number of positively charged particles called protons (the number of which determines its identity as an element; for example, 1 is hydrogen, 2 is helium, and 92 is uranium), and (2) a number of neutral particles (no electrical charge) called neutrons (the number of which may vary slightly from one nucleus of a given element to the next). The number of protons gives us the "atomic number" of an element (it can only have one). The number of neutrons gives us the "atomic weight (or mass)" of a given atom of an element (a given element may have several possibilities). Thus, in addition to ^{238}U one might also find ^{235}U. The difference between the two masses (238 and 235) reflects the number of neutrons that are available to be ejected (possibly with some protons) when the nucleus decays. Thus, the equation above could be diagrammed as follows:

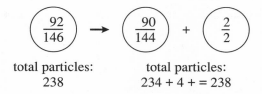

The uranium nucleus has 92 protons (atomic number) and 146 neutrons (for an atomic mass of 238). It decays into (1) a nucleus of thorium with 90 protons (atomic number) and 144 neutrons (for an atomic mass of 234), plus (2) an *alpha*-particle (which consists of 2 protons and 2 neutrons).

Such "radioactive" nuclei are observed to decay at a standard rate, usually expressed in terms of a "decay constant" (more often called its "half-life"). For ^{238}U that half-life is 4.5 billion years, meaning that a pure sample of this form (isotope) of uranium will transform one-half of its atoms into ^{234}Th in that period of time. This can be expressed in the form of a "decay curve" as shown in Figure No. 3. Eight million atoms of ^{238}U would be reduced to four million in 4.5 billion years, to two million in 9 billion years, to one million in 13.5 billion years, to ½ million in 18 billion years, and so on.

There is, then, a direct relationship between (on the one hand) the amount of the "parent" element (uranium) and the amount of the "daughter" element (thorium) in a given rock sample, and (on the other hand) the age of that sample. Thus, a rock containing uranium could be assigned an age if: (1) one could determine the amount of the "daughter" element which was already present when the sample was formed (so that one would be measuring only the amount that has resulted from radioactive decay); (2) the sample had been protected from outside contamination or loss of its contents during its history (so that one would be measuring only the amount of decay); and (3) the rate of decay had remained constant throughout the history of the sample (millions or billions of years).

Radiometric dating usually focuses upon three decay processes: the uranium-thorium-lead sequence (part of which is diagrammed above), the rubidium-strontium sequence, and the potassium-argon sequence. Since it is the last of these that is the least complicated, it will serve hereafter for purposes of illustrations.[2]

Potassium (K; atomic number 19; atomic mass 39, 40, and 41) is widely available in minerals such as feldspar (for example, Orthoclase, $KA1Si_3O_8$) and Mica (for example, Muscovite, $H_2KA1_3[SiO_4]_3$), and thus in igneous rocks in general. Atoms of potassium may decay into argon (Ar; atomic number 18; atomic mass 36, 38, and 40) through a process known as electron capture (which, in effect, transforms a proton into a neutron, leaving the atomic mass the same but reducing the atomic number by one). This can be diagrammed thus:

$$^{40}K + e^- \longrightarrow {}^{40}Ar + \gamma$$

That is, radioactive ^{40}K may add an electron to its nucleus, thus transforming itself into ^{40}Ar with the emission of *gamma*-ray.

$$\left(\frac{19}{21} \right) + e^- \longrightarrow \left(\frac{18}{22} \right) + \gamma$$

At the time when the earth's eldest rocks (igneous rocks) were formed, minerals containing radioactive ^{40}K were contained in them as they solidified from an earlier hot liquid state. As time passed, the ^{40}K began to decay into its stable "daughter" element, ^{40}Ar. Now, an accurate determination can be made in the laboratory of the ratio between the two in a given specimen. Then, a mathematical equation can be used, based upon the half-life (1.25 billion years), to determine the age of that specimen in years before the present. The result has been that the earth's oldest rocks are in the vicinity of four billion years old. Use of the other radiometric techniques (the uranium-thorium-lead sequence and the rubidium-strontium sequence) has led to similar results.

"Creationists," of course, cannot let such findings stand unchallenged. Questions have thus been raised, and legitimately so, concerning the possible presence of a "daughter" element at the time of the formation of the sample, concerning the possibility of contamination or loss of the "daughter" element in the sample since its formation, concerning whether the rate of decay has been constant, and so on.[3] Perhaps it is sufficient, for our present purpose, to respond to these queries from the perspective of the potassium-argon sequence only.

1. Since argon is an inert (exceedingly chemically inactive) element, it was not ordinarily bound into the structure of rocks at their formation. Its presence almost always results, therefore, from the internal decay of the "parent" element, potassium.

2. Contamination of a sample (by argon from the atmosphere) or loss of its argon content (from thermal disturbance) is guarded against by taking samples from deep beneath the earth (as opposed to the surface where they would have been exposed to weathering) and away from fault-zones (where fractures would have allowed disturbance). Otherwise put, acceptable specimens are those which have remained in a "closed" system since their formation.

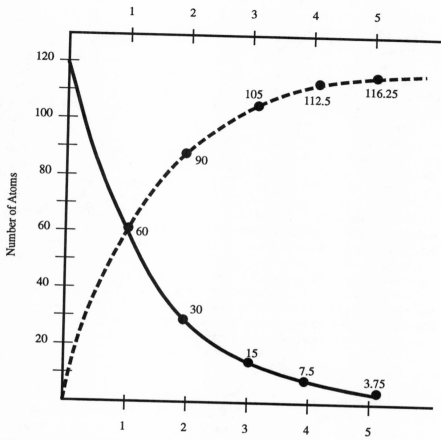

Figure 3. Diagram of the rate of decay of radioactive atoms. As the "parent" element spontaneously decays, the "daughter" element is generated in proportion (the total number of atoms remaining constant). A sample consisting of 120 million atoms of potassium-40 would decay to 60 million atoms of argon-40 in one half-life (1.25 billion years), leaving 60 million atoms of potassium. At the end of two half-lives (2.5 billion years), the potassium would again be halved (to 30 million atoms) and the number of argon atoms would have increased to 90 million. And so on.

In any case, given the inertness of argon, contamination by exposure of a sample may be discounted. On the other hand, loss of argon from the sample would by no means be impossible. In case of such loss, however, the resultant computed age would be in error by appearing to be younger that it actually is. That is, a smaller amount of the "daughter" element would suggest that less time had passed in the process of radioactive decay. Thus, errors in computation caused by exposure of the sample can be of no comfort to "creationists": the true age of the specimen would be even greater than the computation.

3. The question of whether the rate of decay has remained constant throughout the history of the sample (from the formation of the rock to the present) is more serious. While it has remained constant throughout the present century of measurement and while there is no reason intrinsically to suppose that it has changed previously, one would like certitude if it were available. It is interesting to note that samples from radically different sources (the earth, the moon, and meteorites) have approximately the same age (4–4.5 billion years)[4] and this indicates that the rate of decay has been the same, throughout that long span of time, for these respective environments. Furthermore, since the other radiometric techniques have yielded comparable ages for rock samples from earth, one would need to assume that, if all are in error, the rate of decay has changed for each of the three sequences in such a way as to produce the same erroneous result. Given the differences involved in the three sequences (for example, beta decay, alpha decay, and electron capture), this hardly seems even remotely possible.[5]

In sum, it is not merely secular geologists who accept the validity of radiometric dating but devoted Christian ones as well. Davis Young, who belongs to the latter category, puts the consensus succinctly: "No geochronologist will ever take seriously such ["creationist"] arguments."[6]

Appendix VI   Notes

1. Such procedures are quite complicated and can be outlined here in the sketchiest of forms. Those who desire more detail should consult Young, 1982, Chapter 7, and for full discussion, Gunter Faure, 1986.

2. See G.B. Dalrymple and M.A. Lanphere, 1969, *nv.*

3. Rybka, 1982; Morris and Parker, 1982, pp. 242, 250; and a vast array of articles cited by Young, 1982, Chapter 7 and by Strahler, 1987, Chapter 17.

4. To be more precise, the first period of the earth's history cannot be radiometrically dated since its crust was then in the process of formation (5-4 billion years ago?). The oldest earth rocks (formed in the crust) are about 3.8 billion years old. The moon, which cooled a bit more quickly, has yielded rock of an age of approximately 4.5 billion years. See Strahler, 1987, Chapter 20.

5. For further discussion, see the section "Methods of Checking the Integrity of Radiometric Ages" in Strahler, 1987, pp. 132–134.

6. Young, 1982, p. 115. See also Kitcher, 1982, pp. 155–163; S.G. Bush, 1982, pp. 34–58 (*nv*); G.B. Dalyrmple, 1986.

APPENDIX VII

Numbers: Sacred and Symbolic Usage (and the Number Seven in Particular)

IN MODERN western society, characterized as it is by technology and economic concerns, numbers are understood and used almost entirely in a mechanical arithmetic sense. That is, a number is a secular, utilitarian abstraction that enables one to calculate totals or to locate a given item in a sequence. A number is a mere digit with no intrinsic value as opposed to any other. (That is, "first" can be either preferable or non-desirable, depending upon the context.)

Occasionally, however, there survives in modern usage a faint hint of an older system of thought in which numbers also possessed a symbolic value. Consider, for example, that tall buildings (and especially hotels) are often strangely lacking a 13th floor: one goes up a single level from the 12th, and suddenly finds oneself at the 14th! Thirteen, as an "unlucky number," seems especially effective on Fridays that fall on that day of the month (giving rise to a seemingly endless series of movies entitled "Friday the 13th").

Another fossil of symbolic usage of numbers may be encountered in the mountains of western North Carolina where I grew up. The seventh-born son in a family was sometimes given the formal name "Doctor" because he was expected to develop special powers and skills. To such persons (be they named "Doctor" or not) neighbors brought their children who were afflicted with a throat infection known as "thrash." "Doctor" could cure them merely by blowing breath into their throat. Of such children, as well, unusual musical talents were expected (a living case being Doctor Walter Hoppes of Estatoe, N.C.). I am reminded of a line from an operetta concerning gypsies which was performed during my school days: "He's the seventh son of a seventh son, and he can help you vastly!"

The world of the Bible abounds with numbers which have a symbolic, often sacred character. Among the Mesopotamians, for example, various of the deities were so associated with a given number that one of the ways of writing their names was merely to write the number, preceded by the word "god." For example, the moon god (named Sîn by the Semites and Nannar by the Sumerians), because of the monthly cycle of his visible image (the lunar disc), could be designed by the number 30. The goddess Ishtar (Venus) was symbolized by the number 15 (indeed, the number alone could be used as a substitute for the word "goddess"). The weather deity Adad (Hadad, Baal) was sometimes signaled by the number 10, the sun god (Shamash) by 20, the deity of wisdom and fertilizing waters (Ea) by 40, the storm god (Enlil) by 50, and the heavenly father deity (Anu) by 60.

In the Bible, where such supposed deities are denied existence (the forces which they were thought to represent having been reduced to mere "things" [1]), their numbers sometimes retain a special significance. That may help to explain why a few numbers are used over and over again, rather than with the randomness that one might expect in an objective report of the secular "facts." I speak of the amazing frequency with which one encounters the numbers 3, 7, 12, 40, 60, 70, and multiples thereof.[2]

Consider a few instances of the widespread usage of the number forty: age at marriage (Gen 25:20; 26:34); period of Israel's wandering in the Sinai wilderness (Ex 16:35); a period of peace (Jgs 3:11; 8:28; 13:1); length of a monarch's reign (2 Sam. 5:4; 1 Kgs 11:42; 2 Chr 24:1); length of the flood's downpour (Gen 7:4); length of Elijah's journey to Mount Horeb (1 Kgs 19:8); the time remaining for the city of Nineveh to repent (Jon 3:4); the duration of Jesus' temptation (Mt 4:2); and so on.

Apparently, the biblical writers considered this number to be an approximation for the duration of the average generation and thus did not intend it literally for secular chronological purposes.[3] If one had wanted to know, for example, the chronological span from the exodus to the founding of the Solomonic temple, one might have noted that the list of priests within that span was set at eleven (from Aaron to Zadok, 1 Chr 6:3–8). When multiplied by forty, this yields 440 years, precisely the span given at 1 Kings 6:1 in the Greek Bible (LXX; MT, however, has 480 years, apparently assuming twelve priests during that span, patterned after the number of tribes of Israel?).

The massive usage of this number in the Bible (92 instances), as opposed to the much smaller usage of units between 40 and 50), supports its symbolic and non-literal status: six instances of 41, fourteen instances of 42, three instances of 43, five instances of 44, fifteen instances of 45, three instances of 46, three instances of 47, four instances of 48, and one instance of 49.

I turn now to that most frequent of numbers in biblical usage: seven. It occurs about 397 times, sevenfold occurs 9 times, seventh occurs 113 times, for a grand total of 519 times. By contrast, the usages of the number eight total 88.

The sacred character of "seven" may derive from its association with a group of deities called (in Akkadian) the *Sibittu* (literally: "the Seven").[4] Even in Israel veneration of them is attested in such personal names as "Elizabeth" ("My god is the Seven") and "Bathsheba ("Daughter of the Seven") and in such place names as Beersheba ("The Well of the Seven," since they were thought to dwell in the underworld and to manifest themselves at openings in the earth such as springs and wells[5]).

The curiosity remains that one finds a heptad of deities rather than some other number. Correspondingly, why should there be, in semitic cosmology (see Appendix XI), a sevenfold heaven such that Paul could speak of a person who "was caught up to the third heaven" (2 Cor 12:2)? At the opposite cosmological pole, why should there be seven walls around the underworld city?[6] Indeed, so fundamental was the concept of seven in association to the world that the Babylonians could write the word for "world" (*AN.KI*, "sky-earth") as seven cuneiform wedges.[7] From the seven directions of the compass, each represented by a mountain which held up the sky,[8] there could emerge that heptad of deities known as the *Sibittu*, sometimes designated as "the seven gods of the universe."

Such concern for the number seven, especially in connection with deity, may have arisen from human observation of the major celestial bodies (deities[9]): the visible planets (Mercury, Venus, Mars, Jupiter, and Saturn), plus the sun and moon. Hence, the realm of the sky-gods could be perceived to be a sevenfold heaven.

In Israel's monotheistic faith, of course, this polytheistic world was radically transformed (depolytheized, de-"foreignized"): the sole deity (Yahweh) inherits a sevenfold heaven, and the *Sibittu* and others are reduced to mere processes (actions) at Yahweh's bidding. Thus it is that God threatens Israel with sevenfold punishment (Deut 28:22; cf. Job 5:19; Prov 24:16) and desires sacrificial animals in groups of seven (Num 28:11).

One can now better understand how it is that this number has come to symbolize thoroughness or completeness (Gen 4:15, and the addition of 7 to ages of 120 years[10]), or why it may be used to mark that which is exceptional (for example, Lamech as the 7th generation in a genealogy[11]).

Appendix VII Notes

1. See above, Chapter V, Section 3; for details see Lloyd R. Bailey, Sr., 1979, pp. 28–32.

2. See the following *IDB* articles: "Number, Numbering, Numbers" (III, pp. 561–567); "Seven, Seventh, Seventy" (IV, pp. 294–295); "Twelve" (IV, p. 719). For a more comprehensive approach, see Lloyd Bailey, 1988, Appendix Three ("Nonliteral Numbers in the Bible").

3. As a purely mathematical approximation of a generation, it is possibly accurate. See the evidence cited above at Chapter IV, Section 3.

4. A detailed study of these deities may be found in Julius Lewy and Hildegard Lewy, 1942–43.

5. This ancient meaning of the name Beersheba had already been forgotten (or repressed?) by the time of the present form of the stories in Genesis. Hence two folk-explanations are given: "Well of the Oath" (21:31) and "Seven" (26:33; RSV, Shibah).

6. *ANET,* pp. 106–109 (culminating at line 60; cf. Job 38:17; Is 38:10; Jon 2:6).

7. See below, Appendix XI, Section 19.

8. This is the "firmament" of KJV and other translations (e.g. at Gen 1:6–8), described in extra-biblical sources as a hard surface of sufficient strength to contain the waters of the "upper sea" from whence the rains come (Appendix XI). "Creationists" have transformed it into a pre-diluvian "vapor canopy" which created an earthly paradise and which then precipitated the waters of Noah's flood.

9. Since such objects moved against the fixed background of the stars, and descended to the underworld and survived (i.e. their annual period of invisibility), it was assumed that they were the images of immortal deities.

10. See above, Chapter IV.

11. See above, Chapter IV, Section 2.

APPENDIX VIII

Gematria

GEMATRIA IS A system of counting by means of phonemes (letters of the alphabet) rather than by numbers. The word begins with rabbinic Hebrew and is derived from a Greek term that is related to the English word "geometry." In alphabetic languages, it involves assigning a numerical value, in sequence, to each letter. (See Table No. 12.)

In modern Hebrew speech, the system is used in a secular sense, and that but rarely. For example, in order to express "the first day of the week," one might use (instead of the numeral "first") the expression "day 'a'." In earlier Hebrew (biblical and medieval), however, the system was much more elaborate, involving both playfulness and mystic symbolism when the value of the consonants of a word were totaled.

Playfulness apparently is evident when the system is used to arrange the sequence of Jacob's children. That order varies from one list to the next (Gen 49, Num 1, Num 26, Deut 33; cf. Jgs 5). However, at Genesis 29–30, in contrast to the other lists, the son named Gad is listed seventh. Apparently this is because his name, when converted by *gematria* to its numerical value, totals seven. The Hebrew alphabet goes, in effect, a, b, g, d, . . . , so: g = 3 and d = 4, yielding a total consonantal value of 7. Whether Gad was, in fact, the seventh-born and given his name for that reason, cannot be determined.

For many early and medieval interpreters of scripture, *gematria* was more than a matter of playfulness. Their assumption was that nothing in the text is superfluous. Even variations in the spelling of a given word might have significance as part of a code intended by the inspired authors of scripture. For example, how does one know that there should be 613 regulations which were binding for Jewish life?[1] Because the word for scripture itself ("torah") had, as its *gematria,* the value 611, to which were added the first two of the ten commandments.

Intentional use of *gematria* is much older than the text of the Bible, so there is no reason to doubt that, at points, it could have been intended in the scripture of ancient Israel.[2] The most famous example, in the Bible of the

TABLE 12. The Hebrew Alphabet

The Hebrew alphabet consists of 22 consonants. They are:

Form		Name	Transliteration	Numerical Value
	Finals			
א		'Ālep	'	1
ב	ב	Bêṯ	b, ḇ (bh)	2
ג	ג	Gîmel	g, g̱ (gh)	3
ד	ד	Dāleṯ	d, ḏ (dh)	4
ה		Hē	h	5
ו		Wāw	w	6
ז		Zá yin	z	7
ח		Ḥêṯ	ḥ	8
ט		Ṭêṯ	ṭ	9
י		Yôḏ	y	10
כ כ ך		Kap̱	k, ḵ (kh)	20
ל		Lāmeḏ	l	30
מ ם		Mêm	m	40
נ ן		Nûn	n	50
ס		Ṣ̌ameḵ	s	60
ע		'Áyin	'	70
פ פ ף		Pē	p, p̱ (ph)	80
צ ץ		Ṣaḏê	ṣ	90
ק		Qôp̱ of Ḳ ôp̱	q or ḳ	100
ר		Rêš	r	200
ש שׁ		Śîn, Šîn	ś, š	300
ת ת		Tāw	t, ṯ (th)	400

church, occurs at Revelation 13:18. In the previous verse, a world empire, symbolized by "a beast rising out of the sea" and making war on the church, is described. A related "beast" (power), apparently the religious aspect of the empire, is designated by a number concerning which we are specifically told that it is "the number of its *name*." Since other evidence in the book suggests that the "beast" is the Roman empire which was persecuting the church at the time of the author (late first century C.E.), it has long been supposed that the "number of the name," being 666, is a *gematria*. Various possibilities have been suggested,[3] but in view of the alternative value of the "name" in other ancient biblical manuscripts, only one interpretation is likely. (For the alternative 616, see the footnotes in RSV and JB.) The particulars of the *gematria,* using the name of Emperor Nero, are as follows, using the spelling for "Nero Caesar" (*Neron Qesar*).

N (50) − R (200) − W/O (6) − N (200), for a sub-total of 306

Q (100) − S (60) − R (200), for a sub-total of 360

The total value, in an oblique reference to the tyrant, is 666.

With this as the referent, how is the alternative value (616) to be derived? It apparently has resulted from spelling the emperor's name in Latin or Hebrew (which lacks the final "n" of the Greek *Neron*), resulting in the familiar English "Nero." The result, when the value of the "N" (60) is subtracted from 666, is 616!

Another illustration, mentioned in the text above (Chapter IV, Section 1), concerns the derivation of the age of Lamech (777 years) from the *gematria* of his father (Methuselah in Genesis 5, Methushael in Genesis 4). The details are as follows.

Methuselah: M (40) − T(H) (440) − W (6) − SH (300) − L (30) − H (8)
  Total: 784 = 777 + 7
Methushael: M (40) − T(H) (400) − W (6) − SH (300) −' (1) − L (30)
  Total: 777

A final illustration of the power of *gematria* to explain a text concerns the number of persons (specifically, men of fighting age) who left Egypt at the time of the exodus: 603,550 (so Num 1:46; 2:32). This figure (off by one digit) may be derived by placing the *gematria* of two phrases in sequence (rather than totaling them). In order to answer the question "How many such males were there?" the authors of scripture may have resorted to the following *gematria:* "The sons of Israel" + "each male," or *bᵉnê yiśrā'ēl kol rō'š*

B (2) − N (50) − Y (10)/Y (10) − Ś (300) − R (200) −' (1) − L (30)

Total: 62 + 541 = 603
K (20) − L (30)   R (200) −' (1) − SH (300)
Total: 50 + 501 = 551
Sequential configuration of totals: 603,551

What would be the significance of depicting the total of soldiers at 603,550? Not that this was a literal count (as will be suggested below), but rather something like: Every male of the required age, in compliance and readiness.

TABLE 12A. Gematria and Pre-Diluvian Elapsed Time

Chapter 4			Chapter 5	
name	*value*		*name*	*value*
Adam	45		Adam	45
Cain	160		Seth	700
Enoch	84		Enosh	357
'Irad	284		Kenan	210
Mehûya'el	95		Mahalalel	136
Met(h)ûša'el	777		Jared	214
Lamech	90		Enoch	84
			Met(h)ûšelaḥ	784
			Lamech	90
			Noah	58
TOTAL	1535			2678
Jabal	42			
Jubal	48			
Tubal-cain	598			
TOTAL	2223			

MT: Elapsed time from Adam to birth of Shem (first post-flood ancestor):

1556	(see Table No. 14)
- 21	(for three ages to which a seven has been added: see Table No. 8)
1535	

LXX: Elapsed time from Adam to the flood:

2242 (see Table No. 14)

- 14 (for two ages to which a seven has been added: see Table No. 8)

- 8 (for one age to which this may have been added)

2220

Finally, it is necessary to ask: Why should the figure not be taken literally? Consider the fact that only soldiers are counted, neglecting the elderly, women, and children. If those persons were added, the total would be well into the millions, quite astonishing for a community that began 350 years previously as a community of 70 persons (Gen 46:27). Now, if the soldiers alone were arrayed in ranks of ten abreast, with ranks spaced ten feet apart, the resultant line of march would extend for 603,550 feet, or 114 miles. That is more than the direct distance from the border of Egypt to that of the "promised land" (the modern Wadi el-Arish). If a corresponding number of others were added (for each soldier, say, spouse, parents, aunts and uncles, and a half-dozen children), as well as the food-animals necessary for survival for a journey of "forty years," the line of march would be packed "cheek and jowl" from point of departure to point of entry.

Gematria, then, be it in connection with the population that came out of Egypt or in connection with the age of pre-diluvians, is a symbolic way of expressing a truth. It is a mistake for the interpreter, and one never intended by the authors of the biblical text, to shift the focus of such numbers to mere statistics.

Addendum

It is possible, although hardly convincing, that *gematria* has determined the elapsed time from Adam to the flood/in MT (see Tables No. 8 and 14). If modern interpreters are correct that the tradition to which Genesis 4 belongs (the "Yahwist") is much older than that to which Genesis 5 belongs (the "Priestly Code"), then the earliest computation of elapsed time may have involved *gematria* of the Genesis 4 genealogy (see Table No. 12-A). This figure would then have been available for later appropriation by those who supplied ages to the genealogy in Genesis 5, who then supplemented three of the ages by a seven. This almost works for the LXX duration as well.

For more likely derivations of elapsed time, see Chapter IV and Appendix XII.

Appendix VIII Notes

1. Babylonian Talmud, *Makkot,* 23b–24a.
2. See Lieberman, 1987.
3. See the article "Six Hundred and Sixty Six" in *IDB,* Vol. IV (R-Z), pp. 381–382.

APPENDIX IX

Is "Scientific Creationism" Independent of "Biblical Creationism"?

THE CLAIM that the physical sciences and the Bible, both properly understood, lead independently to the same conclusion is a fundamental assertion of "creationism." (See above, Chapter II.) Just as frequently, detractors have claimed that "scientific creationism" has been mandated by that particular interpretation of scripture which has produced "biblical creationism," that is, in reality, "scientific creationism" is an accommodation of the sciences to the Bible.

The issue here is not whether one can interpret the Bible in such a way as to find a report of "creation out of nothing" (for which, see Chapter VI and Appendix X). Nor is the issue whether one can interpret data from geology and paleontology in such a way as to suggest the sudden emergence of matter and life. In formal discussion, the two approaches can indeed be kept apart, just as "creationists" propose to be done. Rather, the issue is whether the ultimate authority for "creationists," the formative beginning of their proposals on creation, resides in two independent realms. The quotations below leave no doubt that such ultimate authority resides in the text of the Bible as interpreted by "creationists." It is at least plausible, then, that this is the source which (consciously or unconsciously) has determined the way that scientific evidence should be interpreted. If so, then the insistence that "creationism" can be taught independently of "biblical creationism" is possibly a legal ploy in order to escape the constitutional issue of the separation of church and state.[1] In the following quotations, emphasis has been added.

Its [the Bible's] unique, plenary, verbal inspiration *guarantees* that these writings, as originally and miraculously given, are *infallible* and completely authoritative *on all matters* with which they deal, free from error of any sort, *scientific* and historical as well as moral and theological.
 Henry Morris, ICR *Impact* Series No. 85 (July, 1980)

. . . the *instructed* Christian knows that the evidences for full divine inspiration of Scripture are *far weightier than the evidences of any fact from science.* When confronted with the consistent Biblical testimony to a universal Flood, the believer *must certainly accept it as unquestionably true.*
 Whitcomb and Morris, *The Genesis Flood,* p. 118

It becomes very important, therefore, for Christians to re-study and to re-think the great mass of geological and paleontological data . . . *to determine clearly wherein . . . it is at variance with the Biblical record of creation* and the Flood. If this [geological and paleontological] scheme is basically fallacious, *as we have had to decide that it must be,* then we need to try to understand why . . . a great body of responsible scientists have accepted it as true.
 Whitcomb and Morris, *The Genesis Flood,* p. 119

Thus the Biblical cosmologist finally must recognize that *the geological ages can have had no true objective existence at all, if the Bible is true.* There must, therefore, be some better explanation for the geological strata and the fossils which they contain.
 Henry M. Morris, *Biblical Cosmology and Modern Science,* p. 24

The Book of Genesis thus is in reality *the foundation of* all true history, as well as of *true science* and true philosophy.
 Henry M. Morris, *The Genesis Record,* p. 21

But the main reason for *insisting* on the universal Flood as a fact of history and as the primary vehicle for geological interpretation is that God's Word plainly teaches it! *No geological difficulties, real or imagined, can be allowed to take precedence* over the clear statements and necessary inferences of Scripture.
 Henry M. Morris, *Biblical Cosmology and Modern Science,* pp. 32–33

The Biblical framework of history into which these data [facts of science] *must* be re-oriented is given in Genesis 1–11.
 Henry M. Morris, *Biblical Cosmology and Modern Science,* p. 68

Evidently most of the scholars attracted to Darwin's ideals were unpracticed in the close study of Genesis . . . *not personally "armed" with* the unchanging and unchangeable answers about ultimate origins in *the Bible;*

hence . . . were "susceptible" and became confused by the various speculative ideas and imaginations of Darwin and his followers.

>   John N. Moore, ICR *Impact* Series No. 52, p. 2

The data of geology, in our view, should be *interpreted in light of Scripture,*
rather than distorting Scripture to accommodate current geological
philosophy.

>   Henry Morris, *Science, Scripture and the Young Earth,* p. 6

The purpose of the present volume is to examine the . . . scientific implications of the Biblical record . . . seeking if possible *to orient the data of these
sciences within this Biblical framework. If this means substantial modification* of the principles of uniformity and evolution . . . then so be it.

>   Whitcomb and Morris, *The Genesis Flood,* p. xx

Here is the greatest fallacy of uniformitarian geology. *Geologists insist* on
applying uniformitarianism to the study of the creation period, *when God
Himself has clearly told them* (e.g., Hebrews 11:3) *it cannot be done!*

>   Henry Morris, *Science, Scripture and the Young Earth,* p. 32

Appendix IX   Note

1. This issue is touched upon in ICR *Acts and Facts,* Vol. 16 No. 12 (December
1987), p. 1. Henry M. Morse (mistake for Morris?) explains why the "creationists' "
defense of the Louisiana Statute before the U.S. Supreme Court made no mention of
the biblical aspect of "creationism." Was the position guilty of "intellectual dishon-
esty" and "deliberate misuse of words," as has been charged? The response:

>   Those "scientific creationists" who wrote and defended the Louisiana bill may have been
>   mistaken in thinking that such a de-Biblicized law would be upheld by the federal judi-
>   ciary, but they knew that no other approach stood any chance at all.

Similar attempts to disguise the religious nature of "creationist" statutes may be
found in documents incorporated into the U.S. District Court decision concerning
McLean versus the Arkansas Board of Education (see Appendix XV).

APPENDIX X

Creation "out of Nothing"?

THE SECTION headings below correspond to those in the main text (Chapter VI), and the purpose of the Appendix is to provide more detail than was given there.

1. *The meaning of the first word of the Bible.* The noun *rē'šît* ("head," "top," "leader," "beginning") has the same form in the absolute and construct states (that it, no special ending and no change of vowels).

Some pre-masoretic vocalizations of the (prefaced) preposition ("b") have a long "a"-vowel, suggesting the definite article (that is, *bārē'šît,* as in Origen's transliteration and the Samaritan Pentateuch). This would yield, "In the beginning." MT, however, has *bᵉrē'šît*), suggesting that the noun is in the construct state, which ordinarily would yield, "In the beginning *of . . .*" or "When God began . . ." Nonetheless, the latter type of construction sometimes appears to have a definite meaning, just as if the article were present. See *mērē'šît* ("from *the* beginning"?) and *miqqedem* ("from *the* ancient times"?) at Isaiah 46:10; *mē'ôlām* ("in *the* times long past"?) and *mērō'š* (at *the* beginning"?) at Proverbs 8:23. (For discussion, see Heidel, *The Babylonian Genesis,* pp. 92–93; Westermann, *Genesis 1–11,* pp. 78, 94–96.)

The first word of Genesis, then, is ambiguous (based upon its form), although one would ordinarily expect the construction to yield "When God began . . ."

2. *The punctuation of the first word of the Bible.* The word *bᵉrē'šît* is accompanied by a common masoretic disjunctive accent called *ṭiphā'.* (For a brief introduction to the system of accents, see the article "Masoretic Accents" in *IDB,* Vol. III, pp. 295–299.) For an illustration of a disjunctive accent amidst a construct relationship (showing that it does not mean to set the construct noun apart as a clause), see Genesis 1:20 (where a *ṭiphā'* occurs at the word *pᵉnê).* That is, the presence of this pausal accent at the first word of Genesis does not *necessarily* mean that the translation should be, "In the beginning . . ."

It would be useful to know how the word *bᵉrē'šît* is used elsewhere in the

Bible: Is it always used as if the definite article were intended, or always as if it were not intended, or sometimes one and sometimes the other? The word occurs but five times, the other four being in Jeremiah (26:1; 27:1; 28:1; 49:34). Every one of them is a construct (as shown by their context), and every one of them has a disjunctive accent. For example, Jeremiah 26:1 reads, "In the beginning of the reign of Jehoiakim . . ."

The famous medieval commentator Rashi thus observed: "Because, whenever the word *rē'šît* occurs in Scripture, it is in a construct state . . . here [Gen 1:1] you must translate it (the same way)." A strong argument indeed, although Westermann (*Genesis 1–11*, p. 95) is strictly correct when he observes that "a word-count cannot solve the problem." He continues, ". . . there is no convincing proof that *bᵉrē'šît* cannot be used in the absolute state at the beginning of a sentence to indicate time." True, as far as the words "proof" and "cannot" are concerned. The available evidence, however, favors Rashi's conclusion.

3. *The syntax of the first verse of the Bible.* The second word of Genesis is a verb, which the Masoretes have vocalized as a finite verb (past tense, 3rd person masculine singular: "he created"). However, since such vocalization was formalized more than a thousand years after the text reached its standardized consonantal form, one may wonder whether the Masoretes vocalized it in the way that the author(s) of Genesis intended. Otherwise put: If the first word is to be a construct, then we would ordinarily expect the next word, if a verb, to be an infinitive (gerund, verbal noun: *bᵉrō'*. The text would then clearly read: "In the beginning of (God's) creating of . . ." or "When God began to create . . ." On the other hand, if the first word is an absolute, then we would expect the next word to be a finite verb (as it is), and thus we would translate, "In the beginning, God created . . ."

However, there are some thirty instances in the Bible where a noun in the construct is followed by a finite verb. (See Genesius-Kautzsch-Cowley, *Hebrew Grammar*, section 130.) An excellent illustration may be found at Hosea 1:2, *tᵉhillat dibber ᵃdōnāy bᵉhôšēᵃᶜ*, "When the Lord first spoke through Hosea . . ." Just so, in Genesis 1:1, *bᵉrē'šît bārā'* may well mean "When God began to create . . ."

4. *The syntax of the first three verses of the Bible.* The ambiguity here is evident from the following conflicting quotes. (1) ". . . a decisive objection [to v. 1 as a temporal clause, as in the NAB and AB] can be raised on the basis of the syntactical construction of v. 2 . . . . The construction . . . proves that v. 2 begins a new subject. It follows, therefore, that the first verse is an independent sentence . . ." (Cassuto, *A Commentary on the Book of Genesis,* I, pp. 19–20). (2) "The parenthetic character of this verse [v. 2] is confirmed by the syntax of Heb. A normal consecutive statement would have begun with *wattᵉhî hā'āreṣ,* not *wᵉhā'āreṣ hāyᵉtā.*" (Speiser, *Genesis,* p. 5). These

conflicting opinions lead Westermann to observe: "The difficulty is compounded when U. Cassuto and E.A. Speiser in their recent commentaries use arguments from syntax to come to quite opposite conclusions" (*Genesis 1–11*, p. 96).

Nonetheless, it may be pointed out that the so-called "Second Story of Creation" (Gen 2:4b–25) may have a similar syntax: a temporal clause (v. 4b), a conditional description beginning with a noun (vv. 5–6), and the concluding main clause beginning with a verb (v. 7). This corresponds to the structure of 1:1, 1:2, and 1:3, respectively, and argues for the AB translation.

"Creationist" Henry Morris, seeking to negate the AB-type translation (which provides no basis for "creation out of nothing"), remarks:

> Furthermore, the conjunction "And" connecting verse 1 and 2 clearly shows sequential action. That is, verse 1 cannot be a sort of modifying clause to verse 2, but rather is a declarative statement followed by a second declarative statement . . . (*The Genesis Record*, p. 42).

The passage would then read, in effect: "In the beginning, God created the heavens and the earth. And (then) . . ."

In actuality, however, the conjunction in Hebrew (ordinarily w^e, as here) may be conjunctive ("and"), disjunctive/adversative ("but"), or conditional ("when," "while," as in AB), according to context. (This may be confirmed by any lexicon/dictionary of Hebrew, e.g. Brown, Driver, and Briggs, *Hebrew and English Lexicon of the Old Testament*, pp. 252–253.) Thus, there is nothing within the word itself to tell us whether the author intended sequential action (contrary to Morris' assertion). If that were the case, then it could be used to support the so-called "gap theory" (see Appendix I), surely a result which Morris did not intend.

APPENDIX XI

The Cosmology of the Ancient Semites

Brief Bibliography:
Article "Cosmogony" in *IDB,* I, 702–709.
Article "World" in *IDB,* IV, 873–878.
Herman Gunkel, *Schopfung und Chaos in Urzeit und Endzeit* (1985).
Peter Jensen, *Die Kosmologie der Babylonier* (1890).
Alexander Heidel, *The Babylonian Genesis* (1951).
Luis I.J. Stadelmann, *The Hebrew Conception of the World* (Ph.D. Thesis, Hebrew Union College, 1967).

Introduction

In any discussion of cosmology, persons will express themselves in terms of the technology and vocabulary of their own day. Modern persons, for example, would refer to the results of spectroscopy, the radio-telescope, seismography, fission, etc., speaking of erosion, evaporation, and evolution. The vocabulary is recognized as transient.

Ancient persons were interested in many of the same problems as we. They wondered about the origin of the world, how it functioned, its purpose, and its destiny. These they tried to "explain" in terms of the knowledge and vocabulary then current. But, lacking the instruments that so aid modern persons, they had to rely largely upon their physical senses to gather the relevant data. In doing so, they were no less "rational" than we, and the conclusions they reached were quite logical.

Let us briefly try to construct a model of the world, using only what our unaided physical senses can observe.

1. The earth is apparently flat (only a few Greeks knew this before the time of Columbus).

2. The earth is apparently a circular disc (the horizon so appears).

3. The earth is surrounded by water. Limitations in travel prevented absolute verification, but the Semite observed, in the various directions, the Mediterranean, Red Sea, Persian Gulf, the Caspian, and the Black Sea. It was a reasonable assumption that all were joined.

4. The earth exists beneath a great reservoir (sea). This was supported by the fact that great amounts of water fell from the sky, sometimes creating floods that threatened to destroy civilization in Mesopotamia. Some strong surface, and the grace of gods, must be operative to prevent the waters from falling down all at once.

5. Since the waters above are so heavy, there must be supports to hold up the container. Thus a series of mountains (usually seven in number) were hypothesized, around the perimeter of the earth.

6. The heavenly bodies are able to move, to effect changes on the earth (we will discuss this below), and are eternal. They are thus gods. Since they can appear and disappear, they must utilize doors in the sky or on the horizon.

7. Since humans were buried in the ground, this was considered the domain of their "spirit." This produced an underworld realm, presided over by deities.

Let us now reconstruct such a universe in graphic form, using the many pieces of evidence from the literary sources (see Figure 4). Two views are given, and the numbers correspond one-with-the-other. The following pages will explain what the numbers represent.

The Babylonian "world map" (shown in the "top view") is not merely a reconstruction from the literary references. Such a map, with details (e.g. the rivers of Mesopotamia), has been found on a cuneiform tablet (c. sixth century B.C.E.), British Museum, no. 92687. (For reproductions, see Edmond Sollberger, 1961, p. 45; G.R. Driver, 1948, Pl. 16.)

The Component Parts of the Universe (the numbers used hereafter correspond to those on the diagrams)

1. The Babylonian Epic of Creation (*Enūma eliš*) relates that when Marduk had slain the dragon, Tiamat (a personification of the sea, *Tiamtu*), he sliced her in half, "like a shellfish" (IV, 135–140). The upper half he fashioned into the "sky," separating the sea (i.e. the Tiamtu/Tiamat) and holding it up. (For the text, see Pritchard, ed., *Ancient Near Eastern Texts* [hereafter cited as *ANET*], pp. 60ff, and the entry by Heidel in the bibliography.)

The Old Testament calls this structure the *Raqia,* "firmament," saying

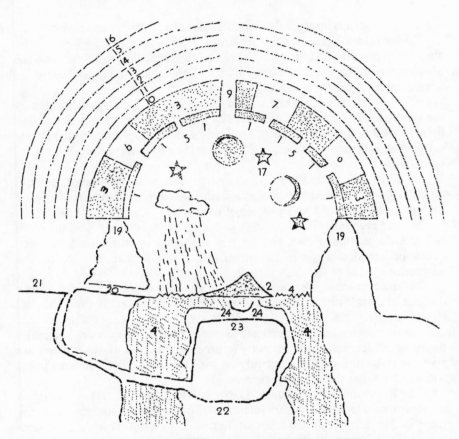

THE UNIVERSE OF THE ANCIENT SEMITES

(VERTICAL SECTION)

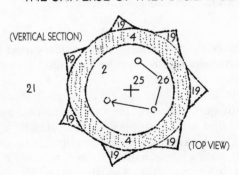

(TOP VIEW)

Figure 4

that it was created by God to separate "the waters from the waters" (Gen 1:6–7). Of what did the OT consider this structure to be made? A hint may be found in Job 37:17–18 (trans. from N.H. Tur-Sinai, *The Book of Job*): "When the waters become forceful and cause the wet clay to fall down (i.e. at the start of the annual rainy season), you (God) patch up the clouds to be strong as a dam." Alternatively, it may have been thought to be a metallic surface (AB on Job 37:18; cf. Deut 28:23). The root-meaning of *Rāqiᵃ* seems to be "to beat, stamp, spread out"; hence it should mean "extended surface, solid expanse." (See *IDB*, "Firmament"; H. Torczyner in *Studia Theologica*, 1 (1948), 188ff. See also Ps 104:2–3; Ez 1:22–23, 26; 10:1; Deut 28:23.)

2. The earth, fashioned from the other half of Tiamat's body (in the Babylonian account). It largely rests above the other half of the sea (*Tiamtu*). On the idea that it is completely surrounded with water, see the Introduction, no. 3. (See the article "Earth," *IDB*, II, 2–3, and "Creation," I, 725–732.)

3. The "upper sea," or half of Tiamat/Tiamtu, called in the OT "the waters above the firmament" (Gen 1:6–7; 7:11–12; Pss 148:4; 104:3; Beresit Rabba 4:4; Jer 10:13).

4. The "lower sea," or half of Tiamat/Tiamtu (the OT *Tᵉhôm*, "deep"). For the earth's resting upon it, see Psalms 24:2; 136:6. Because of the mythic origin of the sea and the fact that the Hebrews were not primarily sea-faring, they always regarded the ocean with fear and reverence. For remnants of the myth of Yahweh's combat with the dragon (which was annually "acted out" in the cult of Israel's neighbors), see Job 26:12–13 (especially in Tur-Sinai's translation); Pss 89:9–10; 74:13–16; Is 51:9; Job 9:7–9, 13; etc. (See the *IDB* articles "Rahab (Dragon)"; "Tiamat"; "Sea"; "Dragon"; and "Leviathan." On the Ugaritic myth of combat between Ba'al and Yam (a personal name of deity and the common word "sea," as in the OT), see *ANET*, pp. 130–131; John Gray, 1956, 268–285; T.H. Gaster's *Thespis*.)

At death, one crossed these waters ("river") to enter the realm of the dead (see nos. 20, 23). The Sumerian hero Gilgames is ferried across it in his quest for eternal life (Gilgameš Epic, table X, (ii), lines 20ff. [*ANET*, pp. 91f]. The seven gallû-demons carry Tammuz across it to the netherworld (see *ANET*, p. 52, n. 6; *Studia Biblica et Orientalia*, III, p. 198, n. 1). Among the Nabateans, as among the Greeks, a coin was placed with the corpse to pay the ferryman at the crossing (see Nelson Glueck, 1965, pp. 339, 374, 381). This is quite similar to the Greek concept of the River Styx. Cf. also the Egyptian solar-barks, buried with the Pharaoh, so that he might cross the river of the netherworld with the sun-god.

5. Openings ("doors"; "windows") in the *Rāqiᵃ* ("firmament," see no. 1), through which rain (no. 18), snow (no. 6), and hail (no. 7) escape and reach the earth. Their opening created the flood (Gen 7:11–12). See also

Anat IV:70 (Ugaritic): "Ba'al sets the (door-)bolts in the heavens; he kindles his lightning." Cf. also Ba'al's fear of placing windows in his heavenly abode (which was re-created each year), lest his enemy, Mot ("death"), enter in (II AB, vi, lines 1–12; vii, lines 17–30 [*ANET*, pp. 134f]). If this does not happen, of course, there will be no rain. Ba'al eventually graciously consents. Note also Ben Sirach (Ecclesiasticus) 43:14, "He (God) has surrounded the heavens with a splendid circle; the hands of the Most High have bent it. By his command he makes the snow to fall [there-through] . . . through this the heavenly chests are opened, and clouds fly out like fowls." See also: Gen 8:2; Is 24:18; Job 37:16 (Tur-Sinai's Commentary).

On the creation of the "doors" (see also those mentioned in nos. 9, 20) in the Babylonian Creation Epic, see *ANET*, p. 67 (Tablet v, line 9). See also Bruno Meissner, 1925, II, 108.

6. Storehouses for snow: Job 38:22.
7. Storehouses for hail: Job 38:22.
8. Storehouses for lightning: Job 38:22.
9. The passageway leading through the *Rāqîaʿ* ("firmament") and upper sea ("waters above the firmament") to the "heavens" beyond, realm of the sky gods. These were the astral deities in particular (see no. 17), who were able to appear (dusk) and disappear (dawn). This is most easily seen in the so-called "Prayer to the Gods of the Night" (*ANET*, pp. 390f; *Studia Biblica et Orientalia*, III, 291):

> The countryside is quiet, the doors (of the houses) are barred;
> The gates (of the city) are closed . . . the land does not utter a sound;
> Only the gates of the Wide Heavens are open,
> And the great Gods of the night that keep watch are (present).
> Come out (now), you great Stars, Gods of the night!

However, not all of the astral bodies were thought to make their entrances and exits at this point. Some appeared (or disappeared) below the horizon as the earth rotated. This gave rise to the belief that there were doors between the mountains upholding the *Rāqîaʿ* (no. 19). In fact, the verbs "to rise" and "to set" in the semitic languages may be "to enter, come in" and "to go out." Many cylinder seals from the Ancient Near East show the sun-god entering through doors (attended by deities) between the cosmic mountains.

Through this passageway also, the devotees of the astral deities hoped to enter and join the immortal realm. On this, see under nos. 10–16.

10–16. The various "heavens" (usually seven in number, but sometimes more), presided over by the Sun-god, Moon-god, and the five major astral deities (Mercury, Venus, Mars, Jupiter, and Saturn). This sevenfold structure of the upper-world was reflected in the seven stages of the Ziqqurrat (on their function, see H. Lewy, 1949, pp. 87–91); Thureau-Dangin, 1907, pp. 76 (statue D, lines 11–12), 84 (statue G, line 13), and 86 (statue I, lines 12–13); Rawlinson, 1861–1884, III, 57:6, line 65; M. Jastrow, 1898, pp. 618ff, 639. Likewise, the city of the underworld (see no. 23) was a seven-walled structure.

On the "seven heavens" in Mesopotamian thought, see also Bruno Meissner, 1925, II, 107–108.

This cosmological view has influenced both Christianity and Judaism. See 2 Corinthians 12:12 (where Paul mentions the "third heaven"); Midrash Konen 32–33; Zohar Hadash, 20b; TB *Hagiga* 12b; II Enoch 3–9; Louis Ginzberg, 1946–1947, V, 158ff; Clement of Alexandria, *Strom.* 4:25; Origen, *Against Celsus,* 6:21 (Ante-Nicene Library, XXIII, 359); and among the medieval Arabs, see Daniel Chwolson, 1856, II, 610.

The Christians, as well as the gnostics, transformed the astral deities ruling the various heavens into demons (thus one society usually tends to so regard the deities of its neighbors). (See Enoch 18:13ff.) Tatian, *Address to the Greeks,* chapter 9, remarks, "Instead of wandering (planetary) demons we have learned to know one Lord who wanders not"; among the Arabs: Chwolson, 1856, II, 400; Scholem, 1965, 1–13.

The gnostics saw the heavens as concentric spheres of evil influence, seeking to imprison the soul of humans within an evil world. It was their hope that the soul might, by the aid of secret knowledge (*gnosis*), rise through these realms to the world of light beyond. Usually the number of such concentric spheres was seven, but some believed in as many as 365. (See J. Behm, 1927; M. Lidzbarski, 1905–1915; Hans Jonas, 1963, esp. pp. 43f.)

What was the means whereby the worshiper reached these various heavens (or beyond them, in the case of the gnostics)? Sumero-Akkadian myth spoke of trying to reach heaven on an eagle (for the myth of "Etana and the Eagle," *ANET,* pp. 114ff; for its interpretation in terms of astral worship, see H. Lewy, *op cit.,* pp. 92f). The famous Assyrian queen Sammuramat was said to have changed to a dove at death and flew away (Diodorus Siculus, II, 20). The eagle was revered throughout the Near East in the Greco-Roman period and frequently found on funerary monuments (F. Cumont, 1910, 119–164; 1959, pp. 157ff). An allusion to this belief may be found in Psalm 90:10.

One should also remark that any sanctuary was regarded as the entrance to the realm of the particular deity worshiped there. Thus the altar of an astral cult was an entrance to the sky through which there might be commerce between the divine and human realm. Thus Jacob sees the deity standing atop steps (RSV: "ladder") reaching from earth to heaven (a ziqqurrat?). Meteorites were thought to reveal such a ladder (among the Egyptians: A.B. Cook, 1914, II, 114–140), and were often incised with a ladder-like design atop which was an astral symbol (E. Douglas Van Buren, 1945, pp. 51ff; Cook, 1914, III, 892; on meteor cults, see H. Lewy, 1950, pp. 346–350; M. Eliade, 1963, sections 79–82). Sometimes the ladder was described as having seven rungs, each made of a different metal (Origen, *Against Celsus,* 6:21). On each god having his own sacred metal, see H. Lewy, 1950, 377–381, and J. Lewy, 1955, 159. On the ladder in "ascension myths," see Mircea Eliade, 1963, sections 32–34.

For the expression "the highest heaven" (denoting a multiplicity?), see Psalm 148:4; 1 Kings 8:27; Nehemiah 9:6. On the idea that the divine residence floats on the water to the upper sea, see Psalm 104:3.

The heavenly dwelling of the deity is described as a "palace" (Mic 1:2, from a Sumerian word meaning "big house"), "house" (Ps 36:8?); "place" (1 Kgs 8:39); "habitation" (Deut 26:15); etc. It seems to have had various compartments (Ps 104:3; cf. Jn 14:2).

In general, the earthly "house" (usually translated "temple") of the deity was considered to be patterned after a heavenly one. Often a Mesopotamian king will record that the deity appeared to him in a dream, commissioning temple construction and giving a blueprint to follow, e.g. Gudea of Lagash (Cylinder A: see the above-mentioned collection by Thureau-Dangin) and Ur-Nammu of the Ur III period (see the famous relief, e.g., in Parrot, 1961, pp. 226–229). T. H. Gaster, 1954, 191. Cf. Ex 25:9, 40.

The ideas that the earthly city of the deity is but a copy of the heavenly one is related both about Babylon (*ANET,* pp. 68b) and Jerusalem (Rev 21:2ff); also Gal 4:26; Heb 12:22; Rev 3:12; 21:10; on "upper and lower Jerusalem," TB *Ta'anit* 5a; *Hagigah* 12b; *Pesikta* 21:144b; Ginzberg, 1946–1947, 5:292; Test. Twelve Patriarchs; Dan 5; Syriac Apocalypse of Baruch 4:3. (On the sacred city as a microcosm, see under no. 25.) Ps 87:3; Gaster, 1954, 195; R.E. Clements, 1965, chapter 5.

On the idea of the heavenly council (the chief deity and his various subordinates) in the OT, see H. Wheeler Robinson, 1944, pp. 151–157; F.M. Cross, 1953, 274–277. See also the article "Hosts of Heaven" in *IDB,* II, 654–656. On the concept of the council of the gods in Mesopotamia, see H. Frankfort, chapter V; *ANET,* p. 93.

17. The astral bodies (sun, moon, five planets, stars, and constellations), which were regarded as images of deities. Some of the reasons for attributing deity to them would include: (a) they did not change, i.e. they were eternal; (b) they had the power of motion, i.e. they were alive; (c) they affected events on earth, since their appearance and disappearance coincided with light and darkness, the seasons, etc. E.g. the heliacal rising of the Hyades always came just before the rainy season, leading the Greeks to call them "the Rainers,"

and the heliacal rising of Sirius always came just before the annual rising of the Nile. Causation was assumed.

For the astronomical knowledge of the ancient Semites, see Franz Kugler, 1924; G. Schiaparelli, 1905; O. Neugebauer, 1962.

Astral worship was basic to the entire Ancient Near East, and Israel was no exception. Her ancestors came from Ur and Harran (the two chief centers of the moon-god Sîn), and remnants of that worship are found throughout the OT. One need merely cite Jeremiah 8:2ff and 44:16ff to demonstrate the traditional worship of Venus, and 2 Kings 23:11 to demonstrate that of the sun. On the pre-Davidic cult at Jerusalem (that of the planet Saturn) and its influence upon Judaism, see H. Lewy, 1950, cited above.

It was to worship them that the ziqqurrats were constructed (the "tower of Babel," in Genesis 11), and they whom one worshiped "on every high hill" (as the prophets often accuse Israel of doing).

Not only were individual stars worshiped, but constellations as well. As early as 2000 B.C.E. they were connected with myths (e.g. Orion is a giant who fought against Yahweh). The Babylonians identified the twelve zodiacal signs with the twelve beasts slain by Marduk, along with Tiamat. He yoked them together, forcing them to circle the sky forever.

Among the gnostics, the signs of the zodiac become demons as well. The Islamic Arabs added them to the seven planets, creating the nineteen guardians of hell (Quran 74:30ff; F. Rosenthal, 1959, 304–318).

18. The clouds, which supply rain for the earth. They posed two logical questions: (a) How could they appear and disappear? (b) How did they obtain water which was stored beyond the *Rāqîᵃʿ*?

For an attempt to identify the role of clouds in the creation myth of Mesopotamia (personified by Mummu?), see Henri Frankfort, pp. 184, 189.

Among the Canaanites (as attested at Ugarit), the god Hadad (better known by the epithet "Ba'al," meaning "Lord") was regarded as the bringer of the fertilizing showers. The clouds were regarded as the chariot and the thunder as the roar of his voice (his very name may be related to "thunder," as we learn from an Arabic cognate). One of his most common epithets is "He who rides upon the clouds."

Whereas the Yahwists at first resisted the attempts of the Israelites to worship Ba'al in the new agrarian setting of Canaan, they later attributed the functions of Ba'al to Yahweh. See e.g. Hosea 2. The extent to which the terminology of the Ba'al cult subsequently influenced Yahwism can be seen, e.g., in Psalms 29:3–6; 68:4; 104:2–3; Deuteronomy 33:26. See the article "Baal" in *IDB,* I, 328–329. The tradition of Yahweh's theophany in a cloud should also be noted (Ex 24:15–18; 33:9–10; Num 12:5–10).

As to the source of the clouds at their appearance, there is no explicit answer. They are said to rise "from the extremities of the earth" (Jer 10:13; Ps 135:7) and "out of the sea" (1 Kgs 18:44). This suggests that they might enter through "doors" at the horizon similar to those used by certain of the astral deities (see nos. 9, 19) and by the "spirit" of the deceased human (see nos. 4, 20). Ben Sirach (Ecclesiasticus) speaks of openings in the *Rāqîaʿ* (43:14), through which "clouds fly out like fowls."

Yet another concept is expressed in the rabbinic period: the clouds function like skin bags (used for carrying water in antiquity), receiving water from the upper sea and pouring it out upon the earth (Rabbi Joshua in Ta'anit 9b; cf. Targum on Job 36:27). Others explain that the *Rāqîaʿ* acts like a sieve, straining the water into drops (Beresit Rabba 13:10), or that the clouds gather the water from the oceans below (Targum Pseudo-Jonathan on Gen 2:6). Cf. Eccl 11:3; Job 38:37; 26:8. See E.F. Sutcliffe, 1953, 99–103.

19. The mountains which encircle the world (note top view), containing the seas, and which hold up the *Rāqîaʿ* (note vertical section). These were conceived as being seven in number, each the home of an ancient wind-god (Gudea, Cylinder A, XI, 19f). These seven winds are called "the gods of the universe," and the Sibittu ("the Seven"). (On these gods, see esp. H. and J. Lewy, 1943, 1ff; A. Deimel, 1914, nos. 1573, 2892; E. Douglas Van Buren, 1939–1941, 277–289.) The Sumerians considered these gods benign, but the invading Semites transformed them into demons, servants of the king and queen of the underworld (no. 23). Hence they were thought to dwell at the entrance to that realm (no. 20), ready to bring destruction upon mankind (see esp. R.C. Thompson, 1903). Later, the Sibittu were transformed into astral deities and identified with the Pleiades.

So fundamental was this idea of seven cosmic mountains that the early compass seems to have had seven directions (see the article by H. and J. Lewy, 1942–43, cited above). In fact, the word for "world" (*AN.KI,* "sky-earth") could be indicated by merely writing the number "7"!

This background of the number seven, both in cosmology and in theology, explains its repetition and almost sacred character in the OT. The Sibittu, as deities, come largely to be sevenfold destruction wrought by Yahweh (Deut 28:22ff; Job 5:19; Prov 24:16; Eccl 11:2; Gen 4:15; Lk 8:2; Rev 8–10, 15–16). Their direct worship is reflected in such names as Sheba (1 Sam 20:1); Elizabeth (Ex 6:23, meaning "My God is the Seven" [Sibittu]); Bathsheba (2 Sam 11:12, meaning "Daughter of the Seven"); Beer-Sheba ("The Well of the Seven"); etc. The Jewish menorah possibly originally goes back to their cult, since Philo identified the seven lamps with the seven planets, and since it is shown on Old Assyrian cylinder seals in an astral context.

Why the number seven, as opposed to another? Probably because of the seven great cities of ancient Sumer (so H. and J. Lewy), forming the basic political and religious structure of the "world," which would be but a reflection of sevenfold nature of the Universe.

The mountains are often graphically depicted on cylinder-seals, where the sun-god is seen entering through doors between them (see no. 9)—e.g. W.H. Ward, 1910, nos. 251–257. Cf. Psalm 19:4b–6.

For biblical mention of these mountains, see Job 26:11; 2 Sam 22:8.

For the Babylonian material, see Jensen, 1890, p. 9.

The Egyptians likewise envisioned the sky as supported by pillars (usually four in number, described as the legs of the heavenly cow, or the arms and legs of Nut, the sky goddess).

It was through these mountains that Gilgamesh journeyed in search of Utnapishtim, who had been granted immortality: *ANET*, 88f.

20. The passageway between the mountains that surround the earth (no. 19). Through it one journeyed to the underworld (no. 23), and through it entered the Sun-god to traverse the sky and exit at the far side through a similar passage (nos. 9, 19). It was not, however, the only means of entering the underworld, as we shall see (nos. 23, 25). It was dark, and through it Gilgamesh journeyed twelve leagues before reaching the immortal realm at the end (no. 21) from which one perhaps continued to the underworld (no. 23). It was guarded by the semi-divine "scorpion men" who attend the entrance and exit of the sun-god (see nos. 9, 19): *ANET*, 88f.

There seems also to have been a chamber for the wind-demons (the Sibittu: see no. 19, and the 1943 article by H. and J. Lewy). Note Gilgamesh's encountering the north wind: *ANET*, 89a, line 8. Cf. Job 37:9; Ps 78:26; and the Greek idea that Hera bound the rebellious winds and kept them locked in a cave.

21. The immortal realm lying beyond the mountains. Gilgamesh journeys there in his search for Ut-napishtim, who survived the flood and was granted immortality by Enlil (Tablet XI, *ANET*, 93–95). He finds a garden filled with precious stones and fruit trees (*ANET*, 89b). On the term "at the mouth of the two rivers" to describe this area (e.g. *ANET*, 95b, line 195), see Albright, 1919, 161–195. In the Sumerian flood story, the survivers are granted immortality in the land of Dilmun, beyond the mountains "where the sun rises" (*ANET*, 44b; see S.N. Kramer, 1944, 18–28; 1963, pp. 147f, 281f).

With this one might compare the Greek idea of the fields of Elysium, where a few mortals and heroes were granted an unending physical existence. One recalls also Heisod's idea that men of the "golden age" did not descend to Hades, unlike the current generation (*Works and Days*, 109ff).

22. The rock surrounding the underworld, separating it from the waters of the sea.

23. The underworld, realm of the dead, was located in a huge under-

ground cavern and could be reached in at least three ways: (a) by crossing the river which surrounds the earth (no. 4), passing between the mountains (no. 19), and following the passageway (no. 20). This was the usual route, and the dead (both among the Semites and the Greeks; see no. 4) were buried with a coin to pay the ferryman. This was the route also taken by Odysseus on his visit. (b) Through fissures in the earth's crust, which seemed to go down to the infernal realm. Note the story of Gilgamesh's drum, which falls to the underworld through one of them (*ANET*, 97f); and the battle report of Shalmaneser III of Assyria, who says that he slew so many of his enemies that "the plain was too small to let (all) their souls descend (into the netherworld)" (*ANET*, 279). Furthermore, such fissures were useful in necromancy: note Enkidu's return (*ANET*, 98), and the visit of Saul to the witch of Endor (1 Sam 28). (On this practice, see Harry Hoffner, 1967, 385ff.) Such openings were especially dangerous in the desert, which was generally regarded as the home of demons (because of its barren and inhospitable nature). On such desert-swelling demons, see Is 13:21; 34:14; A. Haldar, 1950. On the spring and well as such an opening, see no. 26. (c) The sanctuary of a particular deity was regarded as an entrance to his realm (see no. 10–16), and hence the altar of a chthonic deity would lead to the underworld. See Manfred Lehmann, 1953, 361–371. The Bod-Astart Inscription (Phoenician) seems to describe various parts of the temple as such entrances: "In Sidon there is a Sea, a High Heaven, a Land of Shades" (on the latter as a term for the dead, see *IDB*, IV, 301f). The chthonian deities were worshiped in ravines (just as sky-gods were worshiped on "high places"): Is 57:5–6; Jer 7:32; 2 Chr 33:6. One of the most famous of such "low places" was the Valley (of the sons) of Hinnom, just outside Jerusalem. This entrance to the underworld eventually gave its name to the underworld itself, which in the NT is called "Gehenna" (Greek transliteration of Hebrew "Valley of Hinnom") [similarly, Kutu, chief cult-center of the underworld god Nergal, gave its name to that realm: see *ANET*, 107b, line 49]. All three entrances (or places where entrance is possible) to the underworld are mentioned in T. B. *'Erubim* 19a (or: see Hastings, *A Dictionary of the Bible*, II, 386).

The underworld seems to have been a complete city, surrounded by seven walls (*ANET*, pp. 103, 107–109; Job 38:17; Is 38:10; Jon 2:6; cf. B. Meissner, 1925), and presided over by deities (*ANET*, 103–104, 106–109, 109–110; the Ugaritic myths of Mot and Baal, also in *ANET;* the Greek idea of the gods Hades and Pluto; and certain personifications in the OT which may go back to such a deity in Israel: Jon 2:3; Ps 141:7; Prov 1:12; 27:20). [See M. Tsevat, 1954, 41ff; Sarna's 1963 article, 315ff; Albright, 1926 and 1936, 1ff.]

It was very deep within the earth (Is 7:11; Prov 9:18); vast (Hab 2:5; cf. Is 5:14); dark (Job 10:21–22; 17:13); a place of silence (Ps 94:17) and dust (Job

17:16; 20:11); that this does not refer merely to the dust of the grave, or the decomposed body, is shown by many extra-biblical parallels, e.g. Ugaritic (Gordon, text 67), where Mot, god of the underworld, says, "Since when has my appetite failed? Here I have only lavish portions of mud to eat!" See Pope, 1964, 275f; Gaster, 1961, pp. 203f; *ANET,* 107a, line 8. It seems to have various compartments (Prov 7:27; cf. Ez 32:23; Deut 32:22). In the inter-testamental literature it is divided into several distinct departments, according to the future fate of the individual: see the separate treatment of the after-life.

The Hebrew word for this realm is *She'ôl* (the etymology of which is disputed), LXX "Hades," KJV, "hell, grave," but RSV correctly transliterates it as a proper name.

Its inhabitants seem largely oblivious to events on earth (Ps 88:12; cf. vv. 3–5; Job 3:17), although they were sometimes used for necromancy to predict the future (1 Sam 28; Lev 19:31; Is 8:19–20). They are bereft of pleasure (Pss 6:5; 30:9; 115:17; Is 38:18) and seem to be in a state of utter weakness (Ps 88:4; Is 14:10); (the inhabitants are called *R^epā'îm,* "Weak Ones"; see the article "Rephaim," *IDB,* IV, 35). Yet they seem able to recognize each other (Is 14:10) and to converse with the living (1 Sam 28:15ff; *ANET,* 107ff). They seemingly eat (hence the necessity to provide food and drink at the tomb, and if this was not done, the "spirit" was forced to scavenge in the streets of the living [*ANET,* 99a]; one Ugaritic text gives the various menus for underworld meals [none very pleasant!]) and they are always racked with thirst (Is 5:13?; Lk 16:24; Jensen, 1890, p. 233; Ward, 1910, p. 281; also *ANET,* 87a, lines 40–45).

It was a land from which none could return once he had entered (Job 7:10; 16:22). Note in particular the description from the cuneiform epic, "The Descent of Ishtar" (*ANET,* 106ff):

> To the dark house, the abode of Irkal[la],
> To the house which none leave who have entered it,
> To the road from which there is no way back,
> To the house wherein the entrants are bereft of li[ght],
> Where dust is their fare and clay their food,
> (Where) they see no light, residing in darkness,
> (Where) they are clothed like birds, with wings for garments,
> (And where) over door and bolt is spread dust.

The deceased seem to keep their old appearance (i.e. they are recognizable by their form: 1 Sam 28:14), yet seem vaporous in composition (*ANET,* 98b, lines 78–84; *Odyssey,* XI).

In general, the underworld was not regarded as a place of punishment, but as the inevitable destination of all mankind (Job 3:19; cf. Gen 42:38).

There were found great and small, rich and poor, righteous and wicked, infant and adult, without distinction (Job 3:11-19). Justice was rigidly carried out during the lifetime of the individual (hence, the argument of Job's friends). See the article, "Dead, Abode of the," in *IDB,* I, 787f; R.H. Charles, 1913; M. Jastrow, 1898, chapter XXV.

24. The foundations of the earth, sometimes described as "mountains," keeping it from sinking into the sea: Jon 2:6; Pss 104:5; 75:3; Job 9:6; 1 Sam 2:8. The earth is said to be "founded upon the seas" (Pss 24:2; 136:6), and elsewhere to float over a void (Job 26:7). The Ugaritic literature also mentions the "foundations of the earth" (II AB, i. 40). See also Prov 8:29.

25. The geographical center of the earth, or its "navel." See in particular A.J. Wensinck, 1916; Mircea Eliade, 1963, sections 142-145; 1961, chapter 1. The idea that the chief sanctuary of the deity (and, hence, his sacred city) lies at the center of the earth's surface is reflected in the Babylonian "World Map" (for which see the diagram and Introduction). There, of course, it is the city of Babylon. A similar idea is expressed about Jerusalem in the OT: Ez 5:5; 38:12 (context suggests Jerusalem). Shechem was also considered in this fashion: Jgs 9:37, probably in connection with Mount Gerazim as an ancient sanctuary.

Marduk's ziqqurrat at Babylon was called É. TEMEN. AN. KI, "The Temple which is the connecting-link between Heaven and Earth," and other names reflect a similar idea. Nineveh was also regarded by its inhabitants as such a center (W.H. Roscher, 1918, p. 11).

The Egyptians designated such centers, setting up an omphalos to mark the spot (see G.A. Wainwright, 1934, 32ff), as did the Greeks (*Odyssey,* I, 50; H.J. Rose, 1972, pp. 137f), and also the Romans.

The "navel" was usually located on a mountain, since: (a) it reached toward the sky; (b) it was conspicuous on the earth; (c) its foundations reached the underworld. Thus, all sectors of the universe were united by it, and the altar served as an entrance into each realm (see under nos. 10-16, 23 [sub. "c"]; Ez 43:13-17; Albright, 1956, 148ff). Hence, the Semites sometimes conceived of the earth as a mountain and gave their sanctuaries such names as É. KUR, "Mountain House." On the temple as an *imago mundi,* see *VT,* XV (1965), 318f (note also under no. 23c, esp. the Bod-Astart Inscription). Gaster, 1954, pp. 195f.

On Jerusalem in particular as the cosmic mountain (a microcosm), see J. Montgomery, 1908, 24ff.

On the cosmic mountain in the north, see Gaster, 1961, 181f; S.H. Hooke, 1935, pp. 45-70; *JAOS,* XXVI (19), 1-67; Is 14:13-14; Ez 28:11-14; Ps 48:2-3; *JRAS* 1953 (by H.G. Quaritch Wales).

One should also mention that the ziqqurrat, an artificial mountain atop which one worshiped the astral deities, had deep within it a sanctuary to the chthonic deities (i.e. it was a microcosm, a cosmic mountain, the "navel" of the earth).

26. Springs or wells through which water issued forth to enrich the earth. They seem to have been controlled by doors (hence, their dwindling and increasing) which could be opened wide to destroy the earth (as in the flood: Gen 7:11). Through them also the "mist" probably arose which watered the garden of Eden (Gen 2:5–6; the word "mist" is possibly the same as the name of a river-god mentioned in the Mari texts).

Since these water-sources were openings in the earth's crust, and since the waters came from the lower sea which surrounded the underworld, such locations were usually the site of a sanctuary. This was partly because of the blessing of fertility, and fear of the underworld demons who might exit at this point. The Sibittu (see no. 19) are mentioned in particular as living in such places (see H. and J. Lewy, 1943, p. 24): this may allow us to explain the name Beersheba ("The Well of the Sibittu") and Endor ("The Spring of the Pantheon").

Both at Babylon (Hammurabi's code) and Ugarit, the underworld river is personified as a divine judge (Ugaritic "Judge River"). A sacrifice to such a deity lies behind the rites of Deuteronomy 21:1–9, where the blood must flow into a river (see M. Tsevat, 1954, 41ff). This would also explain why sanctuaries at springs became famous for the resolution of legal problems: Meribah (Num 20:13; Ex 17:7; from a root meaning "to institute legal proceedings"), which is also called Kadesh (cf. Num 20:11; "The Sanctuary") and En-mishpat (Gen 14:7; "The Spring of Justice"). See Tsevat, 1954; von Rad, 1962, I, 11–12.

APPENDIX XII

Elapsed Time from Adam to the Flood According to the Greek Bible (LXX)

WHEREAS THE traditional Hebrew text (MT) of Genesis 5 reports a total of 1656 years from the creation of the first human to the coming of the great flood in Noah's time, the traditional Greek text (LXX) gives a total of 2242 years (variation: 2262, perhaps to allow for the lifespan of Methusalah who otherwise would have survived the flood; see Table No. 8). Has the latter total originated as the sum of its parts (individual ages), or was the total an independently derived external figure with the individual ages then tailored to fit? (This is the same question previously asked of the MT total (see Chapter IV, where the latter possibility was proposed).

The third century (B.C.E.) was a time of intense rivalry among the various surviving factions of the empire of Alexander the Great. Historians arose to glorify their particular realm, in part by pointing to the great antiquity of its kingship. Two of these, writing in Greek, are the Babylonian priest Berossos (*Babylonian History*) and the Egyptian priest Manetho (*Egyptian History*). The former work contains a version of the Sumerian King List (see Table No. 6) which provides a basis for understanding the pre-diluvian elapsed time in Genesis 5 (MT). The latter work reports various traditions about divine kingship which provide a basis for understanding that same period of time in Genesis 5 (LXX).

Manetho's work is difficult to use in this regard, on the one hand because it is only partially preserved in summaries which are then quoted by a number of later (sometimes hostile) writers[1] who contradict each other, and on the other hand because his sources (papyri, temple archives, sculptures, wall inscriptions, etc.) already contained errors and contradictions which he

Table 13. Dates From Manetho's *Egyptian History*
1. From the Armenian Version of Eusebius, *Chronica:*

a. Kingship of the Gods:	b. Kingship of the Demi-Gods:
Hephaestus	1255 years
Helios (the sun)	c. "Other Kings":
Sosis	1817 years
Cronos	d. "Thirty More Kings of Memphis":
Osiris	790 years
Typhon	e. "Ten Kings of This":
Orus	350 years
. . . . .	f. "Spirits of the dead and Demi-Gods":
Bydis	5813 years

Total: 13,900 years

Total: 11,025 years
(rounded off to 11,000)

Grand Total: 24,925 years (rounded off to 24,900)

2. From Georgius Syncellus, *Chronicle* (with Manetho's years converted into "lunar years," as if each figure of Manetho were a month of 30 days):

a. Gods:		b. Demi-Gods:	
Hephaestus:	727 3/4	Orus:	25
Helios:	80 1/6	Ares:	23
Agathodaemon:	56 7/12	Anubis:	17
Cronos:	40 1/2	Heracles:	15
Osiris/Isis:	35	Apollo:	25
Typhon:	29	Ammon:	30
		Tithoes:	27
Total: 969 (=11,790 "months")		Sosus:	32
		Zeus:	20

Total: 214 (=2,604 "months")

Grand Total: 1183 (=14,394 "months")

3. From *The Old Chronicle* (as reported by Syncellus):
   a. Kingship of the Gods:

Hephaestus ("has no period assigned, because he shines night and day")	
Helios:	30,000
Cronos ("and the remaining gods, 12 in number")	3,984
b. Kingship of the Demi-Gods: 8 in number	217

Grand Total: 34,201 years

compounded by adding a number of popular traditions. (Two extracts from his work are summarized in Table No. 13.)

Eusebius, in order to reduce the fantastic ages to more reasonable (historical) terms, proposes that "lunar years" be reduced to "solar years": "What we now call a month the Egyptians used formerly to style a year" of thirty days each. (There is no evidence that this was ever the case, however!) The consequence would be that the 24,900 years of Manetho actually indicated "2,206 solar years." In actuality, (24,900) × (30 days/month) ÷ (365 days/ year) = 2046, but then we all have problems with math! Thereby he seeks to bring Manetho's figures into line with "Hebrew chronology" (by which he means the LXX text of Genesis 5) and pronounces that the result is "perfect harmony." The result is not quite "perfect" even in Eusebius' miscalculation, since 2206 is not quite the 2242 of LXX, but close enough for Eusebius to suppose that he had discovered the common ground between Manetho and LXX (if not actually how LXX had derived its figure). Although Manetho's list does not terminate at "the flood," Eusebius observes that, according to scripture, Egypt had its human beginnings with a grandson of Noah, just after that great catastrophe (Gen 10:6). "From him the first Egyptian dynasty must be held to spring."

Syncellus has used a similar calculation to reduce Manetho's figures to what he considers to be more historical years. (It is interesting, although perhaps accidental, that the list of gods which he calls "the first dynasty" totals 969 years, precisely the lifespan of Methuselah.) The grand total of gods and demi-gods is 1183, which is 1059 short of the LXX pre-diluvian period. He then quotes with disfavor an attempt by the Egyptian Christian monk Panodorus (fourth century) to fit this into the biblical chronology: The gods must have reigned 1183 years, with the remainder ("1058") being by humans (beginning with Adam), so that history begins in the year 1058 A.M. (Anno Mundi).

A more exact correlation between ancient Egyptian chronology and the LXX total for pre-diluvians has been proposed by a modern interpreter (Böckh). It is built upon the fact that the ancient Egyptians sometimes reckoned time by Sothic Periods of 1461 years.[2] Such reckoning is evident (among other places) in the Egyptian "Old Chronicle,"[3] which lists 36,525 years of history through the end of the 30th dynasty (which ended with Persian control of the country in 341 B.C.E.). Does that just "happen" to coincide with 25 Sothic Periods exactly, or does it indicate that the total of years has been set so to equal a whole (non-fractional) number of Periods? There seems to me little doubt that it is the latter, since other totals equal multiple Periods.

It would not be implausible to suppose that the LXX figure for pre-diluvian elapsed time since creation had been set to reflect a whole number of Sothic Periods. Now, if one takes the 2242 years of LXX and considers them to be converted from "lunar years" (the reverse of the procedure carried out above by Eusebius and Syncellus), the result is 27,278 years. However, this does not correspond to a whole number of Sothic Periods (being 18.67 instead) or to anything in Manetho (24,925 instead). However, given variations of that figure in Manetho and in the "Old Chronicle" (34,201 for the gods and demi-gods), one could not rule out the possibility of an ancient total which is 19 Sothic Periods (i.e. 27,759). In fact, if one adds Manetho's figure of 24,925 for the pre-historic period to Eratosthenes' figure of 2,075 for the historic period,[4] the total is then 27,000 years, close enough to "round off" (as the ancient often did) to 19 Sothic Periods. That multiple of Periods, when converted in a more refined way (29.5 days/month rather than 30; 365.25 days/year rather than 365) yields 2242.00, *exactly* as in LXX!

It is interesting to note that Eratosthenes' figure for the "historical" period (2,075) is exactly $\frac{1}{12}$ of that of Manetho for the "pre-historic" period (rounded off to 24,900 as did Eusebius). That is, the gods and demi-gods reign as many years as humans do in months (as recognized long ago by Fleay, p. 115). This raises an interesting "chicken and egg" problem with respect to the chronology: Was the human figure multiplied by 12 in order to produce the length of divine rule, or was the human figure derived by dividing the divine period by 12?

Appendix XII   *Notes*

1. *Manetho* (1940). His *History* survives only in quotes from summaries in the Jewish historian Josephus, the Christian chronographers Julius Africanus and Eusebius of Caesarea, the Byzantine historian Georgius Syncellus ("George the Monk"), and a few others. See F.G. Fleay (1899), with comparative information and charts (but exceedingly hard to follow); Wolfgang Helck, (1956); Böckh, (1838).

2. Discussed briefly in the *IDBS* article, "Egypt, Chronology of," pp. 253–255 (at Section 1). "Sothis" is the Greek form of the Egyptian "Sopdet," a name for the "Dog-star" (Sirius, in the constellation Orion). It begins a new cycle (i.e. reaches the same place in the sky on the same day of the year) every 1461 years. See the Egyptian work, "Book of Sothis, or the Sothic Cycle," in *Manetho,* pp. 235–249.

3. *Manetho,* pp. 226–233 (Appendix III).

4. *Manetho,* pp. 213–225.

APPENDIX XIII

The Date of the Second Temple as a Reflection of Calculation in Base-60

EVIDENCE THAT certain mathematical figures in the Bible reflect symbolic thinking (rather than historical and chronological duration in the modern sense of the terms) is seldom clearer than it is in the computation of the date of the founding of the second temple from data in MT. In doing so, it should be remembered that the ages of the pre-diluvians (Gen 5) and the early post-diluvians (Gen 11) are foundational and thus are part of a concern for "truth" that in its non-historical sense it derives from preoccupation with multiples of base-60.

Calculation of the biblical date for the founding of that temple begins with elapsed time from creation to the flood in dates Anno Mundi (i.e. since the creation of the world), as presented in Tables No. 14 and 15.[1]

Elapsed time from Adam to Noah's first-born has been shaped, in SP, by regard for calculation in base-60, and especially in view of the Egyptian ideal lifespan (120 years) which is reflected in Genesis 6:3. That is, the total for 10 generations is 1207 years, or $(60 \times 20) + 7$, or clearer still: $(120 \times 10) + 7$. Thus, not only did these ancestors, in primeval time, far exceed the ideal, but they fostered the next generation, on the average, every 120 years.

MT and LXX, on the other hand, jettison that concern for the total (in contrast to individual ages), apparently deriving that figure instead through modifications of Berossos and Manetho respectively.

In the MT computation, all of Noah's ancestors, save for Methuselah, died prior to the flood (and Methuselah apparently during it). SP has so adjusted its ages that three ancestors expired in the year of that catastrophe (not merely Methuselah, but Jared and Lamech as well). One LXX compu-

TABLE 14. Elapsed Time Since Creation (Dates Anno Mundi)
The Pre-Diluvians

name	elapsed time at birth			elapsed time at death		
	MT	LXX	SP	MT	LXX	SP
Adam	0	0	0	930	930	930
Seth	130	230	130	1042	1142	1042
Enosh	235	435	235	1140	1340	1140
Kenan	325	625	325	1235	1535	1235
Mahalalel	395	795	395	1290	1690	1290
Jared	460	960	460	1422	1922	_1307_
Enoch	622	1122	522	987	1487	887
Methuselah	687	1287	587	_1656_	2256	_1307_
Lamech	874	1454 (1474)	654	1651	2207	_1307_
Noah	1056	1642 (1662)	707	2006	2592	1657
Shem	1556	2142 (2162)	1207	2156	2742	2257
THE FLOOD	_1656_	2242 (2262)	_1307_			

Numbers in parentheses indicate a variant in LXX texts. The higher dates ensure that Methuselah does not survive the flood.
Underlining indicates those persons who died in the flood.

tation has Methuselah die six years before the flood (suggesting that all were righteous?), while the other (through oversight?) has him survive it by fourteen years! Nonetheless, the overall impression is one of careful computation and manipulation.

It is interesting to note that the SP computation allows each ancestor to live to see the birth of Noah, the hero of the flood, upon which the future of the world depends. LXX allows only four to do so, and MT six.

Continuing elapsed time, through the early post-diluvians (Gen 11), is shown in Tables No. 16 and 17.

A crucial moment in the larger biblical story is the call of Abraham (Gen 12:1–3), the beginnings of the elect community to be called "Israel." This is arguably a more important transition than was the flood. It is interesting to see who, in the computations, is allowed to live to witness that decisive moment (which ultimately will produce both synagogue and church). In SP, apparently none of the ancestors were alive at the time of Abraham's summons (father Terah having died the same year). In one LXX computation,

TABLE 15. The first Age of the World: From the Creation to the Flood: This space is called, "Early in the morning," Matt. ii. (Hilar, in loc.)

Ten Fathers Before the Flood.

Annotations (in order along the chart):

- *Adam* hath Cain and Abel, and loseth them both, Gen. iv: unhappy in his children, the greatest earthly happiness, that he may think of heaven the more.
- *Seth* born in original sin, Gen. v. 2, 3: a holy man: and father of all men after the flood, Numb. xxiv 17: to show, all men born in that estate.
- *Enos* born: corruption in religion by idolatry begun, Gen. iv. 25. Enos therefore so named, *Sorrowful*.
- *Cainan* born: a *mourner* for the corruption of the times.
- *Mahalaleel* born: a *praiser of the Lord*.
- *Jared* born: when there is still a *descending* from evil to worse.
- *Enoch* born: and *dedicated* to God: the seventh from Adam, Jude, 14.
- *Methuselah* born: his very name foretold the flood. The lease of the world is only for his life.
- *Lamech* born. A man smitten with grief, for the present corruption and future punishment.
- *Adam* dieth: having lived 1000 years within 70. Now 70 years a whole age, Psal. xc. 10.
- *Enoch* translated: next after Adam's death mortality taught in that, immortality in this.
- *Seth* dieth.
- *Noah* born a comforter.
- *Enos* dieth.
- *Cainan* dieth.
- *Mahalaleel* dieth.
- *Jared* dieth.
- The 120 years begin, Gen. vi. 3.
- *Japheth* born.
- *Shem* born.
- *Lamech* dieth.
- *Methuselah* dieth, and the flood cometh.

Left-margin note: Enoch, the seventh from Adam in the holy line of Seth, prophesied against the wickedness that Lamech, the seventh from Adam in the cursed line of Cain, had brought in.

Year	Adam	Seth	Enos	Cainan	Mahalaleel	Jared	Enoch	Methuselah	Lamech	Noah	Japheth	Shem
130	130											
235	235	105										
325	325	195	90									
395	395	265	160	70								
460	460	330	225	135	65							
622	622	492	387	297	227	162						
687	687	557	452	362	292	227	65					
874	874	744	639	549	479	414	252	187				
930	930	800	695	605	535	470	308	243	56			
987		857	752	662	592	527	365	300	113			
1042		912	807	717	647	582		355	168			
1056			821	731	661	596		369	182			
1140			905	815	745	680		453	266	84		
1235				910	840	775		548	361	179		
1290					895	830		603	416	234		
1422						962		735	548	366		
1536								849	662	480		
1556								869	682	500		
1558								871	684	502	2	
1651								964	777	595	95	93
1656								969		600	100	98

The Whole Works of the Rev. John Lightfoot, D.D. (Edited by the Rev. John Rogers Pitman), Vol. II (London: J.F. Dove, 1822), p. 77. The calculations are based upon MT.

With the story of this fifth chapter, read 1 Chron. i. 1–4, which are an abridgment of it.

Enoch lived as many years as there be days in a year, viz. 365, and finished his course like a sun on earth

TABLE 16.   Elapsed Time Since Creation (Dates *Anno Mundi*)
[The Flood, of one year duration, has not been added]

The Post-Diluvians

name	MT	LXX	SP	MT	LXX	SP
	elapsed time at birth			*elapsed time at death*		
Arpachshad	1658	2244	1309	<u>2096</u>	2809	1747
	(2)	(2)	(2)	(440)	(567)	(440)
Cainan/Kenan		2379			2839	
		(137)			(597)	
Shelah	1693	2509	1444	<u>2124</u>	2969	1877
	(37)	(267)	(137)	(468)	(727)	(570)
Eber	1723	2509	1574	<u>2187</u>	3143	1978
	(67)	(397)	(267)	(531)	(901)	(671)
Peleg	1757	2773	1708	1996	3112	1947
	(101)	(531)	(401)	(340)	(870)	(640)
Reu	1787	2903	1838	<u>2026</u>	3242	2077
	(131)	(661)	(531)	(370)	(1000)	(770)
Serug	1819	3035	1970	<u>2049</u>	3365	2200
	(163)	(793)	(663)	(393)	(1123)	(893)
Nahor	1849	3165	2100	1997	3373	2248
	(193)	(923)	(793)	(341)	(1131)	(941)
Terah	1878	3244	2179	<u>2083</u>	3449	2324
	(222)	(1002)	(872)	(427)	(1207)	(1017)
Abram-Nahor-	1948	3314	2249			
Haran (Gen 11:26)	(292)	(1072)	(942)			
	or	*or*	*or*			
Abram-/Abraham	2008	3374	2249			
(Gen 11:32; 12:1)	(352)	(1132)	(942)			
CALL OF						
ABRAHAM	2023	3389	<u>2324</u>			
(Gen 11:26)	(367)	(1147)	(1017)			
	or	*or*	*or*			
(Gen 11:32;	<u>2083</u>	3449	2324			
12:1)	(427)	(1207)	(1017)			

Figures in parentheses are elapsed time since the flood.

Alternative dates for Abraham's birth and call reflect a difficulty in Genesis 11:26. Were all three sons born in Terah's 70th year (1st option) or Haran only (2nd option)? The latter assumes that the call came after the death of Terah in 2083 A.M. (Gen 11:32; 12:1) when Abraham was age 75 (Gen 12:4).

The LXX figures reflect the lesser figure for Methuselah (see Tables No. 8 and 14). Otherwise add 20 years.

Underlining indicates having lived until the time of Abraham's call. The coincidence of Terah's death (in all three textual traditions) with the date of the call according to Genesis 11:32; 12:1 may suggest that it is the proper option.

TABLE 17.   The second Age of the World: From the Flood to the Promise given to Abraham.

The Ten Fathers After the Flood.

Flood	World	Noah	Shem	Arphaxad born.	Salah born.	Eber born.	Peleg born. Languages confounded about the time of his birth.	Reu born.	Serug born.	Nahor born.	Terah born.	Haran born.	Nahor born.	Abraham born.
2	1658	602	100											
37	1693	637	135	35										
67	1723	667	165	65	30									
101	1757	701	199	99	64	34								
131	1787	731	229	129	94	64	30							
163	1819	763	261	161	126	96	62	32						
193	1849	793	291	191	156	126	92	62	30					
222	1878	822	320	220	185	155	121	91	59	29				
292	1948	892	390	290	255	225	191	161	129	99	70			
340	1996	940	438	338	303	273	239	209	177	147	118	48		
341	1997	941	439	339	304	274		210	178	148	119	49	1	
350	2006	950	448	348	313	283		219	187		138	58	10	
352	2008		450	350	315	285		221	189		140	60	12	
370	2026		468	368	333	303		239	207		148	78	30	18
393	2049		491	391	356	326			230		171	101	53	41
427	2083		525	425	390	360					205	135	87	75

Staircase event labels: Nahor dieth. — Noah dieth. — Abraham born. — Reu dieth. — Serug dieth. — Terah dieth, Gen. xi. 32. The promise given to Abraham, Gen. xii. 1.

With this latter part of the eleventh of Genesis, read 1 Chron. i. 24–27.

The Whole Works of the Rev. John Lightfoot, p. 87. Note that, in calculating the dates of Abraham's birth and call, he has followed the text of Genesis 11:32 and 12:1 rather than 11:26. Consequently, Abraham is born sixty years later than his brother Haran.

Terah alone was then alive; in the other, he apparently was not. In one MT computation, the majority of the ancestors survive until the "call" (Arpachshad, Shelah, Eber, Reu, Serug, and Terah); in the other, Arpachshad, Shelah, and Eber remain. The overall impression from SP and LXX is depiction of a radical transition at the time of Abraham's summons to set out for the "promised land": a new era in human history is opening up. MT, on the other hand, gives the impression of continuity: certain crucial persons were alive to see the beginning of the new era (note especially Eber, apparently understood to be the ancestor of the "Hebrews," with which the chosen community identified itself). Eber, the last to die, even lived to see the birth of Jacob, otherwise known as "Israel," who more precisely was the ancestor of the elect community. So also Shem, born before the flood. Why Shelah was accorded that honor is unclear.

It is interesting to note that a concern for base-60, not evident in MT's elapsed time until the flood, returns in the total of elapsed time since that event: 367 years = (60 × 6) + 7, and 427 years = (60 × 7) + 7. The 1147 of LXX = (60 × 19) + 7.

Computation of elapsed time from Abraham's birth to the founding of the Solomonic (first) temple follows easily from summaries given in the biblical text (see Table No. 18). Thereafter, the matter becomes much more difficult because the books of Kings do not provide totals for the reigns of the monarchs of Israel and Judah. (It should also be stated that whereas the books of Genesis–Numbers have a common editorship and thus an overall chronological scheme, the books of Deuteronomy–2 Kings have a different origin.)

An aberration in the nature of the data (in the leftmost column of Table No. 18) occurs for the period between the two temples. The total of 451 years is not derived by direct statement in the biblical text, contrary to the other figures. Rather, it is a modern calculation based upon a great number of factors in the text, including synchronisms with neighboring monarchies and overlapping reigns (co-regencies). Those who desire to pursue the complicated details should consult the article "Chronology of the OT," in *IDB,* Vol. I (A-D), pp. 580–599, section 3b–3d.

It may be objected that the biblical chronologists possibly would have relied upon overt statements in the text rather than intricate analysis of the type evident in the work of modern chronologists. For example, would they not have utilized the prophetic projection (Jer 25:11; see 2 Chr 36:21) that the period of Judean exile would be 70 years (even if a highly symbolic number), rather than, as it turned out in historical reality, 48 years (587-539 B.C.E.)? Further, rather than speculate the length of a number of co-regencies, would they not have limited their concern to the lengths of reign that are specifically mentioned in the text? If so, they would have begun with the date

Table 18. Elapsed Time After Abraham (Dates Anno Mundi)

All dates have been increased by one year from those in Table No.16 to account for the year of the flood (Gen 7:11; 8:13). LXX figures reflect the lower option from Tables No. 8 and 14 (otherwise add 20 years).

event	range of dates		
	MT	LXX	SP
Abraham's birth	1949	3315	2250
birth of Isaac: + 100 (Gen 17:1, 17)	2049	3415	2350
birth of Jacob: + 60 (Gen 25:26)	2109	3475	2410
Jacob's journey to Egypt: + 130 (Gen 47:9)	2239	3605	2540
exodus from Egypt (Ex 12:40)	2669 (+ 430)	3820 (+ 215)	2755 (+ 215)
arrival at border of Canaan: + 40 (Deut 1:3)			2795
founding of (Samaritan) temple on Mount Gerizim: + 5 (approximate?) (Jos 8:30–33)	2714	3865	2800
founding of Solomon's temple in the 4th year of his reign: + 480 from date of the exodus (1 Kgs 6:1)	3149	4300	3280
from the founding of the Solomonic temple to the founding of the second temple (by calculations of modern chronologists), 967–516 B.C.E.: + 451	3600	4751	3731
TOTAL ELAPSED TIME FROM ABRAHAM'S BIRTH	1651	1436	1481

Note: The LXX figure for the duration of the Egyptian bondage (215 years vs. 430 of MT) is indirectly derived. LXX at Exodus 12:40 states that the 430 years includes the period of patriarchal residence in Canaan. Thus: 430 minus 25 (Abraham arrived at age 75 [Gen 12:4] and Isaac was born in his 100th year [21:5]), minus 60 (Jacob born in Isaac's 60th year [25:26]), minus 130 (Jacob's age when he went to Egypt [47:9]), equals 215. This is the figure quoted by the Jewish historian Josephus (*Antiquities* II.xv.2).

TABLE 19. Chronology of the Judean Monarchy According to the Biblical Text

name	length of reign	source of data		
Rehoboam	17	1 Kgs 14:21	2 Chr 12:13	
Abijam	3	15:2	13:2	
Asa	41	15:10	16:13	
Jehoshaphat	25	22:42		
Jehoram/Joram	8	2 Kgs 8:17	21:20	
Ahaziah	1	8:26	22:2	
Athaliah	6	11:3		
Joash/Jehoash	40	12:1		
Amaziah	29	14:2	25:1	
Uzziah/Azariah	52	15:2		
Jotham	16	15:33	27:1	
Ahaz	16	16:2	28:1	
Hezekiah	29	18:2	29:1	
Manasseh	55	21:1	33:1	
Amon	2	21:19	33:21	
Josiah	31	22:1	34:1	
Jehoiahaz	3 months	23:31	36:2	
Jehoiakim	11	23:36	36:5	
Jehoiachin	3 months	24:8	36:9	
Zedekiah	11	24:18	36:11	
TOTALS	394 years (393.5)			

for the founding of the Solomonic temple (3149 A.M.), added the 36 remaining years of Solomon's reign (1 Kgs 6:1; 11:42), calculated 394 years for the remainder of the monarchy (see Table No. 19), then added 70 more years for the aforementioned prophetic projection of the duration of the exile. The grand total, down to the time of Cyrus the Persian's edict to allow the exiles to return home and rebuild the temple (2 Chr 36:22–23; Ezr 1:1–4), would thus be 500 years, arriving thereby at the year 3649 A.M. In such calculations, it has been proposed that 18 years would have been deducted for overlapping reigns,[2] then 31 years based upon biblical evidence,[3] and thereby one would arrive again at the year 3600 A.M.

It might be argued, of course, that if the date of the founding of the second temple ought to be a highly symbolic number (3600 A.M. = 60^2

years), then biblical chronologists might have proceeded as follows. From the founding of the temple to the birth of Abraham: 1651 years (see Table No. 18); from the birth of Abraham to the flood: 292 years (see Table No. 16); total: 1943 years; 3600 − 1943 = 1657 years remaining since creation; flood of one year's duration; therefore: the flood happened in the year 1656 A.M. In this way of reckoning, the year of the flood (elapsed time since creation) would have been a necessary and derived computation, in which case congruence with the figures of Berossos (conversion of lustra to weeks) would be entirely accidental.

It seems far more likely, however, that the correspondence with Berossos' figure for pre-diluvian reigns is a given datum with which the chronologists worked. It would then be necessary to adjust elapsed time for the early post-diluvians in order to create a grand total of 3600 years.

Modern interpreters have sometimes sought to discover significance in other dates on the scale of elapsed time. Perhaps the most common is that the date of the exodus from Egypt is two-thirds of a world cycle of 4,000 years (100 generations of 40 years each),[4] following which the messiah was to appear. However, such a calculation assumes the correctness of Archbishop Ussher's chronology (Table No. 20), that such a world cycle was projected at the time of the biblical chronologists (in actuality, it seems to be much later), that two-thirds is a significant proportion in biblical reckoning (it isn't), and that there was a well-formed messianic expectation at the time when the chronological system (beginning in Genesis) took shape (in actuality, such expectation belongs to the post-exilic period).

Much more interesting is the proposal of Jepsen (1929) that the earliest reckoning for the pre-diluvians (Gen 5) was that of SP (1307 years to the flood; (see Table No. 14), and that of the early post-diluvians (Gen 11) was MT (1493 years from the flood to the second temple: i.e. 293 [from flood to Abraham: Table No. 16] + 1200 [from Abraham to the fourth year of Solomon: see Table No. 18]). The result would be that Solomon's temple was founded in A.M. 2800 and the Samaritan temple in A.M. 2364. Consequently (he suggests), the Samaritans altered the post-diluvian figures such that their temple was founded in A.M. 2800 (see Table No. 18) and the Judeans altered the pre-diluvian figures such that their second temple was founded in A.M. 3600!

While the occurrence of the year 2800 in each case is indeed striking, this suggestion involves considerable difficulties. (1) Why should 2800 be a significant figure? (It is not a multiple of 60.) (2) Why should the Samaritans have been dissatisfied with absolute dates, since their temple was much older than that of Solomon in any case? (3) If the MT figures are original for the post-diluvian period, and the Judeans then wanted to set a date of 3600 for the second temple, then a date of 1656 would have been *mathematically* man-

TABLE 20. Archbishop Ussher's Chronology
(For Purposes of Comparison with Tables Nos. 14–18)

event	date A.M.	date B.C.E.	date according to modern chronologists, B.C.E. (e.g. in IDB)
creation	1	4004	15,000,000,000 years
the flood	1656	2349	
birth of Abraham (Gen 11:32; 12:1)	2008 (+60)	1996 [2996]	1800s
call of Abraham	2083	1921	
birth of Isaac	2108	1896 [2896]	
birth of Jacob	2168	1836	
Jacob's journey to Egypt	2298	1706	
exodus from Egypt (using LXX figure for duration)	2513 (minus 215)	1491	ca. 1290
founding of Solomon's temple	2993	1012	967
dedication of Solomon's temple	3000	1005	
year 1 of King Evil-Merodach of Babylon	3442	562 [362]	562
founding of the second temple	3485 (+41)	520	537
birth of the messiah (Jesus)	4000	4	7–4

a. Ussher calculated from creation onward (A.M.), using data from the Bible and making choices where the data provided options. (One such instance is the use of Genesis 11:32; 12:1 vs. 11:26, on which see Table No. 16.) He continued this process until he came to an event which could be dated by extra-biblical means to the Julian calendar (and thus assigned a year B.C.E.). That event is the death of Nebuchadnezzar, king of Babylon, and the beginning of the reign of his successor Evil-Merodach in the year 562 B.C.E. (See his "Epistle to the Reader.") Since this happened, in his calculation, in A.M. 3442, the sum of the two figures yields 4004 B.C.E. for elapsed time since creation.

b. The figures in parentheses show the amount of departure by Ussher from the ones that I have utilized for a particular event in Tables Nos. 14, 16, and 18. The combination of +60, minus 215, and +41 yields a total difference of minus 114 years (that is, Ussher dates the founding of the second temple 114 years prior to my date). However, the observant reader will note that A.M. 3600 (Table No. 18) minus 114 yields 3486, one year removed from the 3485 of Ussher! The difference is that I have added the year of the flood's duration (see the heading to Table No. 18).

c. The figures in brackets are those actually listed in the margin of Ussher's text (English edition of 1658). They seem to be typographical errors and I have entered the "corrected" figure above them.

d. In computing elapsed time from the exodus to the founding of the Solomonic temple, Ussher used the LXX datum rather than that of the MT (see the note to Table No. 18). One wonders if those who added Ussher's dates to the margins of the English Bible (giving them a near canonical status) realized this, since the biblical text to which the dates were attached was basically a translation of MT!

e. In his Introduction ("Epistle to the Reader"), Ussher proposes that Jesus was born in the year 4 B.C.E., i.e. A.M. 4000, exactly 1,000 years after the Solomonic temple was completed. This assumes a "world number" of 4,000 years (100 generations of 40 years each), in an overt Christian polemic.

dated for the pre-diluvian period. Once again, congruence with the figures of Berossos would be entirely accidental, and this seems most unlikely. Such derivation from Berossos' ages have been suggested for the post-diluvian period as well (see below, Appendix XVI). (4) One would be left with 1307 years as the initial calculation of the pre-flood period, which seemingly is not derived from any Ancient Near Eastern prototype nor is it a multiple of 60. One could only say that the first ten generations (through Shem's birth) are set at an average of 120 years each, with an additional 7 for complement. That leaves 100 years as a "loose end," with that amount having been added so as to bring about the flood in Noah's 600th year (60 × 10).

Appendix XIII   Notes

1. Calculation of this or any other date from biblical evidence is fraught with difficulties and options. I will give here only a few illustrations. (a) On the one hand, we are told that the waters of the flood began in Noah's 600th year (Gen 7:6, 11; see also 9:28). On the other hand, if Shem was born when Noah was 500 (5:32), and Arpachshad when Shem was 100 ("two years after the flood," 11:10), then the flood should have begun in Noah's 598th year. For a discussion, see Cryer, 1985. (b) Was Abraham born in Terah's 70th year (11:26), or was it 60 years later (see 11:32, where Terah lives for another 135 years, whereupon according to 12:4 Abraham then set out for Canaan at the age of 75)? These two options are reflected in Table No. 16. (c) Is one to reckon the period of Judah's exile literally as "70 years" (Jer 25:11; 2 Chr 36:21), or is one to regard that as a symbolic number (Appendix No. VII) and substitute 48 years as seems to have been the case (see below)? (d) How is one to total the length of reign of the Judean monarchy, in view of overlapping reigns (co-regencies)? (e) Were successive reigns of the monarchs determined by the ante-dating or the post-dating system (see footnote 2)? The following assessment, then, is hardly surprising:

> Every scholar who tries [to assign dates from creation downward] comes to a different result. *L'art de verifier les dates* gives no less than a hundred and eight different views; and the two extremes differ no less than two thousand years from each other. Julius Africanus, from the creation of Christ, 5,500 years; Eusebius, Bede, and the Roman martyrologium, 5,199; Scaliger and Calvisius, 3,950; Kepler and Petavius, 3,984; Ussher, 4004; etc. Uniformity is not to be hoped for under such circumstances . . . (Wieseler, 1882, p. 753).

It is Ussher's date, of course, that has become the most famous one. To be precise, he dated the initial act of creation to "the entrance of the night preceding the twenty third of *Octob.* in the year of the Julian Calendar, 710" (*Annals,* 1658, p. 1). The marginal equivalent is then stated to be 4004 B.C.E. His learning and ecclesiastical stature (archbishop of the Church of England) led to the inclusion of his dates (for the range of events in biblical history) in the margin of the "authorized version" (KJV) beginning with editions in 1701 C.E. (I note that Warfield, 1932, p. 236, remarks: "Usher's own dating was 4138 B.C.," in contrast to the biblical notation of 4004, but I cannot at the moment justify his observation.)

2. So Alfred Jepsen, 1929, pp. 251–255. His proposal is that the biblical chronologists might have *assumed* the text to reflect the ante-dating system, whereby a king was allowed to count the remaining year of his accession to the throne as his first official year, while his predecessor also reckoned it as the last year of his reign. (By contrast, the post-dating system counted such a year only for the former monarch.) The result would be, in terms of the sum of several successive reigns, that one year too many would have been counted for each king. Thus, on Table No. 19, one would deduct a total of 18 years, one for each king who reigned for a full year. On how such reigns were *actually* reckoned in ancient times, see the article "Chronology of the OT," *IDB*, Vol. I (A-D), at p. 586.

3. Jepsen (*ibid.*) suggests deducting 15 years on the basis of 2 Kings 14:18, and 16 years on the basis of 2 Kings 15:5, 33. It must be noted, however, that he has proceeded in a highly compressed and cryptic fashion, and by a slightly different route than the one outlined above.

4. The first to propose this may have been Nöldeke (see the Additional Bibliography below). In such reckoning, the exodus is often dated at 2666 A.M., which is 0.6665 of the supposed world cycle. In Ussher's reckoning, the exodus is 2513 A.M., which would be two-thirds only by rough approximation.

APPENDIX XIV

Anti-Evolutionism
and the Courts

THE FOLLOWING list of legislative actions makes no claim for completeness. It has been assembled primarily from a rapid survey of Larson, *Trial and Error* (1985), and from articles in *Creation/Evolution*.

The legislative history may be divided into two stages: (1) old-time *overtly* religiously based anti-evolutionism (sometimes specified only in terms of human origins) during the period from 1922 (when Kentucky introduced the first bill) to 1970 (when the Mississippi Supreme Court struck down the law of that state following a U.S. Supreme Court decision in 1968), and (2) "creationist" legislation based upon the strategy of "balanced treatment for creation-science and evolution" between the early 1970s and the ruling of the U.S. Supreme Court in 1987 (Louisiana statute negated).

Alabama: "Creationist" statute introduced in 1981 (defeated in committee).

Arizona: A bill was introduced in 1965 (defeated in committee); "creationist" statute enacted in 1983 (vetoed by the governor).

Arkansas: Anti-evolution bill passed by public initiative, 1928; weakened by the state attorney general, 1929; negated by U.S. Supreme Court, 1968 (Epperson vs. Arkansas). Creationist statute enacted in 1981; negated by U.S. District Court, 1982 (McLean vs. the Arkansas Board of Education: see Appendix No. XV).[1]

Colorado: "Creationist" bill introduced in 1981 (defeated in committee).

Connecticut: "Creationist" bill introduced in 1983 (defeated in committee).

Florida: Anti-evolution bill passed in 1923 (did not forbid such teaching as long as it was not stated to be true; provided no penalty for violation). "Creationist" bill, 1980 (defeated in committee).

Georgia: Bill introduced in 1925; "creationist" statute introduced in 1979 and 1980 (did not achieve final passage).

Illinois: "Creationist" bill introduced in 1980 (defeated in committee).

Iowa: "Creationist" bills introduced in 1977, 1979, 1980 (defeated).[2]

Kentucky: Anti-evolution bill introduced in 1922 (the first such bill in the U.S.; narrowly defeated); "creationist" bill introduced but defeated in 1974 and 1980.

Louisiana: "Creationist" bill introduced in 1980 (defeated in committee); passed, 1981 (negated by U.S. Supreme Court, 1987).[3] Previously (1983), the state Supreme Court had upheld the legislature's right to enact such legislation.

Minnesota: "Creationist" bill introduced in 1980 (defeated in committee).

Missouri: The last old-line anti-evolution bill to be introduced in a state legislature: defeated in committee.

Mississippi: Anti-evolution bill passed in 1926 (weakened by state attorney general, 1927; last state law of its type to be struck down (by state Supreme Court, 1970, following a U.S. Supreme Court decision concerning Arkansas in 1968). "Creationist" bill introduced in 1983 (defeated in committee).

New York: "Creationist" bill introduced, 1979 (defeated in committee).[4]

Oklahoma: Anti-evolution statute enacted in 1923 (the first such statute in the U.S.). "Creationist" bill introduced in 1981 (defeated in committee).[5]

Oregon: "Creationist" bill introduced in 1981 (defeated in committee).

South Carolina: Anti-evolution bill introduced in 1922 (narrowly defeated); "creationist" bill introduced in 1980 (defeated).

Tennessee: Anti-evolution bill introduced in 1923 (defeated in committee); passed, 1925 (the famous Butler Act which led to the so-called John Scopes "monkey trial"); repealed in 1967. "Creationist" bill passed, 1973 (negated by Federal Court, 1975; similar rejection in a textbook case in 1988).[6] Bills introduced in 1976 and 1979 (defeated in committee).

Texas: Anti-evolution bill introduced in 1929; state board of education policy allowed the teaching of evolution, provided it was described as one theory among others, 1974 (e.g. a "creationist" approach); negated by the state attorney general following the Arkansas case of 1982.[7]

Washington: "Creationist" bill introduced in 1974 and 1981 (defeated in committee).

West Virginia: "Creationist" bill introduced, 1983 (defeated in committee).

In the following states, among others, there have been controversies concerning the selection of textbooks for the public schools.

California: State Board of Public Instruction directed teachers to present evolution "as a theory only," 1924; textbooks must identify evolution as a "theory" (1963); equal time for creation and evolution (1970; "Science Framework for California Public Schools"), but this policy was dropped in 1972 and concurred with by the state attorney general in 1975 (the result being a return to the "anti-dogmatism policy" of 1963, upheld by the state courts in 1979). A proposed new Science Curriculum Framework (1988) has drawn ICR's ire.[8]

Louisiana and Texas: Commission ordered the deletion of any reference to evolution (1926 and 1925, respectively).

North Carolina: Board forbade the use of any biology text which suggested a non-biblical concept of human origins (1924).

Appendix XIV Notes

1. See Gish, March 1982; Frederick Edwords (Winter 1982), pp. 33–45.
2. Stanley L. Weinberg, 1980, pp. 1–8.

3. See Bird, 1987. For discussion of the anti-creationist brief signed by seventy-two Nobel Laureates, see Sackel, 1986–87, pp. 147–158, and for a positive reaction to the decision, see Gould, 1987–88, pp. 184–187.

4. David Kraus, 1980, pp. 8–9.

5. Frank J. Sonleitner, 1981, pp. 23–27.

6. See George E. Webb, 1988, pp. 37–43.

7. Steven Schafersman, 1982, pp. 30–34; Stuart W. Hughes, 1983, pp. 33–34.

8. Henry M. Morris, December 1988.

APPENDIX XV

McLean vs. the Arkansas Board of Education (U.S. District Court)

IN THE UNITED STATES DISTRICT COURT
EASTERN DISTRICT OF ARKANSAS
WESTERN DIVISION

REV. BILL McLEAN, ET AL.   PLAINTIFFS

VS.   NO. LR C 81 322

THE ARKANSAS BOARD OF EDUCATION, ET AL.   DEFENDANTS

Memorandum Opinion

Introduction

On March 19, 1981, the Governor of Arkansas signed into law Act 590 of 1981, entitled the "Balanced Treatment for Creation-Science and Evolution-Science Act." The Act is codified as Ark. Stat. Ann. §80-1663, *et seq.,* (1981 Supp.). Its essential mandate is stated in its first sentence: "Public schools within this State shall give balanced treatment to creation-science and to evolution-science." On May 27, 1981, this suit was filed[1] challenging the constitutional validity of Act 590 on three distinct grounds.

First, it is contended that Act 590 constitutes an establishment of religion prohibited by the First Amendment to the Constitution, which is made applicable to the states by the Fourteenth Amendment. Second, the plaintiffs argue the Act violates a right to academic freedom which they say is guaranteed to students and teachers by the Free Speech Clause of the First Amendment. Third, plaintiffs allege the Act is impermissibly vague and thereby violates the Due Process Clause of the Fourteenth Amendment.

The individual plaintiffs include the resident Arkansas Bishops of the United Methodist, Episcopal, Roman Catholic and African Methodist Episcopal Churches, the principal official of the Presbyterian Churches in Arkansas, other United Methodist, Southern Baptist and Presbyterian clergy, as well as several persons who sue as parents and next friends of minor children attending Arkansas public schools. One plaintiff is a high school biology teacher. All are also Arkansas taxpayers. Among the organizational plaintiffs are the American Jewish Congress, the Union of American Hebrew Congregations, the American Jewish Committee, the Arkansas Education Association, the National Association of Biology Teachers and the National Coalition for Public Education and Religious Liberty, all of which sue on behalf of members living in Arkansas.[2]

The defendants include the Arkansas Board of Education and its members, the Director of the Department of Education, and the State Textbooks and Instructional Materials Selecting Committee.[3] The Pulaski County Special School District and its Directors and Superintendent were voluntarily dismissed by the plaintiffs at the pre-trial conference held October 1, 1981.

The trial commenced December 7, 1981, and continued through December 17, 1981. This Memorandum Opinion constitutes the Court's findings of fact and conclusions of law. Further orders and judgment will be in conformity with this opinion.

There is no controversy over the legal standards under which the Establishment Clause portion of this case must be judged. The Supreme Court has on a number of occasions expounded on the meaning of the clause, and the pronouncements are clear. Often the issue has arisen in the context of public education, as it has here. In *Everson v. Board of Education,* 330 U.S. 1, 15–16 (1947), Justice Black stated:

"The 'establishment of religion' clause of the First Amendment means at least this: Neither a state nor the Federal Government can set up a church. Neither can pass laws which aid one religion, aid all religions, or prefer one religion over another. Neither can force nor influence a person to go to or to remain away from church against his will or force him to profess a belief or disbelief in any religion. No person can be punished for entertaining or professing religious beliefs or disbeliefs, for church-attendance or non-attendance. No tax, large or small, can be levied to support any religious activities or institutions, whatever they may be called, or whatever form they may adopt to teach or practice religion. Neither a state nor the Federal

Government can, openly or secretly, participate in the affairs of any religious organizations or groups and *vice versa*. In the words of Jefferson,
the clause . . . was intended to erect 'a wall of separation between church
and State.' "

The Establishment Clause thus enshrines two central values: voluntar-
ism and pluralism. And it is in the area of the public schools that these values
must be guarded most vigilantly.

"Designed to serve as perhaps the most powerful agency for promoting
cohesion among a heterogeneous democratic people, the public school
must keep scrupulously free from entanglement in the strife of sects. The
preservation of the community from divisive conflicts, of Government
from irreconcilable pressures by religious groups, of religion from censorship and coercion however subtly exercised, requires strict confinement of
the State to instruction other than religious, leaving to the individual's
church and home, indoctrination in the faith of his choice."

McCollum v. Board of Education, 333 U.S. 203, 216–217 (1948), (Opinion
of Frankfurter, J., joined by Jackson, Burton and Rutledge, J.J.).

The specific formulation of the establishment prohibition has been refined over the years, but its meaning has not varied from the principles
articulated by Justice Black in *Everson*. In *Abbington School District v.
Schempp,* 374 U.S. 203, 222 (1963), Justice Clark stated that "to withstand
the strictures of the Establishment Clause there must be a secular legislative
purpose and a primary effect that neither advances nor inhibits religion."
The Court found it quite clear that the First Amendment does not permit a
state to require the daily reading of the Bible in public schools, for "[s]urely
the place of the Bible as an instrument of religion cannot be gainsaid." *Id.* at
224. Similarly, in *Engel v. Vitale,* 370 U.S. 421 (1962), the Court held that
the First Amendment prohibited the New York Board of Regents from requiring the daily recitation of a certain prayer in the schools. With characteristic succinctness, Justice Black wrote, "Under [the First] Amendment's prohibition against governmental establishment of religion, as reinforced by the
provisions of the Fourteenth Amendment, government in this country, be it
state or federal, is without power to prescribe by law any particular form of
prayer which is to be used as an official prayer in carrying on any program of
governmentally sponsored religious activity." *Id.* at 430. Black also identified the objective at which the Establishment Clause was aimed: "Its first and
most immediate purpose rested on the belief that a union of government and
religion tends to destroy government and to degrade religion." *Id.* at 431.

Most recently, the Supreme Court has held that the clause prohibits a state from requiring the posting of the Ten Commandments in public school classrooms for the same reasons that officially imposed daily Bible reading is prohibited. *Stone v. Graham,* 449 U.S. 39 (1980). The opinion in *Stone* relies on the most recent formulation of the Establishment Clause test, that of *Lemon v. Kurtzman,* 403 U.S. 602, 612–613 (1971):

> "First, the statute must have a secular legislative purpose; second, its principal or primary effect must be one that neither advances nor inhibits religion . . . ; finally, the statute must not foster 'an excessive government entanglement with religion.' "

Stone v. Graham, 449 U.S. at 40.

It is under this three part test that the evidence in this case must be judged. Failure on any of these grounds is fatal to the enactment.

II.

The religious movement known as Fundamentalism began in nineteenth century America as part of evangelical Protestantism's response to social changes, new religious thought and Darwinism. Fundamentalists viewed these developments as attacks on the Bible and as responsible for a decline in traditional values.

The various manifestations of Fundamentalism have had a number of common characteristics,[4] but a central premise has always been a literal interpretation of the Bible and a belief in the *inerrancy* of the Scriptures. Following World War I, there was again a perceived decline in traditional morality, and Fundamentalism focused on evolution as responsible for the decline. One aspect of their efforts, particularly in the South, was the promotion of statutes prohibiting the teaching of evolution in public schools. In Arkansas, this resulted in the adoption of Initiated Act 1 of 1929.[5]

Between the 1920's and early 1960's, anti-evolutionary sentiment had a subtle but pervasive influence on the teaching of biology in public schools. Generally, textbooks avoided the topic of evolution and did not mention the name of Darwin. Following the launch of the Sputnik satellite by the Soviet Union in 1957, the National Science Foundation funded several programs designed to modernize the teaching of science in the nation's schools. The Biological Sciences Curriculum Study (BSCS), a nonprofit organization, was among those receiving grants for curriculum study and revision. Working with scientists and teachers, BSCS developed a series of biology texts which, although emphasizing different aspects of biology, incorporated the theory of evolution as a major theme. The success of the BSCS effort is shown by the fact that fifty percent of American school children currently use BSCS books directly and the curriculum is incorporated indirectly in virtually all biology texts. (Testimony of Mayer; Nelkin, Px 1)[6]

In the early 1960's, there was again a resurgence of concern among Fundamentalists about the loss of traditional values and a fear of growing secularism in society. The Fundamentalist movement became more active and has steadily grown in numbers and political influence. There is an emphasis among current Fundamentalists on the literal interpretation of the Bible and the Book of Genesis as the sole source of knowledge about origins.

The term "scientific creationism" first gained currency around 1965 following publication of *The Genesis Flood* in 1961 by Whitcomb and Morris. There is undoubtedly some connection between the appearance of the BSCS texts emphasizing evolutionary thought and efforts by Fundamentalists to attack the theory. (Mayer)

In the 1960's and early 1970's, several Fundamentalist organizations were formed to promote the idea that the Book of Genesis was supported by scientific data. The terms "creation science" and "scientific creationism" have been adopted by these Fundamentalists as descriptive of their study of creation and the origins of man. Perhaps the leading creationist organization is the Institute for Creation Research (ICR), which is affiliated with the Christian Heritage College and supported by the Scott Memorial Baptist Church in San Diego, California. The ICR, through the Creation-Life Publishing Company, is the leading publisher of creation science material. Other creation science organizations include the Creation Science Research Center (CSRC) of San Diego and the Bible Science Association of Minneapolis, Minnesota. In 1963, the Creation Research Society (CRS) was formed from a schism in the American Scientific Affiliation (ASA). It is an organization of literal Fundamentalists[7] who have the equivalent of a master's degree in some recognized area of science. A purpose of the organization is "to reach all people with the vital message of the scientific and historic truth about creation." Nelkin, *The Science Textbook Controversies and the Politics of Equal Time,* 66. Similarly, the CSRC was formed in 1970 from a split in the CRS. Its aim has been "to reach the 63 million children of the United States with the scientific teaching of Biblical creationism." *Id.* at 69.

Among creationist writers who are recognized as authorities in the field by other creationists are Henry M. Morris, Duane Gish, G.E. Parker, Harold S. Slusher, Richard B. Bliss, John W. Moore, Martin E. Clark, W.L. Wysong, Robert E. Kofahl and Kelly L. Segraves. Morris is Director of ICR, Gish is Associate Director and Segraves is associated with CSRC.

Creationists view evolution as a source of society's ills, and the writings of Morris and Clark are typical expressions of that view.

"Evolution is thus not only anti-Biblical and anti-Christian, but it is utterly unscientific and impossible as well. But it has served effectively as the pseudo-scientific basis of atheism, agnosticism, socialism, fascism, and numerous other false and dangerous philosophies over the past century."

Morris and Clark, *The Bible Has The Answer,* (Px 31 and Pretrial Px 89).[8]

Creationists have adopted the view of Fundamentalists generally that there are only two positions with respect to the origins of the earth and life: belief in the inerrancy of the Genesis story of creation and of a worldwide flood as fact, or belief in what they call evolution.

Henry Morris has stated, "It is impossible to devise a legitimate means of harmonizing the Bible with evolution." Morris, "Evolution and the Bible," *ICR Impact Series* Number 5 (undated, unpaged), quoted in Mayer, Px 8, at 3. This dualistic approach to the subject of origins permeates the creationist literature.

The creationist organizations consider the introduction of creation science into the public schools part of their ministry. The ICR has published at least two pamphlets[9] containing suggested methods for convincing school boards, administrators and teachers that creationism should be taught in public schools. The ICR has urged its proponents to encourage school officials to voluntarily add creationism to the curriculum.[10]

Citizens For Fairness In Education is an organization based in Anderson, South Carolina, formed by Paul Ellwanger, a respiratory therapist who is trained in neither law nor science. Mr. Ellwanger is of the opinion that evolution is the forerunner of many social ills, including Nazism, racism and abortion. (Ellwanger Depo. at 32–34). About 1977, Ellwanger collected several proposed legislative acts with the idea of preparing a model state act requiring the teaching of creationism as science in opposition to evolution. One of the proposals he collected was prepared by Wendell Bird, who is now a staff attorney for ICR.[11] From these various proposals, Ellwanger prepared a "model act" which calls for "balanced treatment" of "scientific creationism" and "evolution" in public schools. He circulated the proposed act to various people and organizations around the country.

Mr. Ellwanger's views on the nature of creation science are entitled to some weight since he personally drafted the model act which became Act 590. His evidentiary deposition with exhibits and unnumbered attachments (produced in response to a subpoena *duces tecum*) speaks to both the intent of the Act and the scientific merits of creation science. Mr. Ellwanger does not believe creation science is a science. In a letter to Pastor Robert E. Hays he states, "While neither evolution nor creation can qualify as a scientific theory, and since it is virtually impossible at this point to educate the whole world that evolution is not a true scientific theory, we have freely used these terms—the evolution theory and the theory of scientific creationism—in the bill's text." (Unnumbered attachment to Ellwanger Depo., at 2.) He further states in a letter to Mr. Tom Bethell, "As we examine evolution (remember, we're not making any scientific claims for creation, but we are challenging evolution's claim to be scientific). . . ." (Unnumbered attachment to Ellwanger Depo. at 1.)

Ellwanger's correspondence on the subject shows an awareness that Act 590 is a religious crusade, coupled with a desire to conceal this fact. In a letter to State Senator Bill Keith of Louisiana, he says, "I view this whole battle as one between God and anti-God forces, though I know there are a large number of evolutionists who believe in God." And further, ". . . it behooves Satan to do all he can to thwart our efforts and confuse the issue at every turn." Yet Ellwanger suggests to Senator Keith, "If you have a clear choice between having grassroots leaders of this statewide bill promotion effort to be ministerial or non-ministerial, be sure to opt for the non-ministerial. It does the bill effort no good to have ministers out there in the public forum and the adversary will surely pick at this point . . . Ministerial persons can accomplish a tremendous amount of work from behind the scenes, encouraging their congregations to take the organizational and P.R. initiatives. And they can lead their churches in storming Heaven with prayers for help against so tenacious an adversary." (Unnumbered attachment to Ellwanger Depo. at 1.)

Ellwanger shows a remarkable degree of political candor, if not finesse, in a letter to State Senator Joseph Carlucci of Florida:

"2. It would be very wise, if not actually essential, that all of us who are engaged in this legislative effort be careful not to present our position and our work in a religious framework. For example, in written communications that might somehow be shared with those other persons whom we may be trying to convince, it would be well to exclude our own personal testimony and/or witness for Christ, but rather, if we are so moved, to give that testimony on a separate attached note." (Unnumbered attachment to Ellwanger Depo. at 1.)

The same tenor is reflected in a letter by Ellwanger to Mary Ann Miller, a member of FLAG (Family, Life, America under God) who lobbied the Arkansas Legislature in favor of Act 590:

". . . we'd like to suggest that you and your co-workers be very cautious about mixing creation-science with creation-religion. . . . Please urge your co-workers not to allow themselves to get sucked into the 'religion' trap of mixing the two together, for such mixing does incalculable harm to the legislative thrust. It could even bring public opinion to bear adversely upon the higher courts that will eventually have to pass judgment on the constitutionality of this new law." (Ex. 1 to Miller Depo.)

Perhaps most interesting, however, is Mr. Ellwanger's testimony in his deposition as to his strategy for having the model act implemented:

Q. You're trying to play on other people's religious motives.

A. I'm trying to play on their emotions, love, hate, their likes, dislikes, because I don't know any other way to involve, to get humans to become involved in human endeavors. I see emotions as being a healthy and legitimate means of getting people's feelings into action, and . . . I believe that the predominance of population in America that represents the greatest potential for taking some kind of action in this area is a Christian community. I see the Jewish community as far less potential in taking action . . . but I've seen a lot of interest among Christians and I feel, why not exploit that to get the bill going if that's what it takes. (Ellwanger Depo. at 146–147.)

Mr. Ellwanger's ultimate purpose is revealed in the closing of his letter to Mr. Tom Bethell: "Perhaps all this is old hat to you, Tom, and if so, I'd appreciate your telling me so and perhaps where you've heard it before—the idea of killing evolution instead of playing these debating games that we've been playing for nigh over a decade already." (Unnumbered attachment to Ellwanger Depo. at 3.)

It was out of this milieu that Act 590 emerged. The Reverend W.A. Blount, a Biblical literalist who is pastor of a church in the Little Rock area and was, in February, 1981, chairman of the Greater Little Rock Evangelical Fellowship, was among those who received a copy of the model act from Ellwanger.[12]

At Reverend Blount's request, the Evangelical Fellowship unanimously adopted a resolution to seek introduction of Ellwanger's act in the Arkansas Legislature. A committee composed of two ministers, Curtis Thomas and W.A. Young, was appointed to implement the resolution. Thomas obtained from Ellwanger a revised copy of the model act which he transmitted to Carl Hunt, a business associate of Senator James L. Holsted, with the request that Hunt prevail upon Holsted to introduce the act.

Holsted, a self-described "born again" Christian Fundamentalist, introduced the act in the Arkansas Senate. He did not consult the State Department of Education, scientists, science educators or the Arkansas Attorney

General.[13] The Act was not referred to any Senate committee for hearing and was passed after only a few minutes' discussion on the Senate floor. In the House of Representatives, the bill was referred to the Education Committee which conducted a perfunctory fifteen minute hearing. No scientist testified at the hearing, nor was any representative from the State Department of Education called to testify.

Ellwanger's model act was enacted into law in Arkansas as Act 590 without amendment or modification other than minor typographical changes. The legislative "findings of fact" in Ellwanger's act and Act 590 are identical, although no meaningful fact-finding process was employed by the General Assembly.

Ellwanger's efforts in preparation of the model act and campaign for its adoption in the states were motivated by his opposition to the theory of evolution and his desire to see the Biblical version of creation taught in the public schools. There is no evidence that the pastors, Blount, Thomas, Young or The Greater Little Rock Evangelical Fellowship were motivated by anything other than their religious convictions when proposing its adoption or during their lobbying efforts in its behalf. Senator Holsted's sponsorship and lobbying efforts in behalf of the Act were motivated solely by his religious beliefs and desire to see the Biblical version of creation taught in the public schools.[14]

The State of Arkansas, like a number of states whose citizens have relatively homogeneous religious beliefs, has a long history of official opposition to evolution which is motivated by adherence to Fundamentalist beliefs in the inerrancy of the Book of Genesis. This history is documented in Justice Fortas' opinion in *Epperson v. Arkansas,* 393 U.S. 97 (1968), which struck down Initiated Act 1 of 1929, Ark. Stat. Ann. §§80-1627-1628, prohibiting the teaching of the theory of evolution. To this same tradition may be attributed Initiated Act 1 of 1930, Ark. Stat. Ann. §80-1606 (Repl. 1980), requiring "the reverent daily reading of a portion of the English Bible" in every public school classroom in the State.[15]

It is true, as defendants argue, that courts should look to legislative statements of a statute's purpose in Establishment Clause cases and accord such pronouncements great deference. See, e.g., *Committee for Public Education & Religious Liberty v. Nyquist,* 413 U.S. 756, 773 (1973) and *McGowan v. Maryland,* 366 U.S. 420, 445 (1961). Defendants also correctly state the principle that remarks by the sponsor or author of a bill are not considered controlling in analyzing legislative intent. See, e.g., *United States v. Emmons,* 410 U.S. 396 (1973) and *Chrysler Corp. v. Brown,* 441 U.S. 281 (1979).

Courts are not bound, however, by legislative statements of purpose or legislative disclaimers. *Stone v. Graham,* 449 U.S. 39 (1980); *Abbington*

School Dist. v. Schempp, 374 U.S. 203 (1963). In determining the legislative purpose of a statute, courts may consider evidence of the historical context of the Act, *Epperson v. Arkansas,* 393 U.S. 97 (1968), the specific sequence of events leading up to passage of the Act, departures from normal procedural sequences, substantive departures from the normal, *Village of Arlington Heights v. Metropolitan Housing Corp.,* 429 U.S. 252 (1977), and contemporaneous statements of the legislative sponsor, *Fed. Energy Admin. v. Algonquin SNG, Inc.,* 426 U.S. 548, 564 (1976).

The unusual circumstances surrounding the passage of Act 590, as well as the substantive law of the First Amendment, warrant an inquiry into the stated legislative purposes. The author of the Act had publicly proclaimed the sectarian purpose of the proposal. The Arkansas residents who sought legislative sponsorship of the bill did so for a purely sectarian purpose. These circumstances alone may not be particularly persuasive, but when considered with the publicly announced motives of the legislative sponsor made contemporaneously with the legislative process; the lack of any legislative investigation, debate or consultation with any educators or scientists; the unprecedented intrusion in school curriculum;[16] and official history of the State of Arkansas on the subject, it is obvious that the statement of purposes has little, if any, support in fact. The State failed to produce any evidence which would warrant an inference or conclusion that at any point in the process anyone considered the legitimate educational value of the Act. It was simply and purely an effort to introduce the Biblical version of creation into the public school curricula. The only inference which can be drawn from these circumstances is that the Act was passed with the specific purpose by the General Assembly of advancing religion. The Act therefore fails the first prong of the three-pronged test, that of secular legislative purpose, as articulated in *Lemon v. Kurtzman, supra,* and *Stone v. Graham, supra.*

III.

If the defendants are correct and the Court is limited to an examination of the language of the Act, the evidence is overwhelming that both the purpose and effect of Act 590 is the advancement of religion in the public schools.

Section 4 of the Act provides:

Definitions. As used in this Act:

(a) "Creation-science" means the scientific evidences for creation and inferences from those scientific evidences. Creation-science includes the scientific evidences and related inferences that indicate: (1) Sudden creation of the universe, energy, and life from nothing; (2) The insufficiency of mutation and natural selection in bringing about development of all living kinds from a single organism; (3) Changes only within fixed limits of originally created kinds of plants and animals; (4) Separate ancestry for man and apes; (5) Explanation of the earth's geology by *catastrophism,* including the occurrence of a worldwide flood; and (6) A relatively recent inception of the earth and living kinds.

(b) "Evolution-science" means the scientific evidences for evolution and inferences from those scientific evidences. Evolution-science includes the scientific evidences and related inferences that indicate: (1) Emergence by naturalistic processes of the universe from disordered matter and emergence of life from nonlife; (2) The sufficiency of mutation and natural selection in bringing about development of present living kinds from simple earlier kinds; (3) Emergence by mutation and natural selection of present living kinds from simple earlier kinds; (4) Emergence of man from a common ancestor with apes; (5) Explanation of the earth's geology and the evolutionary sequence by uniformitarianism; and (6) An inception several billion years ago of the earth and somewhat later of life.

(c) "Public schools" mean public secondary and elementary schools.

The evidence establishes that the definition of "creation science" contained in 4(a) has as its unmentioned reference the first 11 chapters of the Book of Genesis. Among the many creation epics in human history, the account of sudden creation from nothing, or *creatio ex nihilo,* and subsequent destruction of the world by flood is unique to Genesis. The concepts of 4(a) are the literal Fundamentalists' view of Genesis. Section 4(a) is unquestionably a statement of religion, with the exception of 4(a)(2) which is a negative thrust aimed at what the creationists understand to be the theory of evolution.[17]

Both the concepts and wording of Section 4(a) convey an inescapable religiosity. Section 4(a)(1) describes "sudden creation of the universe, energy and life from nothing." Every theologian who testified, including defense witnesses, expressed the opinion that the statement referred to a supernatural creation which was performed by God.

Defendants argue that: (1) the fact that 4(a) conveys ideas similar to the literal interpretation of Genesis does not make it conclusively a statement of religion; (2) that reference to a creation from nothing is not necessarily a religious concept since the Act only suggests a creator who has power, intelligence and a sense of design and not necessarily the attributes of love, compassion and justice;[18] and (3) that simply teaching about the concept of a creator is not a religious exercise unless the student is required to make a commitment to the concept of a creator.

The evidence fully answers these arguments. The ideas of 4(a)(1) are not merely similar to the literal interpretation of Genesis; they are identical and parallel to no other story of creation.[19]

The argument that creation from nothing in 4(a)(1) does not involve a supernatural deity has no evidentiary or rational support. To the contrary, "creation out of nothing" is a concept unique to Western religions. In traditional Western religious thought, the conception of a creator of the world is a conception of God. Indeed, creation of the world "out of nothing" is the ultimate religious statement because God is the only actor. As Dr. Langdon Gilkey noted, the Act refers to one who has the power to bring all the universe into existence from nothing. The only "one" who has this power is God.[20]

The leading creationist writers, Morris and Gish, acknowledge that the idea of creation described in 4(a)(1) is the concept of creation by God and make no pretense to the contrary.[21] The idea of sudden creation from nothing, or *creatio ex nihilo,* is an inherently religious concept. (Vawter, Gilkey, Geisler, Ayala, Blount, Hicks.)

The argument advanced by defendants' witness, Dr. Norman Geisler, that teaching the existence of God is not religious unless the teaching seeks a commitment, is contrary to common understanding and contradicts settled case law. *Stone v. Graham,* 449 U.S. 39 (1980); *Abbington School District v. Schempp,* 374 U.S. 203 (1963).

The facts that creation science is inspired by the Book of Genesis and that Section 4(a) is consistent with a literal interpretation of Genesis leave no doubt that a major effect of the Act is the advancement of particular religious beliefs. The legal impact of this conclusion will be discussed further at the conclusion of the Court's evaluation of the scientific merit of creation science.

IV. (A)

The approach to teaching "creation science" and "evolution science" found in Act 590 is identical to the two-model approach espoused by the Institute for Creation Research and is taken almost verbatim from ICR writings. It is an extension of Fundamentalists' view that one must either accept the literal interpretation of Genesis or else believe in the godless system of evolution.

The two model approach of the creationists is simply a contrived dualism[22] which has no scientific factual basis or legitimate educational purpose. It assumes only two explanations for the origins of life and existence of man, plants and animals: It was either the work of a creator or it was not. Application of these two models, according to creationists, and the defendants, dictates that all scientific evidence which fails to support the theory of evolution is necessarily scientific evidence in support of creationism and is, therefore, creation science "evidence" in support of Section 4(a).

IV. (B)

The emphasis on origins as an aspect of the theory of evolution is peculiar to creationist literature. Although the subject of origins of life is within the province of biology, the scientific community does not consider origins of life a part of evolutionary theory. The theory of evolution assumes the existence of life and is directed to an explanation of *how* life evolved. Evolution does not presuppose the absence of a creator or God and the plain inference conveyed by Section 4 is erroneous.[23]

As a statement of the theory of evolution, Section 4(b) is simply a hodgepodge of limited assertions, many of which are factually inaccurate.

For example, although 4(b)(2) asserts, as a tenet of evolutionary theory, "the sufficiency of mutation and natural selection in bringing about the existence of present living kinds from simple earlier kinds," Drs. Ayala and Gould both stated that biologists know that these two processes do not account for all significant evolutionary change. They testified to such phenomena as recombination, the founder effect, genetic drift and the theory of punctuated equilibrium, which are believed to play important evolutionary roles. Section 4(b) omits any reference to these. Moreover, 4(b) utilizes the term "kinds" which all scientists said is not a word of science and has no fixed meaning. Additionally, the Act presents both evolution and creation science as "package deals." Thus, evidence critical of some aspect of what the creationists define as evolution is taken as support for a theory which includes a worldwide flood and a relatively young earth.[24]

IV. (C)

In addition to the fallacious pedagogy of the two model approach, Section 4(a) lacks legitimate educational value because "creation science" as defined in that section is simply not science. Several witnesses suggested definitions of science. A descriptive definition was said to be that science is what is "accepted by the scientific community" and is "what scientists do." The obvious implication of this description is that, in a free society, knowledge does not require the imprimatur of legislation in order to become science.

More precisely, the essential characteristics of science are:

(1) It is guided by natural law;

(2) It has to be explanatory by reference to natural law;

(3) It is testable against the empirical world;

(4) Its conclusions are tentative, i.e., are not necessarily the final word; and

(5) It is falsifiable. (Ruse and other science witnesses).

Creation science as described in Section 4(a) fails to meet these essential characteristics. First, the section revolves around 4(a)(1) which asserts a sudden creation "from nothing." Such a concept is not science because it depends upon a supernatural intervention which is not guided by natural law. It is not explanatory by reference to natural law, is not testable and is not falsifiable.[25]

If the unifying idea of supernatural creation by God is removed from Section 4, the remaining parts of the section explain nothing and are meaningless assertions.

Section 4(a)(2), relating to the "insufficiency of mutation and natural selection in bringing about development of all living kinds from a single organism", is an incomplete negative generalization directed at the theory of evolution.

Section 4(a)(3) which describes "changes only within fixed limits of originally created kinds of plants and animals" fails to conform to the essential characteristics of science for several reasons. First, there is no scientific definition of "kinds" and none of the witnesses was able to point to any scientific authority which recognized the term or knew how many "kinds" existed. One defense witness suggested there may be 100 to 10,000 different "kinds". Another believes there were "about 10,000, give or take a few thousand." Second, the assertion appears to be an effort to establish outer limits of changes within species. There is no scientific explanation for these limits which is guided by natural law and the limitations, whatever they are, cannot be explained by natural law.

The statement in 4(a)(4) of "separate ancestry of man and apes" is a bald assertion. It explains nothing and refers to no scientific fact or theory.[26]

Section 4(a)(5) refers to "explanation of the earth's geology by catastrophism, including the occurrence of a worldwide flood." This assertion completely fails as science. The Act is referring to the Noachian flood described in the Book of Genesis.[27] The creationist writers concede that *any* kind of Genesis Flood depends upon supernatural intervention. A worldwide flood as an explanation of the world's geology is not the product of natural law, nor can its occurrence be explained by natural law.

Section 4(a)(6) equally fails to meet the standards of science. "Relatively recent inception" has no scientific meaning. It can only be given meaning by reference to creationist writings which place the age at between 6,000 and 20,000 years because of the genealogy of the Old Testament. See, e.g. Px 78,

Gish (6,000 to 10,000); Px 87, Segraves (6,000 to 20,000). Such a reasoning process is not the product of natural law; not explainable by natural law; nor is it tentative.

Creation science, as defined in Section 4(a), not only fails to follow the canons defining scientific theory, it also fails to fit the more general descriptions of "what scientists think" and "what scientists do." The scientific community consists of individuals and groups, nationally and internationally, who work independently in such varied fields as biology, paleontology, geology and astronomy. Their work is published and subject to review and testing by their peers. The journals for publication are both numerous and varied. There is, however, not one recognized scientific journal which has published an article espousing the creation science theory described in Section 4(a). Some of the State's witnesses suggested that the scientific community was "close-minded" on the subject of creationism and that explained the lack of acceptance of the creation science arguments. Yet no witness produced a scientific article for which publication had been refused. Perhaps some members of the scientific community are resistant to new ideas. It is, however, inconceivable that such a loose knit group of independent thinkers in all the varied fields of science could, or would, so effectively censor new scientific thought.

The creationists have difficulty maintaining among their ranks consistency in the claim that creationism is science. The author of Act 590, Ellwanger, said that neither evolution nor creationism was science. He thinks both are religion. Duane Gish recently responded to an article in *Discover* critical of creationism by stating:

"Stephen Jay Gould states that creationists claim creation is a scientific theory. This is a false accusation. Creationists have repeatedly stated that neither creation nor evolution is a scientific theory (and each is equally religious)." Gish, letter to editor of *Discover,* July, 1981, App. 30 to Plaintiffs' Pretrial Brief.

The methodology employed by creationists is another factor which is indicative that their work is not science. A scientific theory must be tentative and always subject to revision or abandonment in light of facts that are inconsistent with, or falsify, the theory. A theory that is by its own terms dogmatic, absolutist and never subject to revision is not a scientific theory.

The creationists' methods do not take data, weigh it against the opposing scientific data, and thereafter reach the conclusions stated in Section 4(a). Instead, they take the literal wording of the Book of Genesis and attempt to find scientific support for it. The method is best explained in the language of Morris in his book (Px 31) *Studies in the Bible and Science* at page 114:

"... it is ... quite impossible to determine anything about Creation through a study of present processes, because present processes are not creative in character. If man wishes to know anything about Creation (the time of Creation, the duration of Creation, the order of Creation, the methods of Creation, or anything else) his sole source of true information is that of divine revelation. God was there when it happened. We were not there. . . . Therefore, we are completely limited to what God has seen fit to tell us, and this information is in His written Word. This is our textbook on the science of Creation!"

The Creation Research Society employs the same unscientific approach to the issue of creationism. Its applicants for membership must subscribe to the belief that the Book of Genesis is "historically and scientifically true in all of the original autographs." [28] The Court would never criticize or discredit any person's testimony based on his or her religious beliefs. While anybody is free to approach a scientific inquiry in any fashion they choose, they cannot properly describe the methodology used as scientific, if they start with a conclusion and refuse to change it regardless of the evidence developed during the course of the investigation.

IV. (D)

In efforts to establish "evidence" in support of creation science, the defendants relied upon the same false premise as the two model approach contained in Section 4, i.e., all evidence which criticized evolutionary theory was proof in support of creation science. For example, the defendants established that the mathematical probability of a chance chemical combination resulting in life from non-life is so remote that such an occurrence is almost beyond imagination. Those mathematical facts, the defendants argue, are scientific evidences that life was the product of a creator. While the statistical figures may be impressive evidence against the theory of chance chemical combinations as an explanation of origins, it requires a leap of faith to interpret those figures so as to support a complex doctrine which includes a sudden creation from nothing, a worldwide flood, separate ancestry of man and apes, and a young earth.

The defendants' argument would be more persuasive if, in fact, there were only two theories or ideas about the origins of life and the world. That there are a number of theories was acknowledged by the State's witnesses, Dr. Wickramasinghe and Dr. Geisler. Dr. Wickramasinghe testified at length in support of a theory that life on earth was "seeded" by comets which delivered genetic material and perhaps organisms to the earth's surface from interstellar dust far outside the solar system. The "seeding" theory further hypothesizes that the earth remains under the continuing influence of genetic material from space which continues to affect life. While Wickramasinghe's theory[29] about the origins of life on earth has not received general acceptance within the scientific community, he has, at least, used scientific methodology to produce a theory of origins which meets the essential characteristics of science.

Perhaps Dr. Wickramasinghe was called as a witness because he was generally critical of the theory of evolution and the scientific community, a tactic consistent with the strategy of the defense. Unfortunately for the defense, he demonstrated that the simplistic approach of the two model analysis of the origins of life is false. Furthermore, he corroborated the plaintiffs' witnesses by concluding that "no rational scientist" would believe the earth's geology could be explained by reference to a worldwide flood or that the earth was less than one million years old.

The proof in support of creation science consisted almost entirely of efforts to discredit the theory of evolution through a rehash of data and theories which have been before the scientific community for decades. The arguments asserted by creationists are not based upon new scientific evidence or laboratory data which has been ignored by the scientific community.

Robert Gentry's discovery of radioactive polonium haloes in granite and coalified woods is, perhaps, the most recent scientific work which the creationists use as argument for a "relatively recent inception" of the earth and a "worldwide flood." The existence of polonium haloes in granite and coalified wood is thought to be inconsistent with radiometric dating methods based upon constant radioactive decay rates. Mr. Gentry's findings were published almost ten years ago and have been the subject of some discussion in the scientific community. The discoveries have not, however, led to the formulation of any scientific hypothesis or theory which would explain a relatively recent inception of the earth or a worldwide flood. Gentry's discovery has been treated as a minor mystery which will eventually be explained. It may deserve further investigation, but the National Science Foundation has not deemed it to be of sufficient import to support further funding.

The testimony of Marianne Wilson was persuasive evidence that creation science is not science. Ms. Wilson is in charge of the science curriculum for Pulaski County Special School District, the largest school district in the State of Arkansas. Prior to the passage of Act 590, Larry Fisher, a science teacher in the District, using materials from the ICR, convinced the School Board that it should voluntarily adopt creation science as part of its science curriculum. The District Superintendent assigned Ms. Wilson the job of producing a creation science curriculum guide. Ms. Wilson's testimony about the project was particularly convincing because she obviously approached the assignment with an open mind and no preconceived notions about the subject. She had not heard of creation science until about a year ago and did not know its meaning before she began her research.

Ms. Wilson worked with a committee of science teachers appointed from the District. They reviewed practically all of the creationist literature. Ms. Wilson and the committee members reached the unanimous conclusion that creationism is not science; it is religion. They so reported to the Board. The Board ignored the recommendation and insisted that a curriculum guide be prepared.

In researching the subject, Ms. Wilson sought the assistance of Mr. Fisher who initiated the Board action and asked professors in the science departments of the University of Arkansas at Little Rock and the University of Central Arkansas[30] for reference material and assistance, and attended a workshop conducted at Central Baptist College by Dr. Richard Bliss of the ICR staff. Act 590 became law during the course of her work so she used Section 4(a) as a format for her curriculum guide.

Ms. Wilson found all available creationists' materials unacceptable because they were permeated with religious references and reliance upon religious beliefs.

It is easy to understand why Ms. Wilson and other educators find the creationists' textbook material and teaching guides unacceptable. The materials misstate the theory of evolution in the same fashion as Section 4(b) of the Act, with emphasis on the alternative mutually exclusive nature of creationism and evolution. Students are constantly encouraged to compare and make a choice between the two models, and the material is not presented in an accurate manner.

A typical example is *Origins* (Px 76) by Richard B. Bliss, Director of Curriculum Development of the ICR. The presentation begins with a chart describing "preconceived ideas about origins" which suggests that some people believe that evolution is atheistic. Concepts of evolution, such as "adaptive radiation," are erroneously presented. At page 11, figure 1.6, of the text, a chart purports to illustrate this "very important" part of the evolution model. The chart conveys the idea that such diverse mammals as a whale, bear, bat and monkey all evolved from a shrew through the process of adaptive radiation. Such a suggestion is, of course, a totally erroneous and misleading application of the theory. Even more objectionable, especially when viewed in light of the emphasis on asking the student to elect one of the models, is the chart presentation at page 17, figure 1.6. That chart purports to illustrate the evolutionists' belief that man evolved from bacteria to fish to reptile to mammals and, thereafter, into man. The illustration indicates, however, that the mammal from which man evolved was *a rat*.

Biology, A Search For Order in Complexity[31] is a high school biology text typical of creationists' materials. The following quotations are illustrative:

"Flowers and roots do not have a mind to have purpose of their own; therefore, this planning must have been done for them by the Creator."— at page 12.

"The exquisite beauty of color and shape in flowers exceeds the skill of poet, artist, and king. Jesus said (from Matthew's gospel), 'Consider the lilies of the field, how they grow; they toil not, neither do they spin . . .' " Px 129 at page 363.

The "public school edition" texts written by creationists simply omit Biblical references but the content and message remain the same. For example, *Evolution–The Fossils Say No!,*[32] contains the following:

Creation. By creation we mean the bringing into being by a supernatural Creator of the basic kinds of plants and animals by the process of sudden, or fiat, creation.

We do not know how the Creator created, what processes He used, *for He used processes which are not now operating anywhere in the natural universe.* This is why we refer to creation as Special Creation. We cannot discover by scientific investigation anything about the creative processes used by the Creator."—page 40

Gish's book also portrays the large majority of evolutionists as "materialistic atheists or agnostics."

Scientific Creationism (Public School Edition) by Morris, is another text reviewed by Ms. Wilson's committee and rejected as unacceptable. The following quotes illustrate the purpose and theme of the text:

Foreword

"Parents and youth leaders today, and even many scientists and educators, have become concerned about the prevalence and influence of evolutionary philosophy in modern curriculum. Not only is this system inimical to orthodox Christianity and Judaism, but also, as many are convinced, to a healthy society and true science as well."

at page iii

"The rationalist of course finds the concept of special creation insufferably naive, even 'incredible'. Such a judgment, however, is warranted only if one categorically dismisses the existence of an omnipotent God."
at page 17.

Without using creationist literature, Ms. Wilson was unable to locate one genuinely scientific article or work which supported Section 4(a). In order to comply with the mandate of the Board she used such materials as an article from *Reader's Digest* about "atomic clocks" which inferentially suggested that the earth was less than $4\frac{1}{2}$ billion years old. She was unable to locate any substantive teaching material for some parts of Section 4 such as the worldwide flood. The curriculum guide which she prepared cannot be taught and has no educational value as science. The defendants did not produce any text or writing in response to this evidence which they claimed was usable in the public school classroom.[33]

The conclusion that creation science has no scientific merit or educational value as science has legal significance in light of the Court's previous conclusion that creation science has, as one major effect, the advancement of religion. The second part of the three-pronged test for establishment reaches only those statutes having as their *primary* effect the advancement of religion. Secondary effects which advance religion are not constitutionally fatal. Since creation science is not science, the conclusion is inescapable that the *only* real effect of Act 590 is the advancement of religion. The Act therefore fails both the first and second portions of the test in *Lemon v. Kurtzman,* 403 U.S. 602 (1971).

IV. (E)

Act 590 mandates "balanced treatment" for creation science and evolution science. The Act prohibits instruction in any religious doctrine or references to religious writings. The Act is self-contradictory and compliance is impossible unless the public schools elect to forego significant portions of subjects such as biology, world history, geology, zoology, botany, psychology, anthropology, sociology, philosophy, physics and chemistry. Presently, the concepts of evolutionary theory as described in 4(b) permeate the public school textbooks. There is no way teachers can teach the Genesis account of creation in a secular manner.

The State Department of Education, through its textbook selection committee, school boards and school administrators will be required to constantly monitor materials to avoid using religious references. The school boards, administrators and teachers face an impossible task. How is the teacher to respond to questions about a creation suddenly and out of nothing? How will a teacher explain the occurrence of a worldwide flood? How will a teacher explain the concept of a relatively recent age of the earth? The answer is obvious because the only source of this information is ultimately contained in the Book of Genesis.

References to the pervasive nature of religious concepts in creation science texts amply demonstrate why State entanglement with religion is inevitable under Act 590. Involvement of the State in screening texts for impermissible religious references will require State officials to make delicate religious judgments. The need to monitor classroom discussion in order to uphold the Act's prohibition against religious instruction will necessarily involve administrators in questions concerning religion. These continuing involvements of State officials in questions and issues of religion create an excessive and prohibited entanglement with religion. *Brandon v. Board of Education,* 487 F. Supp 1219, 1230 (N.D.N.Y.), *aff'd.,* 635 F. 2d 971 (2nd Cir. 1980).

V.

These conclusions are dispositive of the case and there is no need to reach legal conclusions with respect to the remaining issues. The plaintiffs raised two other issues questioning the constitutionality of the Act and, insofar as the factual findings relevant to these issues are not covered in the preceding discussion, the Court will address these issues. Additionally, the defendants raised two other issues which warrant discussion.

V. (A)

First, plaintiff teachers argue the Act is unconstitutionally vague to the extent that they cannot comply with its mandate of "balanced" treatment without jeopardizing their employment. The argument centers around the lack of a precise definition in the Act for the word "balanced." Several witnesses expressed opinions that the word has such meanings as equal time, equal weight, or equal legitimacy. Although the Act could have been more explicit, "balanced" is a word subject to ordinary understanding. The proof is not convincing that a teacher using a reasonably acceptable understanding of the word and making a good faith effort to comply with the Act will be in jeopardy of termination. Other portions of the Act are arguably vague, such as the "relatively recent" inception of the earth and life. The evidence establishes, however, that relatively recent means from 6,000 to 20,000 years, as commonly understood in creation science literature. The meaning of this phrase, like Section 4(a) generally, is, for purposes of the Establishment Clause, all too clear.

V. (B)

The plaintiffs' other argument revolves around the alleged infringement by the defendants upon the academic freedom of teachers and students. It is contended this unprecedented intrusion in the curriculum by the State prohibits teachers from teaching what they believe should be taught or requires them to teach that which they do not believe is proper. The evidence reflects that traditionally the State Department of Education, local school boards and administration officials exercise little, if any, influence upon the subject matter taught by classroom teachers. Teachers have been given freedom to teach and emphasize those portions of subjects the individual teacher considered important. The limits to this discretion have generally been derived from the approval of textbooks by the State Department and preparation of curriculum guides by the school districts.

Several witnesses testified that academic freedom for the teacher means, in substance, that the individual teacher should be permitted unlimited discretion subject only to the bounds of professional ethics. The Court is not prepared to adopt such a broad view of academic freedom in the public schools.

In any event, if Act 590 is implemented, many teachers will be required to teach material in support of creation science which they do not consider academically sound. Many teachers will simply forego teaching subjects which might trigger the "balanced treatment" aspects of Act 590 even though they think the subjects are important to a proper presentation of a course.

Implementation of Act 590 will have serious and untoward consequences for students, particularly those planning to attend college. Evolution is the cornerstone of modern biology, and many courses in public schools contain subject matter relating to such varied topics as the age of the earth, geology and relationships among living things. Any student who is deprived of instruction as to the prevailing scientific thought on these topics will be denied a significant part of science education. Such a deprivation through the high school level would undoubtedly have an impact upon the quality of education in the State's colleges and universities, especially including the pre-professional and professional programs in the health sciences.

V. (C)

The defendants argue in their brief that evolution is, in effect, a religion, and that by teaching a religion which is contrary to some students' religious views, the State is infringing upon the student's free exercise rights under the

First Amendment. Mr. Ellwanger's legislative findings, which were adopted as a finding of fact by the Arkansas Legislature in Act 590, provides:

"Evolution-science is contrary to the religious convictions or moral values or philosophical beliefs of many students and parents, including individuals of many different religious faiths and with diverse moral and philosophical beliefs." Act 590, §7(d).

The defendants argue that the teaching of evolution alone presents both a free exercise problem and an establishment problem which can only be redressed by giving balanced treatment to creation science, which is admittedly consistent with some religious beliefs. This argument appears to have its genesis in a student note written by Mr. Wendell Bird, "Freedom of Religion and Science Instruction in Public Schools," 87 Yale L.J. 515 (1978). The argument has no legal merit.

If creation science is, in fact, science and not religion, as the defendants claim, it is difficult to see how the teaching of such a science could "neutralize" the religious nature of evolution.

Assuming for the purposes of argument, however, that evolution is a religion or religious tenet, the remedy is to stop the teaching of evolution; not establish another religion in opposition to it. Yet it is clearly established in the case law, and perhaps also in common sense, that evolution is not a religion and that teaching evolution does not violate the Establishment Clause, *Epperson v. Arkansas, supra, Willoughby v. Stever,* No. 15 574–75 (D.D.C. May 18, 1973); *aff'd.* 504 F. 2d 271 (D.C. Cir. 1974), *cert. denied,* 420 U.S. 924 (1975); *Wright v. Houston Indep. School Dist.,* 366 F. Supp. 1208 (S.D. Tex. 1978), *aff'd.* 486 F. 2d 137 (5th Cir. 1973), *cert. denied* 417 U.S. 969 (1974).

V. (D)

The defendants presented Dr. Larry Parker, a specialist in devising curricula for public schools. He testified that the public school's curriculum should reflect the subjects the public wants taught in schools. The witness said that polls indicated a significant majority of the American public thought creation science should be taught if evolution was taught. The point of this testimony was never placed in a legal context. No doubt a sizeable majority of Americans believe in the concept of a Creator or, at least, are not opposed to the concept and see nothing wrong with teaching school children about the idea.

The application and content of First Amendment principles are not determined by public opinion polls or by a majority vote. Whether the proponents of Act 590 constitute the majority or the minority is quite irrelevant under a constitutional system of government. No group, no matter how large or small, may use the organs of government, of which the public schools are the most conspicuous and influential, to foist its religious beliefs on others.

The Court closes this opinion with a thought expressed eloquently by the great Justice Frankfurter:

> "We renew our conviction that 'we have staked the very existence of our country on the faith that complete separation between the state and religion is best for the state and best for religion.' *Everson v. Board of Education,* 330 U.S. at 59. If nowhere else, in the relation between Church and State, 'good fences make good neighbors.' " *McCollum v. Board of Education,* 333 U.S. 203, 232 (1948).

An injunction will be entered permanently prohibiting enforcement of Act 590.

It is so ordered this January 5, 1982.

William R. Overton
UNITED STATES DISTRICT JUDGE

Appendix XV   Notes

1. The complaint is based on 42 U.S.C. §1983, which provides a remedy against any person who, acting under color of state law, deprives another of any right, privilege or immunity guaranteed by the United States Constitution or federal law.

This Court's jurisdiction arises under 28 U.S.C. §§1331, 1343(3) and 1343(4). The power to issue declaratory judgments is expressed in 28 U.S.C. §§2201 and 2202.

2. The facts necessary to establish the plaintiffs' standing to sue are contained in the joint stipulation of facts, which is hereby adopted and incorporated herein by reference.

There is no doubt that the case is ripe for adjudication.

3. The State of Arkansas was dismissed as a defendant because of its immunity from suit under the Eleventh Amendment. *Hans v. Louisiana,* 134 U.S. 1 (1890).

4. The authorities differ as to generalizations which may be made about Fundamentalism. For example, Dr. Geisler testified to the widely held view that there are five beliefs characteristic of all Fundamentalist movements, in addition, of course, to the inerrancy of Scripture: (1) belief in the virgin birth of Christ, (2) belief in the deity of Christ, (3) belief in the substitutional atonement of Christ, (4) belief in the second coming of Christ, and (5) belief in the physical resurrection of all departed souls. Dr.

Marsden, however, testified that this generalization, which has been common in religious scholarship, is now thought to be historical error. There is no doubt, however, that all Fundamentalists take the Scriptures as inerrant and probably most take them as literally true.

5. Initiated Act 1 of 1929, Ark. Stat. Ann. §80-1627 *et seq.,* which prohibited the teaching of evolution in Arkansas schools, is discussed *infra* at text accompanying note 15.

6. Subsequent references to the testimony will be made by the last name of the witness only. References to documentary exhibits will be by the name of the author and the exhibit number.

7. Applicants for membership in the CRS must subscribe to the following statement of belief: "(1) The Bible is the written Word of God, and because we believe it to be inspired thruout (sic), all of its assertions are historically and scientifically true in all of the original autographs. To the student of nature, this means that the account of origins in Genesis is a factual presentation of simple historical truths. (2) All basic types of living things, including man, were made by direct creative acts of God during Creation Week as described in Genesis. Whatever biological changes have occurred since Creation have accomplished only changes within the original created kinds. (3) The great Flood described in Genesis, commonly referred to as the Noachian Deluge, was an historical event, worldwide in its extent and effect. (4) Finally, we are an organization of Christian men of science, who accept Jesus Christ as our Lord and Savior. The account of the special creation of Adam and Eve as one man and one woman, and their subsequent Fall into sin, is the basis for our belief in the necessity of a Savior for all mankind. Therefore, salvation can come only thru (sic) accepting Jesus Christ as our Savior." (Px 115)

8. Because of the voluminous nature of the documentary exhibits, the parties were directed by pre-trial order to submit their proposed exhibits for the Court's convenience prior to trial. The numbers assigned to the pre-trial submissions do not correspond with those assigned to the same documents at trial and, in some instances, the pre-trial submissions are more complete.

9. Px 130, Morris, *Introducing Scientific Creationism Into the Public Schools* (1975), and Bird, "Resolution for Balanced Presentation of Evolution and Scientific Creationism," *ICR Impact Series* No. 71, App. 14 to Plaintiffs' Pretrial Brief.

10. The creationists often show candor in their proselytization. Henry Morris has stated, "Even if a favorable statute or court decision is obtained, it will probably be declared unconstitutional, especially if the legislation or injunction refers to the Bible account of creation." In the same vein he notes, "The only effective way to get creationism taught properly is to have it taught by teachers who are both willing and able to do it. Since most teachers now are neither willing nor able, they must first be both persuaded and instructed themselves." Px 130, Morris, *Introducing Scientific Creationism Into the Public Schools* (1975) (unpaged).

11. Mr. Bird sought to participate in this litigation by representing a number of individuals who wanted to intervene as defendants. The application for intervention was denied by this Court. *McLean v. Arkansas,*——F. Supp.,——(B.D. Ark. 1981), *aff'd. per curiam,* Slip Op. No. 81-2023 (8th Cir. Oct. 16, 1981).

12. The model act had been revised to insert "creation science" in lieu of cre-

ationism because Ellwanger had the impression people thought creationism was too religious a term. (Ellwanger Depo. at 79.)

13. The original model act had been introduced in the South Carolina Legislature, but had died without action after the South Carolina Attorney General had opined that the act was unconstitutional.

14. Specifically, Senator Holsted testified that he holds to a literal interpretation of the Bible; that the bill was compatible with his religious beliefs; that the bill does favor the position of literalists; that his religious convictions were a factor in his sponsorship of the bill; and that he stated publicly to the *Arkansas Gazette* (although not on the floor of the Senate) contemporaneously with the legislative debate that the bill does presuppose the existence of a divine creator. There is no doubt that Senator Holsted knew he was sponsoring the teaching of a religious doctrine. His view was that the bill did not violate the First Amendment because, as he saw it, it did not favor one denomination over another.

15. This statute is, of course, clearly unconstitutional under the Supreme Court's decision in *Abbington School Dist. v. Schempp,* 374 U.S. 203 (1963).

16. The joint stipulation of facts establishes that the following areas are the only *information* specifically required by statute to be taught in all Arkansas schools: (1) the effects of alcohol and narcotics on the human body, (2) conservation of national resources, (3) Bird Week, (4) Fire Prevention, and (5) Flag etiquette. Additionally, certain specific courses, such as American history and Arkansas history, must be completed by each student before graduation from high school.

17. Paul Ellwanger stated in his deposition that he did not know why Section 4(a)(2) (insufficiency of mutation and natural selection) was included as an evidence supporting creation science. He indicated that he was not a scientist, "but these are the postulates that have been laid down by creation scientists." Ellwanger Depo. at 136.

18. Although defendants must make some effort to cast the concept of creation in non-religious terms, this effort surely causes discomfort to some of the Act's more theologically sophisticated supporters. The concept of a creator God distinct from the God of love and mercy is closely similar to the Marcion and Gnostic heresies, among the deadliest to threaten the early Christian church. These heresies had much to do with development and adoption of the Apostle's Creed as the official creedal statement of the Roman Catholic Church in the West. (Gilkey.)

19. The parallels between Section 4(a) and Genesis are quite specific: (1) "sudden creation from nothing" is taken from Genesis, 1:1–10 (Vawter, Gilkey); (2) destruction of the world by a flood of divine origin is a notion peculiar to Judeo-Christian tradition and is based on Chapters 7 and 8 of Genesis (Vawter); (3) the term "kinds" has no fixed scientific meaning, but appears repeatedly in Genesis (all scientific witnesses); (4) "relatively recent inception" means an age of the earth from 6,000 to 10,000 years and is based on the genealogy of the Old Testament using the rather astronomical ages assigned to the patriarchs (Gilkey and several of defendants' scientific witnesses); (5) Separate ancestry of man and ape focuses on the portion of the theory of evolution which Fundamentalists find most offensive, *Epperson v. Arkansas,* 393 U.S. 97 (1968).

20. "[C]oncepts concerning . . . a supreme being of some sort are manifestly

religious. . . . These concepts do not shed that religiosity merely because they are presented as philosophy or as a science. . . . " *Malnak v. Yogi,* 440 F. Supp. 1284, 1322 (D.N.J. 1977); *aff'd per curiam,* 592 F. 2d 197 (3d Cir. 1979).

21. See, e.g., Px 76, Morris, *et al, Scientific Creationism,* 203 (1980) ("If creation really is a fact, this means there is a *Creator,* and the universe is His creation.") Numerous other examples of such admissions can be found in the many exhibits which represent creationist literature, but no useful purpose would be served here by a potentially endless listing.

22. Morris, the Director of ICR and one who first advocated the two model approach, insists that a true Christian cannot compromise with the theory of evolution and that the Genesis version of creation and the theory of evolution are mutually exclusive. Px 31, Morris, *Studies in the Bible & Science,* 102–103. The two model approach was the subject of Dr. Richard Bliss's doctoral dissertation. (Dx 35). It is presented in Bliss, *Origins: Two Models-Evolution, Creation* (1978). Moreover, the two model approach merely casts in educationalist language the dualism which appears in all creationist literature—creation (i.e. God) and evolution are presented as two alternative and mutually exclusive theories. See, e.g., Px 75, Morris, *Scientific Creationism* (1974) (public school edition); Px 59, Fox, *Fossils: Hard Facts from the Earth.* Particularly illustrative is PX 61, Boardman, *et al, Worlds Without End* (1971), a CSRC publication: "One group of scientists, known as creationists, believe that God, in a miraculous manner, created all matter and energy. . . .

"Scientists who insist that the universe just grew, by accident, from a mass of hot gases without the direction or help of a Creator are known as evolutionists."

23. The idea that belief in a creator and acceptance of the scientific theory of evolution are mutually exclusive is a false premise and offensive to the religious views of many. (Hicks) Dr. Francisco Ayala, a geneticist of considerable renown and a former Catholic priest who has the equivalent of a Ph.D. in theology, pointed out that many working scientists who subscribed to the theory of evolution are devoutly religious.

24. This is so despite the fact that some of the defense witnesses do not subscribe to the young earth or flood hypotheses. Dr. Geisler stated his belief that the earth is several billion years old. Dr. Wickramasinghe stated that no rational scientist would believe the earth is less than one million years old or that all the world's geology could be explained by a worldwide flood.

25. "We do not know how God created, what processes He used, for *God used processes which are not now operating anywhere in the natural universe.* This is why we refer to divine creation as Special Creation. We cannot discover by scientific investigation anything about the creative processes used by God." Px 78, Gish, *Evolution? The Fossils Say No!,* 42 (3d ed. 1979) (emphasis in original).

26. The evolutionary notion that man and some modern apes have a common ancestor somewhere in the distant past has consistently been distorted by anti-evolutionists to say that man descended from modern monkeys. As such, this idea has long been most offensive to Fundamentalists. See, *Epperson v. Arkansas,* 393 U.S. 97 (1968).

27. Not only was this point acknowledged by virtually all the defense witnesses, it is patent in the creationist literature. See, e.g., Px 89, Kofahl & Segraves, *The*

Creation Explanation, 40: "The Flood of Noah brought about vast changes in the earth's surface, including vulcanism, mountain building, and the deposition of the major part of sedimentary strata. This principle is called 'Biblical catastrophism.' "

28. See n. 7, *supra,* for the full text of the CRS creed.

29. The theory is detailed in Wickramasinghe's book with Sir Fred Hoyle, *Evolution From Space* (1981), which is Dx 79.

30. Ms. Wilson stated that some professors she spoke with sympathized with her plight and tried to help her find scientific materials to support Section 4(a). Others simply asked her to leave.

31. Px 129, published by Zonderman Publishing House (1974), states that it was "prepared by the Textbook Committee of the Creation Research Society." It has a disclaimer pasted inside the front cover stating that it is not suitable for use in public schools.

32. Px 77, by Duane Gish.

33. The passage of Act 590 apparently caught a number of its supporters off guard as much as it did the school district. The Act's author, Paul Ellwanger, stated in a letter to "Dick," (apparently Dr. Richard Bliss at ICR): "And finally, if you know of any textbooks at any level and for any subjects that you think are acceptable to you and also constitutionally admissible, these are things that would be of *enormous* help to these bewildered folks who may be caught, as Arkansas now has been, by the sudden need to implement a whole new ball game with which they are quite unfamiliar." (sic) (Unnumbered attachment to Ellwanger depo.)

Berossos, W-B Text 444, and the Pre-Diluvian Ages in Genesis 5

IN CHAPTER IV (section 2) it was proposed that the total elapsed time from creation to the flood (1656 years in MT; see Table No. 8) had been derived by modification of the Sumerian King List (the total years of reign as recorded by the Babylonian priest Berossos; (see Table No. 6). This was done by dividing the Mesopotamian figure into periods of five years (a lustrum), then treating each of them as if it were a week. Thus, Berossos' total of 432,000 years yields: (432,000 ÷ 5) lustra × 7 days/week ÷ 365.25 days/year = 1655.85 years (i.e. the 1656 years of Genesis 5). This conversion can more simply be done by remembering that 6,000 years in Berossos is equivalent to 23 years in Genesis, or by multiplying a number in Berossos by 0.003833.

While such a conversion seems to explain the total of elapsed time, it is not the case with the derivation of the ages of parents at the time of first-born. Otherwise put: Berossos' first monarch is Alulim, who reigned for 36,000 years. Converted by the formula above, this would be 138 years, which does not correspond to the age of Adam when Seth was born (130 years) or to any other parent in the list. This suggests (as was pointed out above, Chapter IV, Section 2) that the total of elapsed time was computed separately from that of individual ages. The latter were designed to "fit" the prior total figure, with several possibilities for explaining one or more of them. One suggestion was that groups of ages (at time of first-born) might be related to Berossos' figures. Justification of this statement now follows.

Note that the elapsed time between births drops without exception from Adam through Mahalalel (Table No. 5): 130, 105, 90, 70, and 65 years. Then, at the time of Jared, the trend is reversed: 162 years, an all-time high, pass before the birth of Enoch. The figure is still higher for Methuselah (187 years), then drops off. This may indicate that, in a lost narrative about these patriarchs (or their Mesopotamian prototypes), there was a "happening" of some sort: a new situation or condition of humanity which affected the birth rate.[1] This possibility is supported by the fact that the total of elapsed time for parenting, Adam-Mahalalel, is 460 years. This is not an intelligible unit of time, in biblical terms (i.e. not divisible by 60, 40, 12, or 7, the standard "symbolic" numbers). When converted to a Mesopotamian equivalent (original?), in accordance with the formula outlined above, however, the result is 120,000 years (20 periods of 6,000 years each). One is alerted to this possibility more quickly by noting that 460 is a multiple of 23 (20 × 23 years).

One might then look for other blocks of ages that are divisible by 23, and the next three patriarchs are an immediate candidate, just as they should be if there is a transition at that point. The total for Jared (162), Enoch (65), and Methuselah (187) is 414 years, which is (18 × 23), or 108,000 in the Mesopotamian equivalency.

The remaining figures, Lamech (182), Noah (500), and Shem (100 to the time of the flood) total 782 years: (34 × 23), or 204,000 in the Mesopotamian system.

There are, then, three periods of time for the pre-diluvians, discoverable only if the figures were derived from a Mesopotamian prototype. Oppert (1903) was probably right when he remarked: "The three periods correspond to legends now altogether lost" (p. 66).

It would be nice, of course, and confirmation of the proposal, if there were groups of monarchs within the King List whose total length of reign corresponded to the aforementioned biblical figures. In one case, there is such a confirmation, and for the same number of individuals: Alulim, Dumuzi, and Ensipazianna reigned for 36,000 each, a total 108,000 years, comparable to Jared, Enoch, and Methuselah's figures (above). The two remaining groups from Genesis are close to sub-totals in Berossos, but not quite: (1) the 120,000 years of Genesis (Adam-Mahalalel) approximates 118,800 for Alalgar, Enmengalanna, and Ammenon; and (2) the 204,000 of Genesis (for Lamech-Shem) approximates 205,200 for Enmenluanna, Evedoragxos, Ubartutu, and Ziusudra.

The biblical text gives two ages for the pre-diluvians: time between generations (used above to compute elapsed time), and the lifespan (age at death). Correspondence with Mesopotamian data has, thus far, centered upon the former. Is there a similar connection for the latter? Otherwise put: How was it decided that Adam lived a total of 930 years (see Table No. 8)? The source cannot be Berossos' figures, since they have been utilized already. A possibility to be investigated would be the other versions of the King List: Weld-Blundell Texts 62 and 444 (see Table No. 6). A quick test to determine candidacy would be to divide the Genesis ages by 23 (as previously discussed). None of them "fits" for an individual age, just as they did not for age-at-time-of-first-born. What, however, about overall totals, e.g. 9175 years in MT? There would be a basic difference, of course, since the King List means for its reigns (figures) to be consecutive whereas Genesis means for its lifespans to overlap. Nonetheless, Oppert (1903) has observed that an MT total of 9177 years[2] conforms to the scheme (being 399×23). This would suggest a Mesopotamian prototype of 2,394,000 years (or $60^2 \times 655$). He goes on to observe that the total of lifespans from Adam to Jacob is 12,075 years (525×23), or 3,150,000 ($60^2 \times 875$) in the Mesopotamian system. Such fantastic figures may be compared with the Babylonian reckoning of 215 myriads of time (10,000 years each) from the beginning of the world to the time of Alexander the Great, being 2,150,000 years (curiously, not a multiple of 60^2).

A more interesting possibility emerges when comparison is made with W-B Text 444. While its total conforms to the sexagesimal system (241,200 being $60^2 \times 67$), it does not conform to the conversion formula outlined above (yielding a mere 925 years rather than 9175/9177). However, Walton (1981) has proposed a different conversion formula. He correctly observes that W-B 444 lists eight generations (whereas the other two versions list ten). This conforms, incidentally, to the parallel genealogy in Genesis 4: eight generations from Adam to Lamech, omitting the flood-hero Noah (just as W-B 444 does not include the flood-hero Ziusudra). See Table No. 21. Walton proposes that the proper parallel in Genesis 5 would be to omit Adam's 930 years (since W-B 444 does not suggest "that it begins with the first man") as well as Noah-Shem's 1550, leaving a total of 6695 (which he "rounds off" to 6700).[3] One may then observe the following correspondence: W-B's $241,200 = 67 \times 60^2$, and Genesis 5's $6700 = 67 \times 10^2$. To him, this suggests that an antecedent (ancestor) text gave rise to ambiguity: ". . . a scribe read a perhaps ambiguous notation as one number system (e.g. sexagesimal) when the document actually intended the other system (e.g. decimal)." That is, suppose the sign "Z" represents 10^2 in one system (base-10 system which the Bible usually uses) and 60^2 in another (sexagesimal). Then (according to Walton's system) ZZ would be either $10^3 + 10^2$ (i.e. 1100) or $(60^2 \times 10) + 60^2$ (i.e. 39,600). That is, place-notation increases by a multiple of 10 in each system. (Unfortunately, however, this does not conform to the Mesopotamian way of reading such sequences.)

For them, ZZ would be $60^3 + 60^2$ (i.e. 219,600). It is more likely, therefore, that the biblical figures are a deliberate modification (reduction), as was the case with ages at first-born, rather than an accident resulting from ambiguity in writing. It would amount to dividing the Mesopotamian figure by 36 (6×6).

TABLE 21. Sequence of Names in Pre-Diluvian Genealogies

	Genesis 4	Genesis 5	Sumerian King List (W–B 444, the prism)	Sumerian King List (W–B 62)	Berossos
1.	Adam	Adam ("Man")—Seth	alulim	alulim	Aloros
2.	Cain (Qayin) Seth	Enosh—Enosh ("Man") Kenan (Qenan)	Alalgar	Alalgar ...kidunnu	Alaparos
		Mahalalel Yared	Enmenluanna	...alima	Ammelon Ammenon
			Enmengalanna		Ammegalanos
			Dumuzi	Dumuzi Emmenluanna	Daonos poimen
3.	Enoch	Enoch			Evedoragxos
4.	'Irad				
5.	Mehuya'el				
6.	Metuša'el	Metušelah	Ensipazianna	Ensipazianna	Amempsinos
7.	Lamech	Lamech	Enmendurana	Enmendurana	
8.	Jabal/Jubal/Tubal		Ubartutu	Ubartutu	Otiartas
9.					
10.		Noah	Ziusudra	Ziusudra	Xisouthros

THE FLOOD

Once the sum of the lifespans was determined in one of the fashions outlined above (Oppert vs. Walton, or some other), then individual ages were set in order to reach that pre-determined total. Some of the factors in those decisions are suggested above (Chapter IV, Section 2).

Appendix XVI   Notes

1. Such descriptions may be found in the King List for the post-flood monarchs and in the genealogy in Genesis 4.

2. The total accumulation in Genesis 5 is 9175 years (Table No. 8). There is, however, a tension with Genesis 11:10, where Shem becomes a father "two years after the flood" rather than before it. It is the latter tradition (yielding 9177 years) that "fits" the Mesopotamian prototype pointed out by Oppert. (Still, the one year duration of the flood is ignored.) On the tension cited, see Cryer (1985).

3. It might be preferable, in terms of genealogies of eight generations (W-B 444 and Genesis 4), to wonder if the earliest genealogy in Genesis 5 began with Enosh (yielding a parallel with W-B 444). Curiously, the Hebrew word *enosh* means "human being; man," as does *adam*. This may suggest that two genealogies have been combined in the course of Israel's sociological growth (uniting of various "tribes"), each tracing history back to the "first" human. In the final union, one first human (*adam*) becomes the grandfather of the other first human (*enosh*). In such a case, the total of lifespans from Enosh through Noah is 6733 (still to be rounded off to 6700?).

ESSENTIAL BIBLIOGRAPHY

I. *In order to understand "creationism":*

Morris, Henry M. *The Genesis Record.* San Diego: Creation-Life Publishers, 1976. Although not addressed to defining biblical creationism per se, this is an excellent example of how that approach works out in practice as the author comments upon the biblical text in a seriatim fashion.

Morris, Henry M., and Gary E. Parker. *What Is Creation Science?* San Diego: Creation-Life Publishers, Inc., 1982.

II. *In order to evaluate scientific "creationism":*

Kitcher, Philip. *Abusing Science.* Cambridge: The MIT Press, 1982. A wide-ranging, penetrating denunciation.

Strahler, Arthur N. *Science and Earth History: The Evolution/Creation Controversy.* Buffalo: Prometheus Books, 1987. Astonishing in its range of coverage and informed contents (552 pages); filled with illustrations; *must* reading.

Van Till, Howard J. *The Fourth Day.* Grand Rapids: William B. Eerdmans Publishing Company, 1986. Focuses upon astronomical and geological issues.

Van Till, Howard J., Davis A. Young, and Clarence Menninga. *Science Held Hostage: What's Wrong with Creation Science and Evolutionism.* Downers Grove: InterVarsity Press, 1988. Expertly and clearly written.

Wonderly, Daniel E. *Neglect of Geological Data: Sedimentary Strata Compared with Young-Earth Creationist Writings.* Hatfield: Interdisciplinary Biblical Research Institute, 1987.

Young, Davis A. *Christianity and the Age of the Earth.* Grand Rapids: Zondervan Publishing House, 1982.

III. *In order to understand the legal history of the anti-evolution movement:*

Larson, Edward J. *Trial and Error: The American Controversy Over Creation And Evolution.* New York: Oxford University Press, 1985.

IV. *In order to understand how modern historical-critical scholars*
interpret the text of Genesis:

Anderson, Bernhard W. (ed.). *Creation in the Old Testament.* Philadelphia: Fortress Press, 1984.
Bailey, Lloyd R. *The Pentateuch.* Nashville: Abingdon Press, 1981.
Hyers, Conrad. *The Meaning of Creation: Genesis and Modern Science.* Atlanta: John Knox Press, 1984.

V. *In order to understand the history of Christian thought*
about creation and evolution:

Frye, Roland Mushat (ed.). *Is God a Creationist? The Religious Case Against Creation-Science.* New York: Charles Scribner's Sons, 1983.
McMullin, Ernman (ed.). *Evolution and Creation.* Notre Dame: University of Notre Dame Press, 1985.

VI. *In order to understand how astronomers view the beginning of the universe:*

Weinberg, Steven. *The First Three Minutes.* Updated edition. New York: Basic Books, Inc., 1988.

BIBLIOGRAPHY OF
SOURCES CITED

(excluding *IDB, IDBS, IB, IO-VC,* and *JBC* articles)

Acts and Facts. "Evolutionists Attack ICR and Creation-in-School Movement," Vol. IX, No. 5 (May 1980).

———. "The ICR Position on Creationist Litigation and Legislation," Vol. X, No. 5 (May 1981).

———. "ICR Graduate School under Attack!" Vol. XVIII, No. 2 (February 1989).

———. "Nova Program Attacks Creationism," Vol. XVIII, No. 4 (April 1989).

Albright, William F. "The Mouth of the Two Rivers," *American Journal of Semitic Language,* XXXV (1919), 161–195.

———. "Mesopotamian Elements in Canaanite Eschatology," *Oriental Studies Dedicated to Paul Haupt.* Baltimore: Johns Hopkins Press, 1926, 143–154.

———. "The Canaanite God Hauron (Horon)," *American Journal of Semitic Language,* LXXX (1936), 1–12.

———. *Archaeology and the Religion of Israel.* Baltimore: Johns Hopkins Press, 1956.

Archer, Gleason L. *A Survey of Old Testament Introduction.* Chicago: Moody Press, 1974.

Armstrong, Herbert W. *Did God Create a Devil?* Pasadena: Worldwide Church of God, 1978.

———. *Mystery of the Ages.* Pasadena: Worldwide Church of God, 1985.

Armstrong, John Reginald. "The Evolution of Creationism," *Earth Sciences History,* VII, No. 2 (1988), 151–158.

Awbrey, Frank. "Evidence of the Quality of Creation Science Research," *Creation/Evolution,* II (Fall 1980), 40–43.

———. "Space Dust, the Moon's Surface, and the Age of the Cosmos," *Creation/Evolution,* XIII (Summer 1983), 21–29.

Awbrey, Frank T., and William M. Thwaites. "A Closer Look at Some Biochemical Data That 'Support' Creation," *Creation/Evolution,* VII (Winter 1982), 14–17.

Badash, Lawrence. "The Age-of-the-Earth Debate," *Scientific American,* 261, No. 2 (August 1989), 90–96.

Bailey, Lloyd R. *Biblical Perspectives on Death.* Philadelphia: Fortress Press, 1979.

———. *The Pentateuch.* Nashville: Abingdon Press, 1981.

————. "Words and the Translator," *Word and World,* VI (1986), 266–277.

————. *Leviticus.* Atlanta: John Knox Press, 1987.

————. *Noah: The Person and the Story in History and Tradition.* Columbia: University of South Carolina Press, 1989.

Baumgarten, Albert I. *The Phoenician History of Philo of Byblos.* Leiden: E.J. Brill, 1981.

Behm, Johannes. *Die mandäische Religion und das Christentum.* Leipzig: A. Deichert, 1927.

Bird, Wendell. "The Supreme Court Decision and Its Meaning," ICR *Impact* No. 170 (August 1987).

Bliss, Richard B. "Good Science: A K-6 Plan for Excellence," ICR *Impact* No. 182 (August 1988).

Böckh, August. *Manetho und die Hundssternperiode.* Berlin: Veit and Co., 1838.

Brown, Raymond E. *The Birth of the Messiah.* Garden City: Image Books, 1979.

Burnham, Robert, Jr. *Burnham's Celestial Handbook.* Volume Three. New York: Dover Publications, Inc., 1978.

Burstein, Stanley Mayer. *The Babyloniaca of Berossus.* Malibu (California): Undena Publications, 1978.

Bush, S.G. "Finding the Age of the Earth: By Physics or by Faith?" *Journal of Geological Education,* 30 (1982), nv.

Cassuto, Umberto. *Commentary on Genesis,* I. Jerusalem: Magnes Press, 1961.

Castellino, G.R. "Les origines de la civilisation selon les textes bibliques et les textes cuneiformes," *Supplements to Vetus Testamentum,* IV (1957), 116–137.

Charles, R.H. *A Critical History of the Doctrine of a Future Life in Israel.* 2nd edition. London: A. and C. Black, 1913.

Chwolson, Daniel. *Die Ssabier und der Ssabismus.* 2 vols. St. Petersburgh: Buchdruckerei der Kaiserlichen Akademie der Wissenschaften, 1856.

Clements, Ronald Ernest. *God and Temple.* Oxford: B. Blackwell, 1965.

Cole, John R. "Misquoted Scientists Respond," *Creation/Evolution,* VI (Fall, 1981), 34–44.

Cole, John R., and Laurie R. Godfrey (eds.). "The Paluxy River Footprint Mystery—Solved," Special Issue of *Creation/Evolution* (XV; Vol. 5, No. 1), 1–56.

Cook, A.B. *Zeus.* 3 vols. Cambridge: Cambridge University Press, 1914.

Cox, Harvey. *The Secular City.* New York: Macmillan Paperback, 1965.

"Creationism in Schools: The Decision in McLean versus the Arkansas Board of Education," *Science,* 215 (February 19, 1982), 934–943.

Cross, F.M. "The Council of Yahweh in Second Isaiah," *Journal of Near Eastern Studies,* XII (1953), 274–277.

Cryer, Frederick H. "The Interrelationships of Gen. 5, 32; 11, 10–11 and the Chronology of the Flood (Gen. 6–9)," *Biblica,* 66 (1985), 241–261.

Cumont, Franz. "L'aigle funéraire des Syriens et l'apothéose des empereurs," *Revue de l'histoire des religions,* LXII (1910), 119–164.

————. *After Life in Roman Paganism.* New York: Dover Publications, Inc., 1959.

Dalrymple, G.B. *Radiometric Dating, Geological Time, and the Age of the Earth: A Reply to "Scientific Creationism."* Menlo Park: U.S. Geological Survey, 1986.

Dalrymple, G.B., and M.A. Lanphere. *Potassium-Argon Dating.* San Francisco: W.H. Freeman, 1969.

Deimel, Antonius. *Pantheon Babylonicum.* Roma: Sumptibus Pontificii Instituti Biblici, 1914.

Delitzsch, Franz. *A New Commentary on Genesis.* Translated by Sophia Taylor. Edinburgh: T. and T. Clark, 1899.

Driver, G.R. *Semitic Writing From Pictograph to Alphabet.* London: The British Academy, 1948.

Edwords, Frederick. "Creation-Evolution Debates: Who's Winning Them Now?" *Creation/Evolution,* VIII (Spring 1982), 30–42.

————. "Victory in Arkansas: The Trial, Decision, and Aftermath," *Creation/Evolution,* VII (Winter 1982), 33–45.

Eichrodt, Walther. "In the Beginning: A Contribution to the Interpretation of the First Word of the Bible," in *Creation in the Old Testament* (Bernhard W. Anderson, ed.). Philadelphia: Fortress Press, 1984, 65–73.

Eliade, Mircea. *The Sacred and the Profane.* New York: Harper Torchbooks, 1961.

————. *Patterns in Comparative Religion.* Cleveland and New York: Meridian Books, 1963.

Faure, Gunter. *Principles of Isotope Geology.* New York: John Wiley and Sons, 2nd edition, 1986.

Ferris, Timothy. *The Red Shift.* New York: Quill, 1983 (*nv*).

Fleay, F.G. *Egyptian Chronology.* London: David Nutt, 1899.

Frankfort, Henri, *et al. Before Philosophy.* Baltimore: Penguin Books (no date).

Frye, Roland Mushat. "The Religious Case Against Creation-Science," *Reports from the Center,* Number 1. Princeton: Center of Theological Inquiry, 1983. (Apparently a fascicle of the volume, *Is God a Creationist?*)

Gardner, Martin. "Modern Creationism's Debt to George McCready Price," *The Skeptical Inquirer,* X, No. 3 (Spring 1986), 202–205.

Gaster, Theodor H. "Myth and Story," *Numen,* I (1954), 184–212.

————. *Thespis.* Garden City: Doubleday Anchor Books, 1961.

————. *Myth, Legend, and Custom in the Old Testament.* New York: Harper and Row, 1969.

Gilkey, Langdon. "The Creationist Issue: A Theologian's View," *Cosmology and Theology* (David Tracy and Nicholas Lash, eds.). *Concilium: Religion in the Eighties.* New York: Seabury Press, 1983, 55–69.

Ginzberg, Louis. *The Legends of the Jews.* 7 vols. Philadelphia: The Jewish Publication Society of America, 1946–1947.

Gish, Duane T. "The Arkansas Decision on Creation-Science," ICR *Impact* No. 105 (March 1982).

————. "It Is Either 'In the Beginning, God'—or . . . 'Hydrogen,' " *Christianity Today,* XXVI, No. 16 (October 8, 1982), pp. 28–33.

Gish, Duane T., and Richard B. Bliss. "Summary of Scientific Evidence for Creation," ICR *Impact* No. 96 (June 1981). See also No. 95 (May 1981).

Glueck, Nelson. *Deities and Dolphins.* New York: Farrar, Straus and Giroux, 1965.

Gould, Stephen J. "The Return of Hopeful Monster," *Natural History,* LXXXVI, No. 6 (June–July 1977), 22, 24, 28, 30.

————. "Is a New and General Theory of Evolution Emerging?" *Paleobiology,* VI, No. 1 (Winter 1980), 119–130.

————. "The Verdict on Creationism," *The Skeptical Inquirer,* XII, No. 2 (Winter 1987–1988), 184–187.

Gould, Stephen J., and Niles Eldridge. "Punctuated equilibria: the tempo and mode of evolution reconsidered," *Paleobiology,* III, No. 2 (Spring 1977), 115–151.

Gray, John. "The Hebrew Conception of the Kingship of God," *Vetus Testamentum,* VI (1956), 268–285.

Gunkel, Herman. *Schopfung und Chaos in Urzeit und Endzeit,* 1895.

Haldar Alfred O. *The Notion of the Desert in Sumero-Akkadian and West Semitic Religions.* Uppsala, 1950.

Ham, Ken. "Five Vital Questions To Ask Your Church Or School," ICR *Back to Genesis* (May 1989).

Harrison, Roland Kenneth. *Introduction to the Old Testament.* Grand Rapids: William B. Eerdmans, 1969.

Hastings, Ronnie J. "Tracking Those Incredible Creationists—The Trail Goes On," *Creation/Evolution,* XXI (1987).

Heidel, Alexander. *The Babylonian Genesis.* Chicago: Phoenix Books, 1951.

————. *The Gilgamesh Epic and Old Testament Parallels.* Chicago: Phoenix Books, 1963.

Helck, Wolfgang. *Untersuchungen zu Manetho und den ägyptischen Königsslisten.* Berlin: Akademie Verlag, 1956.

Hoffner, Harry. "Second Millennium Antecedents to the Hebrew *'ÔB,*" *Journal of Biblical Literature,* LXXXVI (1967), 385–401.

Hooke, Samuel Henry. *The Labyrinth.* New York: Macmillan Co., 1935.

Hoyle, Fred. "The Steady State Universe," in *The Universe, a Scientific American Book.* New York: Simon and Schuster, 1956, 1957, 77–86.

Hughes, Stuart W. "Textbook Publishers Face Scientists and Educators," *Creation/Evolution,* XII (Spring 1983), 33–34.

Humber, Paul G. "The Ascent of Racism," ICR *Impact* No. 164 (February 1987).

————. "Hitler's Evolution Versus Christian Resistance," ICR *Impact* No. 181 (September 1988).

Hyers, Conrad. *The Meaning of Creation: Genesis and Modern Science.* Atlanta: John Knox Press, 1984.

Jacobsen, Thorkild. *The Sumerian King List.* Assyriological Studies No. 11. Chicago: University Press, 1939.

Jastrow, Morris, Jr. *The Religion of Babylonia and Assyria.* Boston: Ginn and Company, 1898.

Jensen, Peter. *Die Kosmologie der Babylonier,* 1890.

Jepsen, Afred. "Zur Chronologie des Priesterkodex," *Zeitschrift für die Alttestamentliche Wissenschaft,* 47 (1929), 251–255.

Johanson, Donald C. "Ethiopia Yields First 'Family' of Early Man," *National Geographic,* 150 (December 1976), 790–811.

Johanson, D.C., and Maitland A. Edey. *Lucy: The Beginnings of Humankind.* New York: Simon and Schuster, 1981.

John Paul II, Pope. Address to Scientists and Members of the Pontifical Academy of Sciences. *Origins,* 11, No. 18 (October 15, 1981), 277, 279.

Jonas, Hans. *The Gnostic Religion.* Boston: Beacon Press, 2nd edition, 1963.

Journal of the General Convention of the Protestant Episcopal Church in the United States of America . . . 1982.

Kitcher, Philip. *Abusing Science.* Cambridge: The MIT Press, 1982.

Knaub, Clete, and Gary Parker. "Molecular Evolution?" ICR *Impact* No. 114 (December 1982).

Koestler, Arthur. "Is Man's Brain an Evolutionary Mistake?" *Horizon,* X, No. 2 (Spring 1968), 34–43.

Kramer, Samuel Noah. "Dilmun, the Land of the Living," *Bulletin of the American Schools of Oriental Research,* XCVI (1944), 18–28.

———. *The Sumerians.* Chicago: University Press, 1963.

Kraus, David. "The New York Creation Battle," *Creation/Evolution,* II (Fall 1980), pp. 8–9.

Kugler, Franz Xaver. *Sternkunde und Sterndienst im Babel.* 2 vols. Münster: Aschendorff, 1907–1924.

Lambert, W.G., and A.R. Millard. *Atra-hasis: The Babylonian Story of the Flood.* Oxford: Clarendon Press, 1969.

Larson, Edward J. *Trial and Error: The American Controversy Over Creation and Evolution.* New York: Oxford University Press, 1985.

Lehmann, Manfred. "A New Interpretation of the Term שׁדּמות," *Vetus Testamentum,* III (1953), 361–371.

Lewy, Hildegard. "The Babylonian Background of the Kay Kâûs Legend," *Archiv Orientální,* XVII, No. 3–4 (1949), 28–109.

———. "Origin and Significance of the Mâgên Dâwîd," *Archiv Orientální,* XVIII, No. 3 (1950), 330–365.

Lewy, Julius, and Hildegard Lewy. "The Origin of the Week and the Oldest West Asiatic Calendar," *Hebrew Union College Annual,* 17 (1942–43), 1–152.

Lewy, Julius. "Old Assyrian Ḥusârum and Sanchunyâtôn's Story about Chusor," *Israel Exploration Journal,* 5 (1955), 154–162.

Lidzbarski, Mark. *Das Johannesbuch der Mandäer.* 2 vols. Giessen: A. Topelmann, 1905–1915.

Lieberman, Stephen J. "A Mesopotamian Background for the So-Called *Aggadic* 'Measures' in Biblical Hermeneutics?" *Hebrew Union College Annual,* 58 (1987), 157–225.

Lightfoot, John. *The Whole Works of the Rev. John Lightfoot, D.D.* (ed. John Rogers Pitman). Volume II. London: J.F. Dove, 1822.

Manetho. Loeb Classical Library. Cambridge: Harvard University Press, 1940.

McIver, Tom. "Formless and Void: Gap Theory Creationism," *Creation/Evolution,* XXIV (Fall 1988), 1–36.

Meissner, Bruno. *Babylonien und Assyrien.* Vol. II. Heidelberg: Carl Winters Universität Buchhandlung, 1925.

Minutes of the General Assembly of the United Presbyterian Church in the United States of America. Part I, Journal of the One Hundred and Ninety-Fourth General Assembly, Seventh Series, Volume XVI (1982).

Montgomery, James. "The Holy City and Gehenna," *Journal of Biblical Literature,* XXVII (1908), 24–47.

Moore, George Foot. *Judaism,* I. Cambridge: Harvard University University Press, 1927.

Moore, John N. "The Impact of Evolution on the Social Sciences," ICR *Impact* No. 52 (October 1977). Continued in No. 53 (November 1977).

Morris Henry M. *Biblical Cosmology and Modern Science.* Grand Rapids: Baker Book House, 1970.

———. *The Remarkable Birth of Planet Earth.* San Diego: Creation-Life Publishers, 1972.

———. *Scientific Creationism.* General Edition. San Diego: Creation-Life Publishers, 1974 (*nv*).

———. *The Troubled Waters of Evolution.* San Diego: Creation-Life Publishers, 1974 (*nv*).

———. *The Genesis Record.* San Diego: Creation-Life Publishers, 1976.

———. "The Religion of Evolutionary Humanism and the Public Schools," ICR *Impact* No. 51 (September 1977).

———. "Thermodynamics And The Origin of Life," ICR *Impact* Nos. 57 (March 1978) and 58 (April 1978).

———. "Revolutionary Evolutionism," ICR *Impact* No. 77 (November 1979).

———. "The Tenets of Creationism," ICR *Impact* No. 85 (July 1980).

———. "Evolution Is Religion, Not Science," ICR *Impact* No. 107 (May 1982).

———. *Science, Scripture and the Young Earth.* El Cajon: Institute for Creation Research, 1983.

———. "Does Entropy Contradict Evolution?" ICR *Impact* No. 141 (March 1985).

———. "Evolution and the New Age," ICR *Impact* No. 165 (March 1987).

———. "Is Creationism Scientific?" ICR *Acts and Facts* XVI No. 2 (December 1987).

———. "The Heritage of the Recapitulation Theory," ICR *Impact* No. 183 (September 1988).

———. "Proposed California Science Framework," ICR *Impact* No. 186 (December 1988).

Morris, Henry M., and Gary E. Parker. *What Is Creation Science?* San Diego: Creation-Life Publishers, 1982.

Morris, John D. *Tracking Those Incredible Dinosaurs and the People Who Knew Them.* San Diego: Creation-Life Publishers, 1980 (*nv*).

———. "The Paluxy River Mystery," ICR *Impact* No. 151 (January 1986).

———. "How Do the Dinosaurs Fit In?" ICR *Back to Genesis* (May 1989).

Neiman, David. "The Polemical Language of the Genesis Cosmology," *The Heritage of the Early Church.* Orient. Christ. Analecta 195 (1973), 47–63.

Neugebauer, O., and A. Sachs. *The Exact Sciences in Antiquity.* New York: Harper, 1962.

News Notes. "Redshift Anomaly Resolved?" in *Sky and Telescope,* 79, No. 1 (January 1990), 9–10.

Nickels, Martin K. "Creationists and the Australopithecines," *Creation/Evolution,* XIX (Winter 1986–1987), 1–15.

Niessen, Richard. "Theistic Evolution and the Day-Age Theory," ICR *Impact* No. 81 (March 1980).

———. "Starlight and the Age of the Universe," ICR *Impact* No. 121 (July 1983).

Oppert, Jules. "Chronology," in *The Jewish Encyclopedia* (1903), Vol. IV, 64–68.

Parrot, André. *Sumer: The Dawn of Art.* New York: Golden Press, 1961.

Patrick, Dale. *Old Testament Law.* Atlanta: John Knox Press, 1985.

Patterson, John W. "Thermodynamics and Evolution," in *Scientists Confront Creationism* (ed. Laurie R. Godfrey). New York: W.W. Norton and Co., 1983.

Pope, Marvin H. "The Word שחת in Job 9:31," *Journal of Biblical Literature,* LXXXIII (1964), 269–278.

Pritchard, James B. *Ancient Near Eastern Texts Relating to the Old Testament.* Second edition. Princeton: University Press, 1955.

Rawlinson, H. C. *The Cuneiform Inscriptions of Western Asia.* 5 vols. London: R.E. Bowler, 1861–1884.

Rice, Stanley. "Scientific Creationism: Adding Imagination to Scripture," *Creation/Evolution,* XXIV (Fall 1988), 25–36.

Robinson, H. Wheeler. "The Council of Yahweh," *Journal of Theological Studies,* XLV (1944), 151–157.

Roscher, Wilhelm Heinrich. *Der Omphalosgedanke bei verscheidenen Völkern.* Leipzig: B.G. Teubner, 1918.

Rose, Herbert Jennings. *A Handbook of Greek Mythology.* London: Methuen, 1972.

Rosenthal, Franz. "Nineteen," *Studia Biblica et Orientalia,* III (1959), 304–318.

Rybka, Theodore W. "Consequences of Time Dependent Nuclear Decay Indices on Half Lives," ICR *Impact* No. 106 (April 1982).

Sagan, Carl. *Cosmos.* New York: Random House, 1980.

Sandage, Allan. "The Red Shift," in *The Universe, a Scientific American Book.* New York: Simon and Schuster, 1956, 1957, 89–98.

Sarna, Nahum M. "The Mythological Background of Job 18," *Journal of Biblical Literature,* LXXXII (1963), 315–318.

Schadewald, Robert J. "Six 'Flood' Arguments Creationists Can't Answer," *Creation/Evolution,* IX (Summer 1982), 12–17.

Schafersman, Steven. "Censorship of Evolution in Texas," *Creation/Evolution,* X (Fall 1982), 30–34.

Schiaperelli, Giovanni Virginio. *Astronomy in the Old Testament.* Oxford: Clarendon Press 1905.

Schnabel, Paul. *Berossus und die babylonisch-hellenistische Literatur.* Hildesheim: Georg Olms, 1968.

Scholem, G. "Some Sources of Jewish-Arabic Demonology," *The Journal of Semitic Studies,* XVI (1965), 1–13.

Schramm, David N. "The Age of the Elements," *Scientific American,* 230 (1974), 69–77.

Seckel, Al. "Science, Creationism, and the U.S. Supreme Court," *The Skeptical Inquirer,* XI, No. 2 (Winter 1986–1987), 147–158.

Shore, Steven N. "Footprints in the Dust: The Lunar Surface and Creationism," *Creation/Evolution,* XIV (Fall 1984), 32–35.

Sollberger, Edmond. *The Babylonian Legend of the Flood*. London: Trustees of the British Museum, 1961.

Sonleitner, Frank J. "Creationists Embarrassed in Oklahoma," *Creation/Evolution*, IV (Spring 1981), 23–27.

Speiser, E.A. *Genesis*. Anchor Bible 1. Garden City: Doubleday and Co., Inc., 1964.

Stadelmann, Luis I.J. *The Hebrew Conception of the World*. Ph.D. Dissertation, Hebrew Union College, 1967.

Stambaugh, James S. "How Long Was the Seventh Day?" ICR *Impact* No. 197 (November 1989).

Strahler, Arthur N. *Science and Earth History: The Evolution/Creation Controversy*. Buffalo: Prometheus Books, 1987.

Sutcliffe, E.F. "The Clouds as Water-Carriers in Hebrew Thought," *Vetus Testamentum*, III (1953), 99–103.

Thompson, R. Campbell. *The Devil and Evil Spirits of Babylonia*. London: Luzac and Company, 1903.

Thureau-Dangin F. (ed.). *Die Sumerischen und Akkadischen Königs-inschriften*. Leipzig: J.C. Hinrichs'sche Buchhandlung, 1907.

Tsevat, Matitiahu. "The Canaanite God Šälaḥ," *Vetus Testamentum*, IV (1954), 41–49.

Tur-Sinai, N.H. *The Book of Job: A New Commentary*. Jerusalem: Kiryath Sepher Ltd., 1957.

Ussher, James. *The Annals of the World*. London: E. Tyler, 1658.

Van Buren, E. Douglas. "The Seven Dots in Mesopotamian Art and Their Meaning," *Archiv für Orientforschung*, XIII (1939–1941), 277–289.

———. *Symbols of the Gods in Mesopotamian Art*. Analecta Orientalia XXIII. Roma: Pontificum Institutum Biblicum, 1945.

Van Till, Howard J. *The Fourth Day*. Grand Rapids: William B. Eerdmans Publishing Co., 1986.

Van Till, Howard J., Davis A. Young, and Clarence Menninga. *Science Held Hostage: What's Wrong with Creation Science and Evolutionism*. Downers Grove: InterVarsity Press, 1988.

Vawter, Bruce. *On Genesis: A New Reading*. Garden City: Doubleday and Company, Inc., 1977.

von Rad, Gerhard. *Old Testament Theology*, I. New York: Harper and Row, 1962.

Wainwright, G.A. "Jacob's Bethel," *Palestine Exploration Fund Quarterly Statement*, 1934, 32–44.

Wales, H.G. Quaritch. "The Sacred Mountain in Old Asiatic Religion," *Journal of the Royal Asiatic Society of Great Britain and Ireland*, 1953 (Parts 1 and 2), 23–30.

Ward, William Hayes. *The Seal Cylinders of Western Asia*. Washington: Carnegie Institute, 1910.

Warfield, Benjamin Breckinridge. "On the Antiquity and the Unity of the Human Race," *Studies in Theology* (New York: Oxford University Press, 1932), 235–258.

Webb, George E. "Demographic Change and Antievolution Sentiment: Tennessee as a Case Study, 1925–1975," *Creation/Evolution*, XXIV (Fall 1988), 37–43.

Weinberg, Stanley L. "Reactions to Creationism In Iowa," *Creation/Evolution,* II (Fall 1980), pp. 1–8.

Weinberg, Steven. *The First Three Minutes: A Modern View of the Origin of the Universe.* Updated edition. New York: Basic Books, 1988.

Wensinck, A.J. *The Ideas of the Western Semites Concerning the Navel of the Earth.* Amsterdam: J. Müller, 1916.

Wessetzki, V. "Alter," in *Lexikon der Ägyptologie,* I (1972), 154–156.

Westermann, Claus. *Genesis 1–11.* Minneapolis: Augsburgh Publishing House, 1984.

Whitcomb, John C., Jr., and Henry M. Morris. *The Genesis Flood.* Philadelphia: Presbyterian and Reformed Publishing Co., 1961.

Wieseler, K. "Era," in the *Schaff-Herzog Encyclopedia of Religious Knowledge.* Volume I. New York: Funk and Wagnalls, 1882, 7–753.

Wolff, Hans Walter. "Problems Between the Generations in the Old Testament," in *Essays in Old Testament Ethics* (Crenshaw and Willis, eds.). New York: KTAV Publishing House, 1974, 77–95.

Wonderly, Daniel E. *Neglect of Geological Data: Sedimentary Strata Compared with Young-Earth Creationist Writings.* Hatfield: Interdisciplinary Biblical Research Institute, 1987.

Woosley, Stan, and Tom Weaver. "The Great Supernova of 1987," *Scientific American,* 261, No. 2 (August 1989), 32–40.

Works of the Emperor Julian, The. Vol. III. Loeb Classical Library. New York: G.P. Putman's Sons, 1923.

Young, Davis A. *Creation and the Flood,* 1977 (*nv*).

———. *Christianity and the Age of the Earth.* Grand Rapids: Zondervan Publishing House, 1982.

ADDITIONAL BIBLIOGRAPHY

The following items, relevant for an understanding of chronology in the book of Genesis, either came to my attention too late for incorporation in the present volume, or they were not available to me. Some of them were cited in other works in such incomplete or erroneous form that it has been difficult to recover a reliable bibliographical entry. Summaries of some of them have been taken from such sources and I cannot guarantee their accuracy.

Bertheau, (Ernest?). Article in the Jahresbericht of *Deutsche Morgenländischen Zeitung,* 1845. According to Delitzsch (1899, p. 207), Bertheau assumed that the ten generations in Genesis 5 lived an average of 160 years each (reduced to 120 after the flood; both multiples of 60), for a total of 1600 years of elapsed time. When converted to lunar years (of 365 days each), the 1656 years of MT results. (See above, Chapter IV, note 28.)

Bertheau, E. (Ernest?). "Die Zahlen der Genesis in Cap. 5 und Cap. 11," *Jahrbucher für deutsche Theologie,* XXIII (1878), 657–682. Observes that the lifespans in Genesis 5 (SP, and in some cases MT) apparently were derived by adding the ages for certain other persons in the genealogy at the time of their first-born. Thus Adam's 930 years equals the 105 of Seth, plus the 90 of Enosh, plus the 70 of Kenan, plus the 65 of Mahalalel, plus the 500 of Noah, plus the 100 of Shem. (The choice of names does not follow any particular pattern, however.) Delitzsch (1899, pp. 208–209) dismisses this as "a curious trick of accident," and gives priority to the SP figures.

Bosse, (Alfred?). "Die chronologischen Systeme im A.T. und bei Josephus," *Mittheilungen der vorderasiatischen Gesellschaft,* 1908. Suggests that two chronological systems are at work in the text of the Hebrew Bible: (1) using generations of 40 years each, yielding 4,000 years from Shem to the end of the exile, and (2) using solar cycles of 260 years each, yielding 3,166 years from creation to the consecration of Solomon's temple. (See the article, "Time, Biblical Reckoning of," in *The New Schaff-Herzog Encyclopedia.*)

Bousset, D.W. "Das chronologische System der biblischen Geschichtsbücher," *ZAW,* XX (1900), 136–147. Sets the dedication of the Solomonic temple at A.M. 3001, i.e. at three-fourths of a world cycle of 4,000 years, based upon evidence in Josephus (*Antiquities*) and the Apocalypse of Ezra (9:38ff).

Budd, Theodore. *The Modern-Hebrew Numbers.* London: John F. Shaw and Co., 1880. (A copy of this item, cited in Delitzsch, 1899, p. 206, does not seem to be available in the U.S., and I finally received a copy from Cambridge University, England.) One of a number of British publications of the period which argues that the MT figures are "modern" in the sense that the Jewish scribes of the early rabbinic period changed them to disguise the fact that the messiah was born in the 6th millennium since creation (as part of a world week of 1,000 years each). He thinks that, originally, the MT figures were identical to those of LXX. (A clearer illustration of blind Christian polemic and misunderstanding of sources would be difficult to find.)

Budde, Karl. *Die biblische Urgeschiche (Gen. 1–12, 5).* Giessen: J. Ricker, 1883. Supports the originality of the SP figures.

Cassuto, Umberto. עשרה דורות שמאדם ועד נח ("The Ten Generations from Adam to Noah"), *Louis Ginzberg Jubilee Volume.* New York: American Academy of Jewish Research, 1945. An expansion of his ideas as presented in *A Commentary on the Book of Genesis,* I (1978).

Clémencet, Charles, and Ursin Durand. *L'art de vérifier les dates.* 42 volumes (?). Paris: Moreau, 1783–87 (3rd edition?). Reveals more than one hundred different computations for biblical chronology. (See above, Appendix XIII, footnote 1.)

Euringer, Sebastian. *Die Chronologie der biblischen Urgeschichte* (Gen. 5 und 11). Biblische Zeitfragen. Münster: Aschendorff, 1909.

Fisher, O. "Die Chronologie der Priesterkodex und ihre Umgestaltung," *ZAW,* XXXI (1911), 241–255.

Gehringer, (?), in *Tübinger Programm,* 1842 (cited by Delitzsch, 1899, p. 206). Suggests that the SP figures resulted "from accidental errors in reading and writing in the years of Methuselah and Lamech."

Green, William Henry. "Primeval Chronology," *Bibliotheca Sacra,* 47 (April 1890), 285–303. Argues that the genealogies in Genesis 5 were not intended for chronological purposes. Cited with great approval by Warfield (1932, p. 237).

König, Eduard. "Beiträge zur biblischen Chronologie, I," *Zeitschrift für kirchliche Wissenschaft und kirchliches Leben,* 1883. Argues that MT has preserved the authentic form of the genealogies in Genesis 5 and 11.

Kuenen, Abraham. *Les origines du Text Masoréthique de l'Ancien Testament.* Paris: E. Leroux, 1875. Contains a refutation of the article (below) by Lagarde. (See Delitzsch, 1899, pp. 207–208.)

Lagarde, Paul Anton de. According to Delitzsch (*ibid.*), he suggests that the MT figures have been shortened by about 1,000 years in an attempt to deprive Christians "of the proof that the Messiah really appeared in the year of the world 5500." (See the entry by Budd.)

Lederer, Carl. *Die biblische Zeitrechnung.* Erlangen: F. Kleeberger, 1888.

Lynn, William Thynne. *Bible Chronology.* London: Bagster and Sons, 1905.

Mahler, Eduard. *Biblische Chronologie und Zeitrechnung der Hebräer.* Vienna: C. Konegan, 1887.

Merx, Adabert. "Der Messias oder Ta'eb der Samaritaner," *Beihefte zur ZAW,* XVII. Giessen, 1909 (pp. 80–91). Asserts the independence of SP figures from those of LXX.

Meysing, J. "The Biblical Chronologies of the Patriarchs," *Christian News From Israel,* 13 (1962), 3–12.

Nöldeke, Theodor. "Die s.g. Grundschrift des Pentateuchs," in *Untersuchungen zur Kritik des Alten Testaments.* Kiel: Schwers, 1869, pp. 1–144. Suggests that the exodus was set at A.M. 2666 so as to fall at two-thirds of a world cycle of 4,000 years (100 generations of 40 years each).

Oppert, Jules. "Über die Daten der Genesis," *Göttingische Gelehrte Anzeigen,* No. 10 (1877), 201–223. Argues that the MT total for the pre-diluvians is a modification of Berossos' total for the Sumerian King List.

Toffteen, Olaf Alfred. *Ancient Chronology.* Chicago: University of Chicago Press, 1907 (new edition, 1909).

Young, Dwight W. "A Mathematical Approach to Certain Dynastic Spans in the Sumerian King List," *Journal of Near Eastern Studies,* 47 (1988), 123–129. Concentrating upon the Mesopotamian Post-diluvians, Young cogently suggests that the total years of dynastic spans not only were calculated prior to the individual reigns, but also that such totals reflect either the square or quartic of an integer plus the square of ten (e.g. Mari's 136-year span = $6^2 + 10^2$).

————. "On the Application of Numbers from Babylonian Mathematics to Biblical Life Spans and Epochs," *Zeitschrift für die alttestamentliche Wissenschaft,* 100 (1988), 331–335. The author points to correspondences between ages of the Pre-diluvians and answers to foundational problems in Babylonian mathematical texts.

————. "The Influence of Babylonian Algebra on Longevity among the Antediluvians," *Zeitschrift für die alttestamentliche Wissenschaft,* 102 (1990), 321–335. A study of the importance of the numbers 10, 20, and 30 in the biblical life spans, in view of the central role of those numbers in Babylonian calculations.

SUBJECT INDEX

AUTHOR INDEX